THE WORKS OF SRI CHINMOY

POETRY

VOLUME VI

THE WORKS OF SRI CHINMOY

POETRY

VOLUME VI

★

WHEN GOD LOVE DESCENDS
LORD, I ASK YOU FOR ONE FAVOUR
LORD, RECEIVE THIS LITTLE UNDYING CRY • LORD, I NEED YOU
MY LIFE-TREE • MY PROMISE TO GOD
SOUND BECOMES, SILENCE IS • THE SILENCE-SONG
SILENCE-SEED AND SOUND-FRUIT • THIS IS GOD'S HOME
DEDICATION-DROPS • UNION AND ONENESS
THREE SOULFUL PRAYERS • MY FIFTY GRATITUDE-SUMMERS
THE LOSER AND THE WINNER • I MEDITATE SO THAT
I PRAY SO THAT • I AM READY
MY HEART'S THIRTY-ONE SACRED SECRETS
MY GOD-HUNGER-DREAMS,
THE GOD OF THE MIND
O MY HEART • O MY MIND
MY LORD SUPREME, DO YOU HAVE A MOMENT?
GOD IS KIDNAPPED • EUROPEAN POEM-BLOSSOMS
EVERY DAY A NEW CHANCE
GOD MINUS • GOD PLUS

LYON · OXFORD
GANAPATI PRESS
XC

THE WORKS OF SRI CHINMOY

POETRY

VOLUME VI

★

(CONTINUED)

TWENTY-SEVEN HEART-FRAGRANCE-DREAMS
EACH HOUR IS A GOD-HOUR • MY LIFE-BOAT'S DREAM-REALITY-SHORE
WAR: MAN'S ABYSMAL ABYSS-PLUNGE • I KNOW WHY I AM HELPLESS
THE BEGINNING AND THE ARRIVING • BEAUTY-DISCOVERY
BEAUTIFUL IS MY WHISPERING SOUL • FRIENDSHIP-BIRDS FLY
GOD THE EYE AND GOD THE HEART • MY GOD-MASTER
MY GOD-PRAYERS AND MY GOD-MEDITATIONS • I AM SURE
MY MIND-CONFUSION OUT, MY MIND-ILLUMINATION IN
MY GOD-COMMITMENTS
MORNING INVITES MY HEART • EVENING INVITES MY LIFE
THE ONENESS-HEART-UNIVERSITY • PEACE: GOD'S FRAGRANCE-HEART
YESTERDAY, TODAY, TOMORROW • IMMEDIATELY START!
IMMEDIATELY START AGAIN! • IMMEDIATELY STOP!
MY BONDAGE-LIFE IS MY SELF-INVENTION • MY EAGERNESS-HEART
MY GRATITUDE-HEART-GARDEN
MY GRATITUDE-TEARS AND GOD'S SATISFACTION-SMILES
GOD THE MOTHER AND GOD THE FATHER • A LOVE-BATHED HEART
LOVE, COMPASSION, FORGIVENESS

© 2021 THE SRI CHINMOY CENTRE

ISBN 978-1-911319-35-1

See appendix for notice regarding this edition.

FIRST EDITION WENT TO PRESS ON 1 JULY 2021

POETRY

VOLUME VI

PART I

WHEN GOD-LOVE DESCENDS

WHEN GOD LOVE DESCENDS

1. CONTAGIOUS

Frustration is contagious;
Therefore, be careful.
Happiness is contagious;
Therefore, be happy,
And see, by spreading your
 happiness,
You increase your happiness.

Suspicion is contagious;
Therefore, be careful.
Faith is contagious;
Therefore, have faith,
And see, by spreading your faith,
You increase your faith.

2. THE LISTENER IN YOU

The speaker in you tells you
That you and he can transform
The length and breadth of the
 world.

The listener in you tells you
That you and he can manifest
God-Light, God-Truth and
God-Perfection on earth.

I tell you,
The listener in you is sincere and
 genuine.
Give him a chance.
He will do everything to please you,
To fulfil you.
Just give him a chance.

3. THE RESTING PLACE WITHIN

Are you looking for the resting
 place within?
Then ask God where the
 hallowed door is.
If you cannot ask Him,
If you do not know who God is,
Then ask your humility-friend,
Ask your sincerity-friend.
They know where the resting
 place within you abides.
They know; ask them!
They are eager to tell you.

4. GOD'S FUTURE

God's future
Nobody knows
But me.
His future
Shall win
My life's
Surrender
Unconditional.

5. DREAM-LIFE, REALITY-LIFE

You know what your dream-life is,
But you know not what your
　reality-life is.
Your dream-life is an assuring life
　of promise,
A life of joy.
Your reality-life is a God-life
　of love-perfection
And oneness-satisfaction on earth.
Therefore, stay not always in the
　dream-life.
Come out.
Embrace the reality-life.

6. GOD'S SATISFACTION-CHOICE

You were the son of God.
You didn't know it.

You are the friend of God.
You don't know it.

You shall be the satisfaction-choice
　of God.
You will not know it.
Alas, alas, alas.

7. WHAT DID GOD TELL YOU?

When did I love you?
I loved you when God loved you.
Where did I see you?
I saw you where God saw you.
What did I tell you?
I told you what God told you.

What did God tell you?
God told you that
He does not believe
In the existence of death,
He does not believe
In the existence of ignorance.
He does not believe
In death-dart,
He does not believe
In ignorance-clay.

8. HE PLAYS FOR YOU

When does the Supreme play?
The Supreme plays
Only when you appreciate
　His Play,
Only when you want to learn from
　Him,
Only when you want to become a
　player like Him,
Only when you want to make
　friends with Eternity like Him.
When you feel that
　His cosmic Play
Is all that you want,
He plays,
He plays for you.

9. LOVE IS A THING TO BECOME

Love is not a thing to understand.
Love is not a thing to feel.
Love is not a thing to give and
 receive.
Love is a thing only to become
And eternally be.

10. LOOK UP, LOOK BELOW

Look up.
Your grasp will exceed your reach,
I assure you.
Look below.
Your grasp will never attain your
 reach,
Needless to say.

11. THREE APOSTLES

Three apostles of atheism:
A sleeping body,
A strangling vital,
A doubting mind.

Three apostles of theism:
A believing heart,
A loving life,
A serving soul.

12. GROWING BETTER

Every day I am growing better.
This is what I hear from my
 Inner Pilot.
Every day I am getting worse.
This is what I hear from the
 human beings around me.
Who is telling me the truth?
Is it my Inner Pilot or the
 human beings?
My Inner Pilot is telling me
 the truth,
For I know there was a time
When I wanted to devour
 the world;
But now I want to feed the world.

13. FATHER AND SON

It is the father who first loves
 the son.
It is the son who first seeks
 the father.
It is the father who first tells
 the son
That his son is the son of
 greatness.
It is the son who first tells
 the father
That his father is the father of
 greatness.

14. THE WORLD THAT I HAVE DISCOVERED

The new world of Columbus
Likes to be loved first,
And then it wants to love.
But my new world,
The world that I have discovered,
Wants only to love and thus become
What love eternally is.

15. EARTH'S MUSIC

O earth, you tell me
That God does not love
　your music.
But how can God love your music
Since your music does not
　love God?
It only loves the pleasure-vital
　in itself.
If your music loved God,
God would not only love
　your music,
But also tell the world that
　your music
Is His immediate Perfection-
　Manifestation on earth,
The manifestation of His
　universality's Height on earth.

16. TRY THIS HELPER

When other helpers fail you,
Try this one:
His name is earth-patience.

When other helpers fail you,
Try this one:
His name is Heaven-Compassion.

When other helpers fail you,
Try this one:
His name is surrender-beauty.

17. SWEET HOPE

Sweet hope,
You are not the product of
　earth-desire,
But the blossom of
　God-aspiration.
O sweet hope,
Therefore
I am in love with you.

18. GOD AND HIS LOVERS

God and His seekers know,
God and His seekers glow,
God and His seekers grow.
But God and His lovers
Eternally are.

19. WHO NEVER SMILES, WHO NEVER CRIES

Who never smiles?
You?
Not true.
I have seen you smile
Inside the Heart of God,
At the Feet of God.

Who never cries?
You?
Not true.
I have seen you cry
Inside earth-hunger heart,
At the thunderous destruction-feet of earth.

20. SOMETHING IS GOING ON

Something is going on in your inner world,
My friend: doubt.
I am telling you why.
I see clearly that you are not satisfied
With what you have and what you are.
What you have is frustration;
What you are is deception.

21. PERFECTION-MOON, PERFECTION-SUN

Insincerity is the disease
Of your thought-life.
Sincerity is the cure
Of your will-life.
Humility's beauty and surrender's duty
Are the perfection-moon and perfection-sun
Of your soul-life.

22. OUR WEAKNESSES

You talk and never stop.
That is your weakness.

He never talks.
That is his weakness.

I talk only to myself,
Not to God.
That is my weakness.

23. SOMETIMES I WONDER WHY

Earth does not need me.
Sometimes
I wonder why
I still stay on earth.

Heaven does need me.
Sometimes
I wonder why
I still do not go to Heaven.

24. BELIEVE IT OR NOT

Believe it or not,
Although you do not love God,
God does not hold anything
   against you.

Believe it or not,
Although you serve ignorance,
Ignorance does not trust you.

25. THERE IS YET TIME

There is yet time.
You are destined to see God.
Don't believe your earthly eyes.

There is yet time.
You are destined to realise God.
Don't believe your earthly friends.

There is yet time.
You are destined to become God.
Don't believe your
   earth-bound self,
But believe your Heaven-free
Divinity and Immortality.

26. LITTLE TROUBLES AND BIG TROUBLES

Your little troubles are:
You do not care for God,
You do not love God.
But your big troubles are:
God smiles at somebody else,
God takes the service of
   somebody else.

27. DO YOU CARE FOR GOD'S SMILE?

Do you care for God's rare Smile?
Then call on Him
And love Him with your heart's
 love.

Do you care for God's
 constant Smile?
Then become what He wants
 you to be:
A surrender-flower at His
 Transcendence-Feet.

28. NEVER BELIEVE WHAT YOUR MIND SAYS

Never believe what your mind says.
Your mind is a liar.

Never believe what your mind says.
Your mind is a beggar.

Never believe what your mind says.
Your mind is secretly digging your
 grave.

Never believe what your mind says.
Your mind tells you that God is
 somewhere else,
That God is someone else other
 than you.

29. WHEN GOD-LOVE DESCENDS

When God-Love descends,
Beauty appears from nowhere.
When God-Compassion descends,
Delight appears from nowhere.

30. THE LATECOMER

O world-ignorance,
You are a latecomer.
Yet God will consider your case,
God will grant your choice,
God will offer you
 His heavenly Voice
And He will use your
 earthly years.
God will fulfil you,
God will make you perfection's
Immortality.
O latecomer, God is still yours
And you are still His.

31. WHAT I HAVE FOUND

What I have found in Heaven,
I tell you:
Heaven knows how to smile,
Heaven knows how to dance,
Heaven knows how to enjoy.

What I have found in earth,
I tell you:
Earth knows how to cry,
Earth knows how to sigh,
Earth knows how to die.

What I have found in God,
I tell you:
God knows how to forget
 world-torture,
God knows how to forgive
 world-ignorance.

32. NO TIME TO WORRY

No time to worry
If you want to serve God.

No time to worry
If you want to love God.

No time to worry
If you need God.

No time to worry
If you really want to be the God
 of tomorrow.

33. HEAVEN-SILENCE

Heaven-silence loves ignorance,
For by loving alone
Can Heaven transform ignorance.

Ignorance loves Heaven-silence,
For by giving what it has,
What it is,
Ignorance becomes
 Heaven-silence.
What ignorance has
Is the message of
 life-transformation.
What ignorance is
Is the message of God-preparation
 for perfection's Light.

34. YOU ARE THE ANSWER

"Lord, I am determined to love
 You."
Son, I am determined to free you.
"Lord, I am determined to fulfil
 You."
Son, I am determined to offer you
To quench the thirst of humanity
And to feed the hunger of
 divinity.
You are the answer to humanity's
 thirst for God-realisation.
You are the answer to Divinity's
 hunger for God-manifestation.

35. I AM NOT

The hour is coming.
The hour is approaching fast.
God will tell me
What I am not,
Who I am not,
Where I am not.

What am I not?
I am not ignorance.
Who am I not?
I am not God's slave,
I am not a stranger to God.
Where am I not?
I am not in the mouth
Of a devouring ignorance-tiger.

36. NOTHING IS REALLY LOST

Nothing is really lost.
No, not even my long-forgotten
   peace.

Nothing is really gained.
No, not even my constantly used
   dedication-body.

37. IS YOUR SOUL TROUBLED?

Is your soul troubled?
Then I tell you,
Think of your claim:
Your God's Greatness-Height.
Is your life troubled?
Then I tell you,
Think of your life's
   nothingness-might.

38. PLEASED WITH ME

Sound-life
Was pleased with me
When I said
God is great.

Silence-life
Was pleased with me
When I said
God is good.

Perfection-life
Was pleased with me
When I said
God is becoming.

39. THE SIMPLE ONES

My Lord preserves the simple ones.
My Lord fulfils the sincere ones.
My Lord becomes the humble ones.

40. I AM WHERE I AM

I am from above,
Believe it or not.
For God's sake I am on earth.

I am from below,
Believe it or not.
For man's sake I am in Heaven.
No preference have I
For the highest Height
Or the abysmal depth.
For God's sake,
For man's sake,
I am where I am.

41. ONLY TWO THINGS

Lord, I am ready to receive.
What do You have for me?
"Son, I have only two things
To give you:
The Crown of
   My Heaven's Vision,
And the frown of ignorance-force
At My whole universal Mission."

42. WHY MEN CRY

I tell you in supreme secrecy,
God will become a man,
God will cry like a man.
God will become a man
To see what man needs most.
God will cry like a man
To see why men cry.

43. TWO HOPES OF GOD

Two hopes of God:
Man will take His place,
Man will give Him rest,
Eternity's rest.

44. DO NOT FLATTER ME ANY MORE

O Heaven,
For God's sake
Do not flatter me any more.
I am sick of your flattery,
Totally sick of your flattery.
I am unimaginably sick of your
   flattery.

O earth,
For God's sake
Do not torture me any more.
I am sick of your torture,
Totally sick of your torture.
I deserve better treatment
   from you.

45. A GOD-INVOKING WORK

A soulful work is the first reward.
A surrender-work is the best
  reward.
A God-invoking work
Is the first and best dream-reward
  of God,
The first and best
  reality-achievement of man.

46. ADDITION AND SUBTRACTION

While loving
He subtracts himself;
Therefore, he is really great.

While serving
He adds God to his service-seed;
Therefore, he and his action
Are supremely perfect.

47. DIVINE NECESSITIES

Surrender-fruit
Is my first necessity.
Devotion-flower
Is my second necessity.
Love-leaf
Is my third necessity.
But God the Compassion-Tree
Is my supreme necessity.

48. DIVIDED SINCERITY

Your outer life
Is multiplied indifference;
Therefore, my soul does not like
  you.

Your inner life
Is divided sincerity;
Therefore, my heart does not love
  you.

49. WILL-SEA

Thought-waves caught me;
Therefore, I lived in
  possibility-world.
Will-sea has freed me;
Therefore, I am in reality-world.

50. THREE SUBLIME THINGS

He always does
Not one, but three sublime things:
He loves God openly,
He keeps God's Blessing-Fruit
  safely,
He distributes God-Delight
  unreservedly.

PART II

LORD, I ASK YOU FOR ONE FAVOUR

LORD, I ASK YOU FOR ONE FAVOUR

1. REMINDERS

Earth reminds me
Of my outer duty:
God-dedication.

Heaven reminds me
Of my inner beauty:
God-compassion.

God reminds me
Of my supreme necessity:
God-manifestation.

2. DREAMS

Earth-dreams are black;
Therefore, I devour them.

Heaven-dreams are white;
Therefore, I need them.

God-dreams are gold;
Therefore, I treasure them.

3. DEBTS

I owe my earth
My simplicity-sea.

I owe my Heaven
My beauty-wave.

I owe my God
My humility-drop.

4. SONGS OF THE HEART

The song of the bleeding heart:
"Save me!"

The song of the crying heart:
"Take me!"

The song of the surrendering
    heart:
"I am Yours!"

5. IF I HAD THE LIBERTY

If I had the liberty to die
I would have already died,
For what is earth
If not the destruction-life
Of excruciating pangs?

If I had the liberty to live
I would have lived eternally on earth,
And offered Mother-earth
My Eternity's gratitude-life.

6. SELECTIONS

The soul divine selects its own
Perfection-goal.

The heart divine selects in own
Realisation-soul.

The body divine selects its own
Dedication-role.

7. SWEET PARTING, SAD PARTING

Sweet parting pure:
Our earth-bound journey
From Heaven-height.
Sad parting pure:
Our Heaven-bound journey
From earth-core.

8. BE TRUTHFUL AS THE SUN

Be truthful as the sun.
Earth will admire you.

Be soulful as the moon.
Earth will claim you.

Be fruitful as the stars.
Earth will treasure you.

9. PERFECTION

Silence is perfect
When it commands.

Sound is perfect
When it obeys.

I am perfect
When I cry.

10. JUST TRY ONCE MORE

O my helpless soul,
Look around.
I tell you, God-manifestation
Is not so difficult a thing
As you imagine.
Just try only once more.
You will be crowned with
    success-heights.

11. GIFTS TO GOD

Earth gives to God
Its frustration-vital.

Heaven gives to God
Its dedication-soul.

I give to God
My imagination-life.

12. OUR KNOWLEDGE

Heaven knows that Heaven
Is not really great.

Earth knows that earth
Is not really pure.

I know that I
Am not really perfect.

13. HEART-DOOR AND MIND-DOOR

Shut not your heart-door.
God the universal Beauty
May come in.

Open not your mind-door.
Teeming ignorance-night
May slip in.

14. STRENGTH

Union is strength.
Love-light knows it.

Disunion is strength.
Hate-night believes it.

15. DARING SOUL-FEET

All your danger
Is in your delaying life-train.

All your safety
Is in your daring soul-feet.

16. ALL WE KNOW

Beauty's smile
Is all we know of Heaven.

Duty's cry
Is all we know of earth.

Necessity's life
Is all we know of God.

17. THREE DEATHS

You died
For beauty's charming body.
You are dying
For beauty's loving heart.
You shall die
For beauty's serving life.

18. I EXAMINE WITH THE MIND OF LEISURE

I examine with the mind of leisure.
I study with the heart of labour.
I stay not with the vital of
   frustration.
I dance not with the body of
   pleasure.

19. TWO BEGGARS

A beggar before the Door of God.
Who is he?
The man who thinks
That he needs.

A beggar before the door of man.
Who is he?
The man who does not know
Who he himself is.

20. BEFORE YOU SEEK TO GET RID OF ME

Bless me, my Lord,
Before You seek
To get rid of me.

Love me, my Lord,
Before I get rid of
My imperfection-choice
And destruction-voice.

21. MY WAYS TO LOVE GOD

These are my ways
To love God:
I am giving Him
What I have —
Silence-smile;
I am giving Him
What I am —
Sound-cry.

22. GOD'S FEET

I dreamed
That I was nearing God's Feet.

I see
That I am God's Feet.

I know
That I am for God's Hour.

23. ELDEST AMONG ALL MORTALS

Eldest among all mortals:
Compassion-king.
Youngest among all mortals:
Depression-prince.

24. QUESTIONS

Reality, where are you?
Why are you hiding?

Divinity, how far are you?
Why are you so slow?

Immortality, who are you?
Do you really belong to God?

25. THE SONG

He sang the song;
Therefore,
He is mortal.

The song sang him;
Therefore,
He is immortal.

God sang the song for him;
Therefore,
He is supremely divine
And
Eternally perfect.

26. GOD-MANIFESTATION ON EARTH

Disunion: a soulless falsehood.
Union: a soulful truth.
Oneness: a fruitful life.
Satisfaction: God-manifestation
   on earth.

27. MY LIFE IS DEATH

My life is death
When I think that God
Does not care for me.

My death is life
When I know that God
Will employ me.

28. OF ME YOU KNOW LITTLE

Of me you know little;
Therefore,
My gratitude loves you.

Of you I know much;
Therefore,
My earth-existence needs you,
Only you.

29. ONE THING WE NEED

Heaven needs one thing:
Preparation-seed.

Earth needs one thing:
Purification-flower.

I need one thing:
Perfection-fruit.

30. I WAS GOD'S HUMAN EFFORT

I was God's human effort.
I am now God's divine Grace.
I shall be God's effortless case
And graceful perfection.

31. TORTURES

Heaven's superiority
Tortures my realisation.

Earth's inferiority
Tortures my compassion.

My impurity
Tortures my dedication.

32. GOD-SECRECY

Concentration
Is God-secrecy's daring body.

Meditation
Is God-secrecy's illumining life.

Contemplation
Is God-secrecy's fulfilling soul.

33. MIND-KNOWLEDGE IS EARNED

Mind-knowledge is earned
And hoarded.

Heart-wisdom is achieved
And distributed.

Soul-light is revealed
And manifested.

34. WHO I SHALL BE

Do you know
Who I was?
I was an intellectual fool.

Do you know
Who I am?
I am an intuitive rogue.

Do you know
Who I shall be?
I shall be an innocent saint.

35. NOT WHAT I THOUGHT

I saw the face
Of my vital.
It is not as ugly
As I thought.

I felt the love
Of my heart.
It is not as pure
As I declared.

36. MY DIFFERENT GODS

My mind
Is my conscious God.

My heart
Is my auspicious God.

My soul
Is my precious God.

My life
Is my prosperous God.

37. CONSCIOUS AND UNCONSCIOUS

Man, an unconscious God.
God, a conscious man.
I, an unconscious man
And a conscious God.

38. MY HEART BECAME GOD

My heart became God
Out of pure necessity.
My mind became man
Out of sheer curiosity.

39. MY LIFE

My silence-life
Is the dawn of my dream.

My sound-life
Is the doom of my bloom.

My surrender-life
Is the birth of my God.

40. LIVE LIKE A SEED

Live like a seed.
God loves secrecy.

Live like a plant.
God loves innocence.

Live like a tree.
God loves beauty's ascension
And duty's expansion.

41. I KNOW SOMETHING

God knows everything;
Therefore,
He is Perfection-Smile.

I know only something;
Therefore,
I am imperfection-cry,
Plus
Frustration-sigh.

42. I AM AFRAID OF THEM

Death is an elephant.
I am afraid of elephant-strength.

Life is an ant.
I am afraid of ant-impotence.

Man is a king.
I am afraid of king-importance.

43. MY LIFE, MY LOVE

God-love loves me;
Therefore
God needs me.

Man-life needs God;
Therefore,
Man needs God.

My life has God the necessity,
My love is God the Reality.

44. MY ASPIRATION LOVES MY BODY

My aspiration loves my body
Because it obeys my soul.
My realisation loves my soul
Because it perfects my body.

45. TO DIVINITY'S SILENCE

Divine, to divinity's silence
He is.

Human, to humanity's sound
He is.

Animal, to animal's hunger
He is.

46. NOT YET FORSAKEN

Life does not want me.
Death does not need me.
I do not love me,
Yet I dare not forsake me.

47. THEY NEVER DIE

Your inner beauty
Never dies.

Your outer duty
Never dies.

Your supreme Reality
Cannot die,
Even after time itself is dead.

48. KNOW AND CONFESS

None but the good can be good:
My soul and my God
Definitely know it.

None but the bad can be bad:
My body and my vital
Confess it.

49. FAITHFUL

Faithful to the end
My heart shall be.

Faithful from the beginning to
   the end
My life shall be.

Faithful from before the
   beginningless beginning
To long after the endless end
My soul shall be.

50. LORD, I ASK YOU FOR ONE FAVOUR

"Lord, I ask You for one favour.
Tell me what You think of me."

Son, I ask you for one favour.
Believe me,
My Vision and Reality
Are eternally for You.

PART III

LORD, RECEIVE THIS
LITTLE UNDYING CRY

LORD, RECEIVE THIS LITTLE UNDYING CRY

1. LORD, RECEIVE THIS LITTLE UNDYING CRY

Lord, receive this little life.
It is all Yours.

Lord, receive this little world.
It is all Yours.

Lord, receive this little undying cry.
It is all Yours.

2. I ASSURE YOU

Love earth.
I assure you,
The world will not
Disappoint you.

Love Heaven.
I assure you,
Heaven will not
Desert you.

Love the inner man in yourself.
I assure you,
He alone can and will
Fulfil you.

3. DO YOU WANT TO BE

Do you want to be a ruler?
Then be just.

Do you want to be a lover?
Then be pure.

Do you want to be a teacher?
Then be sure.

Do you want to be another God?
Then be perfect.

4. HE IS WRONG

Who told you
That Heaven is indifferent?
He is totally wrong.

Who told you
That earth is weak?
He is completely wrong.

Who told you
That God does not have
The same concern
For earth-reality
And Heaven-dream?
He is absolutely wrong.

Who told you
That I do not love you most?
He is shamelessly wrong.

5. THEY PLEASE ME

Earth pleases me
With its stark hunger.

Heaven pleases me
With its giant feast.

God pleases me
With His stupendous Satisfaction.

6. POWER

You had occult powers;
Therefore
I adored you.

You have spiritual powers;
Therefore
I love you.

You will have love-power,
Therefore
I shall need you,
I shall need you only.

7. NATURALLY, I WAS FLABBERGASTED

My occultist friend
Told me that he could run
Faster than a deer.
Naturally, I was flabbergasted.

My yogi friend
Told me that he could
Make himself stronger
Than an elephant.
Naturally, I was fascinated.

My avatar friend
Told me that he became
A faithful dog
To carry my message to God
And God's Message to me.
Naturally, I was happy
   and grateful.

8. SHOW ME

Show me one beautiful thing
In the physical world.
I shall love you.

Show me one useful thing
In the vital world.
I shall love you.

Show me one fruitful thing
In the mental world.
I shall love you.

Show me one soulful thing
In the psychic world.
I shall love you.

9. DREAMERS AND LOVERS

Dreamers are lovers,
Lovers are dreamers.

Dreamers are lovers
In the world of light.

Lovers are dreamers
In the world of night.

Dreamers are lovers
In the world of perfection.

Lovers are dreamers
In the world of preparation.

10. A BIRD OF THE EAST

A bird of the East
Told me that God is beautiful
And that God loves singing.
I believed the bird.
I am now trying to be beautiful
    myself
In order to sing with God.

A bird of the West
Told me that God is powerful
And that God loves dancing.
I believed the bird.
I am now trying to be powerful
    myself
In order to dance with God.

11. THERE WE ARE FREE

In the heart of gratitude-sky
My body, my soul and I are free.
My body freely serves God.
My soul freely manifests God.
I freely enjoy God.

12. WE ARE UNKIND

The clouds are simply unkind
When they cover the face
Of the beautiful moon.

I am mercilessly unkind
When I ridicule the suffering
   world's
Bleeding swoon.

13. COMPLAINERS

Who complained?
The hungry animal in me.
Who complains?
The ugly human in me.
Who will complain?
The desperate divine in me.

14. INNER PROGRESS

My Lord is satisfied
With my inner progress,
But I am not.
My Lord is satisfied
With my outer success,
But I am not.

Why? Why?

I am not satisfied
Because
I am still unkind to my Lord.
I have not given Him
An opportunity to rest,
Which He so rightly deserves.

15. RENUNCIATION

Earth, I have renounced Heaven
Only to love you.
Heaven, I have renounced earth
Only to satisfy you.
I have renounced myself
Only to serve God.
Alas,
It seems I have not pleased
Any of them.
Alas,
Is it my poor fate
Or
Is it God's wise Choice?

16. GRATITUDE

He covered the length
   and breadth
Of the world
To see the face of gratitude.
What he saw
Everywhere
Was ingratitude-trees.

17. OUR NEEDS

I need patience-light.
You need tranquility-height.
I need forgiveness-might.
You need perfection-white.

18. INNER VISION

My inner vision tells me
That I am nearer than the nearest
To my Lord Supreme.

My outer sight tells me
That I am farther than the farthest
From my Lord Supreme.

Whom to believe?

If I believe my inner vision,
Pride tortures my heart.
If I believe my outer sight,
Frustration tortures my mind.

Therefore
I am not going to believe either.

19. HOPE

Sweet is my hope.
Pure is the life of my hope.

With my sweet hope
I try to reach the higher worlds.
With my pure hope
I try to fathom my inner worlds.

But alas,
In neither way do I succeed.
I fail,
I miserably fail.

20. PURITY

In purity's heart
Earth's saint-life grows.

In purity's soul
God-vision expands.

In purity's goal
Heaven and earth together dance.

21. HUMILITY

Humility
Is divinity
On the earth-plane.

Humility
Is perfection
In earth-achievements.

Humility
Is God's Satisfaction
In His cosmic Game, His
    universal Game,
His human and divine
    Self-transcendence Game.

22. JOY

Give joy;
Earth will be yours.

Take joy;
Heaven will be yours.

Become joy;
God will claim you,
Earth will need you,
Heaven will treasure you.

23. SELFLESSNESS

I had a dream.
In my dream
I became selflessness.
My dream disappeared
And
I became reality-story.
In my reality-story
I discovered myself
As the perfect perfection of
Earth-possessiveness,
Heaven-possessiveness,
God-possessiveness,
And
Self-possessiveness.

24. SURRENDER

To earth
I have surrendered my wisdom
So that earth-heart can be flooded
With my wisdom-light.

To Heaven
I have surrendered my
　ignorance-night
So that Heaven can claim me
And Heaven can utilise me
As its very own.

To God
I have surrendered my 'I-ness';
Therefore
God declares
Not only with His infinite Bounty,
But with His utmost Sincerity,
That I am another God.

25. PERFECTION

On earth
Perfection-plant grows.

In Heaven
Perfection-river flows.

In God
Perfection-sky glows.

26. ASPIRATION

There was a time
When I and my aspiration
Tried and cried
To see the Face of God.

But now my aspiration-God and I
Try and cry and cry and try
To see the face of one single real
　man.

27. ILLUMINATION

Earth-illumination is another
　name
For earth-transformation.

Heaven-illumination is another
　name
For Heaven-transcendence.

God-illumination is another name
For the liberation of earth-bound
　consciousness
And
The perfection of Heaven-free
　concern.

28. COMPASSION

He answered
Millions and millions of questions,
Earthly questions
And
Heavenly questions.
But one day
He was asked
What compassion was.
He remained silent,
For compassion is
God-property
And
God-reality.

29. INNER BEAUTY

Your inner beauty
Lies in your surrendering to God,
Your Beloved Supreme,
All that you are:
Gratitude-sea.

Your outer beauty
Lies in your unconditional smile
For suffering earth-life
And
Bleeding world-heart.

30. CONCERN

With my unlit and unconscious
Human concern
I break God's cosmic Rhythm
And ruin His cosmic Game.

With my illumined and conscious
Divine Concern
I not only serve God in
   His cosmic Game
But also add beauty and
   satisfaction
To His cosmic Game.

31. SIMPLICITY

Simplicity
Is God-Quality
In our inner life.

Simplicity
Is God-Capacity
In our outer life.

Simplicity
Is God-Beauty
In God's own Life.

32. DELIGHT

My body's delight
Is my ignorance-sleep.

My vital's delight
Is my aggression-sword.

My mind's delight
Is my suspicion-eye.

My heart's delight
Is my oneness-embrace.

My God's delight
Is the message of
My Self-transcending Beyond.

33. HEAVEN-RELUCTANCE

Earth is the mother
Of four billion things.
She gladly gives them away
To Heaven.

Heaven is the father
Of only one thing: smile.
He is reluctant to give it away
To earth.

34. LET ME LOVE

Let me love.
God will give me
His eternal Name.

Let me serve.
God will make me
A member of His Eternity's
   Game.

35. WHAT NEVER DIES?

What never dies?
The dissatisfied animal in me.

What never lives?
The satisfied human in me.

36. I CALL THEM SOMETHING ELSE

What you call
An emancipated life,
I call that very thing
God's Compassion-Smile.

Whom you call
A realised man,
I call that very man
God's Concern-Experience.

37. WE ARE GREAT

Heaven has received
My aspiration;
Therefore
Heaven is great.

Earth has received
My dedication;
Therefore
Earth is great.

My life has received
My liberation;
Therefore
My life is great.

38. FOLLOWERS

Earth follows Heaven;
Therefore
Earth is entitled to be happy.

Heaven follows earth;
Therefore
Heaven is entitled to be brave.

39. HEART-CONCLUSION

Mind-seclusion
Is not heart-conclusion.
Heart-conclusion
Is life's realisation
And
God's Victory-Satisfaction.

40. UNPLEASANT TRUTH

Unpleasant truth exposed:
You are reviled.
Unpleasant truth concealed:
You are revered.
Therefore
Be wise.
Act not like a first-class fool.

41. IF YOU HAVE TO FLY

If you have to fly,
Then fly for the highest Truth.

If you have to run,
Then run for the brightest Light.

If you have to dive,
Then dive for the deepest Delight.

42. AGES IN HIS FACE

When I saw
Age in his face
I cried and cried
Because
It was I who was responsible
For the age in his face.

When I saw
Ages in his face
I danced and danced
Because
It was I who had helped him
And made him the possessor of ages.

43. DO YOU HAVE ANYTHING ELSE?

O earth,
Do you have anything else
Save and except
Your blind God?

O Heaven,
Do you have anything else
Save and except
Your callous indifference?

O God,
Do You have anything else
Save and except
Your unknowable Sacrifice-Life?

44. YOURS IS THE GOD

Yours is the body
That sleeps.

Yours is the vital
That strikes.

Yours is the mind
That envies.

Yours is the heart
That bears.

Yours is the soul
That dreams.

Yours is the God
Who has a quenchless thirst.

45. TEARS

Tears that reveal your heart
Thrill God's Heart,
For that is the only time
When God can make you feel
That you are His own,
Very own.

46. HOW FAR CAN YOU TAKE ME?

O hope,
How far can you take me?

O faith,
How deep can you take me?

O cry,
How high can you take me?

O God,
How near can You make me?

47. NO DIFFERENCE

Where is the difference
Between
My earth and a warrior?
No difference,
Absolutely none.

Where is the difference
Between
My Heaven and a dreamer?
No difference,
Absolutely none.

Where is the difference
Between
My God and a lover?
No difference,
Absolutely none.

48. CHOICES

Here on earth
I had to choose either
The soul or material wealth.
I chose the soul.

There in Heaven
I had to choose either
God-manifestation on earth
Or
God-enjoyment in Heaven.
I chose God-manifestation on
    earth.

49. ALWAYS BE BUSY

Always be busy.
Earth's indolence
Will surrender to you;
Heaven's superiority
Will surrender to you.

50. BE PURE

Are you not sure
That God is everywhere?
Then just do one thing:
Try to be pure.
If you become pure,
Then you will see
That it is not just God
Who is everywhere
But
You, too, are everywhere.
Be pure, like God.
Your existence-light
Shall shine everywhere.

PART IV

LORD, I NEED YOU

LORD, I NEED YOU

1. NOT A FICTION

O aspiring humanity,
Liberation is not a fiction
Of your Heaven-imagination.

O illumining divinity,
Perfection is not a fiction
Of your earth-realisation.

2. TWO PLACES TO LIVE

Live in the doubting mind.
Yours is the torture of the
 sound-life.

Live in the crying heart.
Yours is the rapture of the
 silence-life.

3. HISTORICAL ACHIEVEMENTS

Yesterday's
Greatest historical achievement:
Man doubted God.

Today's
Greatest historical achievement:
Man loves God.

Tomorrow's
Greatest historical achievement:
Man shall become God.

4. GREATNESS AND GOODNESS

You are great
Only when you illumine
Your darkened mind.

You are good
Only when you feed
Your hungry heart.

5. DONKEYS AND TIGERS

O talkative humanity,
Your donkey-stupidity
Is torturing your soul.

O silent divinity,
Your tiger-cruelty
Is devouring your life.

6. JUST BECAUSE

Just because
You do not love God
You are ruthlessly challenged.

Just because
You love yourself
You are embarrassingly exposed.

7. EDUCATE YOURSELF

Educate your thoughts;
Earth-infancy will appreciate you.

Educate your mind;
Earth-maturity will admire you.

Educate your heart;
Earth-divinity will not only love
    you,
But need you, too.

8. WHERE IS YOUR COMPASSION-FLOOD?

O indifferent Heaven,
Where is your Compassion-flood
When I pass through death-pangs?

O jealous earth,
Where is your oneness-blood
When world-prosperity embraces
    my life,
Inner and outer?

9. LORD, I NEED YOU

Lord, I adore You
Because You are great.

Lord, I love You
Because You are good.

Lord, I need You
Because You are
My Eternity's All.

10. WHO ALWAYS SMILES?

Who always smiles?
Heaven-prince?
Not true.
Heaven cries for
    God-manifestation
On earth.

Who always cries?
Earth-beggar?
Not true.
Earth smiles at God
For God's sake.

11. MY LORD'S COMPASSION-FEET

Lord, I love Your Compassion-Feet
More than I love Your
   Illumination-Heart.
Why?
Because Your Compassion-Feet
Touch my ignorance-head
Long before Your
   Illumination-Heart.

12. JUST TELL ME ONCE

Lord, even if You have to tell me
   a lie
I won't mind.
I assure You I shall not be angry
   with You.
Just tell me once,
Only once,
That I am Your best instrument,
That I am Your most perfect child.

13. JOURNEY'S START, JOURNEY'S CLOSE

My Heaven-dreams are totally
   shattered,
My earth-realities are aimlessly
   scattered.
Yet
I love both Heaven and earth
Because
Heaven was my journey's start,
Earth is my journey's close.

14. IN SILENCE

In silence I grieve.
No, not even God consoles me.

In silence I smile.
No, not even ignorance-prince
ignores me.

15. SLEEP WITH A PRAYER

Sleep with a prayer.
You will wake up
At God's choice Hour;
You will grow into
God's highest Tower.

16. MY LOVE CROWNS YOU

My love crowns you,
My crown honours you,
My God needs you
And
Claims you.

17. MY SEARCH

My mind is in search of something
Great, very great.

My heart is in search of something
Good, very good.

My soul is in search of something
Perfect, absolutely perfect.

18. A FULFILLING PERFECTION

Heaven-beauty
Is an encouraging thought.

Earth-duty
Is an illumining will.

God-Compassion
Is a fulfilling perfection.

19. THE LIFE THAT IS STILL BECOMING

Earth's is the soul
That is still pursuing.

Heaven's is the goal
That is still achieving.

God's is the Life
That is still becoming.

20. FEARS

You are afraid to die.
I am afraid to live.
Earth is afraid to smile.
Heaven is afraid to share.

21. THE ETERNAL MASTER

I do not know
Who I am.
I do not know
Why I am not another God.
But I do know
That I can really love and serve
God
If I want to.
From now on
Let me love my God,
The eternal Beloved,
And
Serve my God,
The eternal Master.

22. I SHALL NOT BURY YOU

Darkness, I shall not bury you.
I shall ask light to transform you.

Ignorance, I shall not bury you.
I shall ask wisdom to befriend you.

Death, I shall not bury you.
I shall ask life to illumine you.

23. LORD, I SHALL SPEAK

Lord, I shall speak
Because You are divinely great.

Lord, I shall listen
Because You are supremely good.

Lord, I shall become
Because You are my Eternity's All.

24. ACROSS THE AGES

Across the ages
The human in us
Tried and failed.

Across the ages
The divine in us
Willed and became.

Across the ages
The Supreme in us
Cried and smiled,
And smiled and cried.

25. I REFUSE TO SPEAK

I refuse to speak to myself
Because I overestimate myself.

I refuse to speak to you
Because I underestimate you.

I refuse to speak to God
Because I have nothing new to say.

26. WAITING

What was I waiting for?
I was waiting for man to cry.

What am I waiting for?
I am waiting for God to smile.

What shall I be waiting for?
I shall be waiting for man
And God to barter their
    possessions.

27. I WANTED SOMETHING ELSE

This is not something I wanted;
I wanted something else.
I wanted God-Compassion.

This is not something I wanted;
I wanted something else.
I wanted earth-perfection.

28. I TELL THEM WHAT TO DO

I tell my inner world what to do:
Aspire and inspire.

I tell my outer world what to do:
Love God and become God.

29. JUST A THOUGHT

Just a thought of perfection
Can easily raise
Earth's God-Height.

Just a thought of satisfaction
Can easily transform
Earth's ceaseless pangs
Into Heaven's endless rapture.

30. I NEED THE DELIGHT

Oh let me serve!
I need the delight of service.

Oh let me love!
I need the delight of oneness.

Oh let me become!
I need the delight of
　God-satisfaction.

31. OPINIONS OF THE MIND

An old opinion of the mind:
God is great and complicated.

A new opinion of the mind:
God can be given
The supreme chance to say
　His say.

32. VISION, MISSION, PERFECTION

Vision wants to rest.
Mission wants to work.
Perfection wants to smile,
Perfection wants to serve and
　become
And become and serve.

33. LITTLE, LESS, LEAST

Little we see:
God-Truth.
Less we feel:
God-Love.
Least we are:
God-Perfection.

34. IN YOUR LIFE

It is in your face:
Earth-deception.

It is in your heart:
Heaven-Compassion

It is in your life:
God-Perfection.

35. BATTLES

Battles to be fought:
Self-immolation
And
Self-glorification.

Battles to be won:
Ignorance-frustration
And
God-Compassion.

36. LITTLE SORROWS, BIG SORROWS

His little sorrows:
He is unrealised,
He is imperfect.

His big sorrows:
God does not love him,
God does not need him.

37. ALTERNATIVES

Another place to stay
Is in humanity's heart.

Another thing to do
Is to love God.

Another way to realise God
Is to perfect oneself.

38. TWICE I WAS MISUNDERSTOOD

Twice I was misunderstood.
Once when I said to earth:
Heaven is my realisation-height;
Once when I said to Heaven:
Earth is my preparation-light.

39. I AM THINKING OF QUITTING THE WORLD

Why are you thinking of quitting
   the world?
Because the world does not need
   you?
Because the world does not love
   you?

"No. I am thinking of quitting
   the world
Because I see the world has
   no need for God,
For His Life of Light
And for His Heart of Love."

40. THE REALISATION OF IMPARTIALITY'S SUN

If you are greedy in your demands,
God will forgive you
And the world will forgive you.
But you will not forgive yourself
When the realisation of
   impartiality's sun
Dawns in your devoted mind
And surrendered oneness-heart.

41. YOUR BEST AND ONLY FRIEND

Your best friend is your
   only friend.
Your only friend is he who
   tells you
That you are not only of God
   for God
But you are unmistakably
The God of tomorrow.

42. WHEN GOD HIDES HIMSELF

When God hides Himself
You cry.
You try to find Him.
But do you know
That you have been trying
To hide from God for countless
   centuries?
What has God been doing?
He has been pleading with you
To come to the fore and replace
   Him
For He is tired.
He wants you to play His role.

43. CONFESS YOUR FOLLY

You confess your folly.
The world neither ridicules you
Nor appreciates you.
But God in you gets the
　opportunity
To help you in emptying yourself,
Your unconscious bondage-night.

44. A HEAVY WEIGHT

O earth, your weight of
　forgetfulness
Is considerably heavy;
Yet I try to lift you
　and your weight.

O Heaven, your weight of
　indifference
Is unimaginably heavy;
Therefore, I dare not lift you
　and your heaviest weight.

45. MY PILGRIM DAYS ARE OVER

My pilgrim days are over.
My days of searching are over.
My days of surrendering have
　begun.
My days of smiling and dancing
　have begun.
My days of God-service and
God-manifestation have begun.

46. ONE SOULFUL SMILE

One brave step is not too much
　to take.
Take one brave step toward
　your destined goal.

One kind word is not too much
　to say.
Say one kind word to the lost,
　orphaned world.

One soulful smile is not too much
　to offer.
Offer one soulful smile and
　transform the face of the world,
Within and without.

47. TRANSPORTATION OF LIFE

Transportation of life from below
　to above
Is the transformation of life,
Within and without.

Transportation of earth-cry from
　below to above
Is the perfection-manifestation of
　God's Smile,
Within and without.

48. NO U-TURNS

In the desiring life
There can be and there are
 U-turns.
But in the life of aspiration
There can be no U-turns.
Once you leave your earth home,
You have to reach your
 Heaven-home without fail,
For there is no U-turn,
Nothing of the sort.

49. INDIAN HOMES

There was a time when each
 Indian home
Cried for liberation from
 bondage-night.
But now each Indian home
Cries for freedom from
 starvation-hole.
There shall be a time when each
Indian home
Shall cry only for
God-Compassion,
God-Invocation
And God-Manifestation.

50. TRY, YOU CAN EASILY DO IT

Before another God manifests
 Himself,
Why don't you try to manifest
 yourself?
Before another God can love
 the world,
Why don't you try to love
 the world?
Before another God is needed
 by the world,
Why don't you try to offer your
 service to the world?
Try,
You can easily manifest yourself.
Try,
You can easily love the world.
Try,
You will be sorely needed by
 the world.

PART V

MY LIFE-TREE

MY LIFE TREE

1. MY LIFE-TREE

My life-tree
Is made up of my earth-hopes.

My life-leaves
Are made up of my earth-cries.

My life-flowers
Are made up of my earth-sighs.

My life-fruits
Are made up of my earth-failures.

2. THEY NEVER GET TIRED

My feet never get tired
No matter how many miles I walk.

My hands never get tired
No matter how long I work.

My heart never gets tired
No matter how many people
  I love.

But my mind always gets tired
The moment it tries to chase away
A fraction of a doubt.

3. NOT SUCH A DIFFICULT TASK

Try to arrange your thoughts.
It is not such a difficult task.

Try to control your thoughts.
It is not such a difficult task.

Try to conquer your thoughts.
It is not such a difficult task.

Try to surrender your thoughts
To the inner Pilot.
It is the easiest thing.
If you do it,
Then you do not have to
Arrange, control and conquer
Your thoughts.
It is all done.

4. THERE IS A DIFFERENCE

Love is love,
But there is a difference
Between my love for God
And my love for man.
My love for God
Is for my perfection light.
My love for man
Is for my expansion-right.

5. ARE THEY HAPPY?

Is your earth happy?
Not exactly,
But it tries to be happy.

Is your Heaven happy?
Yes, it is.
It is always happy.
It seems it can never be otherwise.

6. TWO EXCEPTIONS

Man is an exception.
He does not have to be
As beautiful as an angel
In God's Vision-Light.

Angels are exceptions.
They do not have to be
As responsible as man
In God's Creation-Reality.

7. THOUGHTS

A God-lover's thoughts:
Acceptance-light,
Rejection-night.

A God-server's thoughts:
Service-opportunity,
Satisfaction-necessity.

My thoughts:
Transformation-duty,
Perfection-beauty.

8. I WILL DO IT FOR YOU FREE

I will do it for you free:
I will help you realise God.

I will do it for you free:
I will help you reveal God.

I will do it for you free:
I will help you manifest God.

9. FOUR STRANGERS

A stranger to my will:
Failure.
A stranger to my thought:
Success.
A stranger to my life:
Rejection.
A stranger to my death:
Acceptance.

10. HOW CAN I FORGET YOU?

How can I forget you?
It was you who told me
About God.

How can I forget you?
It was you who told me
That God loves me deeply.

How can I forget you?
It was you who told me
That God needs me sincerely.

11. BELIEVE IT OR NOT

Believe it or not,
You are all I know.

Believe it or not,
You are the only one I love.

Believe it or not,
You are the only one to care
   for me.

Believe it or not,
My soul and my body
Exist only to please Your Feet.

12. WHAT MORE DO I NEED?

You love my heart.
What more do I need?

You feed my soul.
What more do I need?

You transform my body.
What more do I need?

You cancel my death.
What more do I need?

13. NO OTHER CHOICE

I have no other choice
Save Yours, my Lord!

I have no other voice
Save Yours, my Lord!

I have no other bondage-night
Save Yours, my Lord!

I have no other freedom-light
Save Yours, my Lord!

I have no other Perfection-Depth
    or Satisfaction-Height
Save Yours, my Lord!

14. WE TOUCH

Lord, I touch You
Only when I feel that You are
    proud of me.

Lord, You touch me always,
Even when You are not
Proud of me at all.
Lord, Your kindness
Fascinates my heart
And
Baffles my mind.

15. WHAT PULLED YOU DOWN?

What pulled you down?
Your wild vital-horse.

What pulled him down?
His stupid donkey-mind.

What pulled me down?
My blind insecurity-cat.

16. MY CREATOR

Who made my heart?
God the Lover.

Who made my soul?
God the Seer.

Who made my life?
God the Knower.

17. WHEN I HEAR TIME

When I hear time's footsteps,
I ignore them.

When I hear time's call,
I ignore it.

When I hear time's threat,
I ignore it.

But when I hear time's pitiful cry,
I love it
And
Die with it.

18. I SPEAK FORTHRIGHTLY

I speak without being biased:
You are not meant for
    God-realisation.

I speak without being prejudiced:
He is not meant for God-journey.

I speak without being falsely
    modest:
My realisation will take care
Of you both.

19. TWO ERRORS

A very common error:
When people say that they do not
Need God.

A very uncommon error:
When people think and declare
That they are all
    God-realised souls.

20. A DEATHLESS MEMORY

Your life's gratitude
Has a bad memory.

Your heart's gratitude
Has a short memory.

Your soul's gratitude
Has a deathless memory.

21. A LIFE OF INNOCENCE-FUN

A life of innocence-fun
I love.

A life of wisdom-light
I love.

A life of perfection-service
I love.

A life of gratitude-song
I love.

22. HE WHO IS

He who thinks
Is great.
He who acts
Is good.
He who loves
Is perfect.
He who is
Is Eternity's
   Transcendence-Beyond.

23. TWO MOST DEPLORABLE MISTAKES

You achieved your God-realisation
Far too soon;
Therefore, it was not as mature
As it could have been.

You started your
   God-manifestation
Far too soon;
Therefore, you are encountering
Too many uncompromising,
Undivine and hostile forces.

So you see, you have not made
   one,
But two most deplorable mistakes
In this life.

24. A WORLD UNQUIET

Three things have made your
   world unquiet:
Doubt-net,
Jealousy-cloud,
Anxiety-arrow.

Only two things can save you
And your world:
Your love of God-Compassion,
Your surrender to God-Decision.

25. ONE MAN IN A HUNDRED

One man in a million
Cares to hate me.
Am I not lucky?

One man in a thousand
Cares to love me.
Even a little is better than
   nothing.

One man in a hundred
Cares for my advice.
Unlike billions and trillions,
I, at least, am needed.

26. FOUR CURSES

Four tremendous curses:
God does not need me really.
Ignorance loves me mercilessly.
My mind leads me ceaselessly.
I hide my imperfections
　shamelessly.

27. THREE INNER MEALS

God-Light feeds me;
Therefore
I am strong.

God-Delight feeds me;
Therefore
I am dynamic.

God-Compassion feeds me;
Therefore
I am perfect.

28. NOTHING BUT AMAZEMENT

Nothing but bewilderment
When I look at earth-face.

Nothing but suspicion
When I look at human race.

Nothing but amazement
When I look at
　God's unconditional Grace.

29. I LOVE MY LIFE

I love my service-life
Because it is pure.

I love my oneness-life
Because it is sure.

I love my satisfaction-life
Because it is perfect.

30. MY EARTH-FACE

My dream-journey
I have begun.
My reality-shore
I shall soon reach.
And then I shall value
My earth-face:
God-Grace.

31. I TOLD YOU

I told you,
No dependence on human
    tongues,
You fool.

I told you,
No independence of God-Grace,
You fool.

I told you,
Do not go elsewhere for
    God-realisation;
Stay with me through Eternity.
You disobeyed me,
You fool.

32. NOT OUR FAULT

Your heart is precious.
Who does not know it?
Not your fault,
If others do not know it.

His soul is gracious.
Who does not know it?
Not his fault,
If others do not know it.

My life is prosperous.
Who does not know it?
Not my fault,
If others do not know it.

33. IT REQUIRES NO EFFORT

It requires a superhuman effort
To elevate one's consciousness.
It requires no effort,
One can do it with effortless ease,
To love God
And surrender oneself to God
And finally to become
    God Himself.

34. BORN IN HIS DIVINITY-EYE

All saints were born
Here, in his purity-heart.
All Yogis were born
Here, in his luminosity-soul.
All Avatars were born
Here, in his divinity-eye.

35. IN MY CAREER

In my career as a human being
I loved God,
The unrealised man.

In my career as a divine being
I love man,
The unmanifested God.

36. WHY WASTE YOUR TIME?

Why waste your time on earth?
Earth is so unreceptive!

Why waste your time in Heaven?
Heaven is so indifferent!

Why waste your time with
   yourself?
You are so afraid of
   self-transcendence!

37. HOW MANY CAN BOAST?

How many can boast?
Not you in the least.
You do not love God.
Not he in the least.
He does not serve God.
Not I in the least.
I do not think of God.

38. THE SERMON

The God-sermon for yesterday:
Give and give.

The man-sermon for today:
Take and take.

The God-and-man-sermon for
   tomorrow:
Give and take.

39. YOU WILL BE HAPPY

Step beyond your mind.
You will be really happy.

Remain inside your heart.
You will be divinely happy.

Fly with your soul.
You will be supremely happy.

40. GOD BLESSED MY JOURNEY

En route to earth
I met God.
He blessed my brave journey
With His Pride supreme.

En route to Heaven
I met God.
He blessed my fruitless journey
With a heavy sigh.

41. AN EXIT EVERYWHERE

There is an exit
Everywhere on earth
When I cry and surrender.

There is an exit
Everywhere in Heaven
When I dream and promise.

42. HIDE NOT

Hide not, my soul.
I have to see your God-Beauty.

Hide not, my heart.
I have to see your God-Grace.

Hide not, my God.
I have to see my own
Perfection-Face.

43. MY BONDAGE

I am heart-tied;
Therefore
I cannot speak.

I am mind-tied:
Therefore
I cannot teach.

I am vital-tied;
Therefore
I cannot breathe.

I am body-tied;
Therefore
I never dare to leave.

44. I DREAMT

Lord,
I dreamt I saw Your Face.
It was really beautiful.

Lord,
I dreamt I loved Your Smile.
It was really meaningful.

Lord,
I dreamt I felt Your Grace.
It was really fruitful.

45. WHAT SHALL I DO?

What shall I do with my
　　leisure-life?
It has shortened my life.

What shall I do with my
　　pleasure-life?
It is killing my life.

What shall I do with my
　　doubt-life?
It has kept my Lord
Away from my life.

46. MORNING PRAYERS, EVENING GIFTS

My morning prayers to God:
Give me and satisfy me.
God's evening gifts to me:
His Satisfaction-Smile
And
His Perfection-Height.

47. ATTACHMENTS

One hundred attachments —
How can I love God?

One thousand attachments —
How can I see God?

One million attachments —
How can I think of God?
I really do not know.

48. UNHELPED BY MAN

Unfrequented by man:
My heart-door.
Unchallenged by man:
My spirit's height.
Unhelped by man:
My God-manifestation —
Dream
   and
Promise.

49. WHERE DO MY HEAVEN-DREAMS DWELL?

Where do my
   Heaven-dreams dwell?
They dwell in my
   heart's glowing ecstasy.

Where do my earth-realities live?
They live in my mind's
   fruitless secrecy.

50. NO DIFFERENCE

The difference
Between man and animal
Lies in the kindness-life.

The difference
Between God and man
Lies in the forgiveness-life.

I see no difference
Between an animal and me
When I live in the body.
I see no difference
Between God and me
When I live in the soul.

PART VI

MY PROMISE TO GOD

MY PROMISE TO GOD

1. MY PROMISE TO GOD

My promise to God
I tell you in secret supreme.
Don't let anybody else know.
If they hear, they will laugh and
    laugh.
My promise is God-manifestation.
And I tell you,
This promise of mine
Has been a steady,
Illumining
And fulfilling relationship with
    God.

2. AN AUTHENTIC POWER

The peace-voice that breaks
Is an unauthentic power.
I knew it and I know it.

The love-choice that builds
Is an authentic power.
I knew it and I know it.

3. YOUR HEART WAS ECLIPSED

Your heart was eclipsed by sin;
Therefore
Your body is exposed by failure.
And what is sin?
The strangling waves of your
    imagination-clouds.

4. TWO BETRAYERS

You are betrayed
By two things.
Do you know what they are?
They are your imagination-hunger
And
Your temptation-choice.

5. DRUNK WITH JOY

Drunk with joy
I saw the Face of God.

Drunk with love
I touched the Heart of God.

Drunk with peace
I sat
Plus
Stayed at the Feet of God.

6. MY DAWN DIED WITH ME

My dawn died.
My dawn died with me
Reluctantly.

My noon dies.
My noon dies with me
Dauntlessly.

My evening shall die.
My evening shall die with me
Cheerfully.

7. GOD'S GOD-COMPASSION

God calls it my divinity;
I call it God's God-Reality.

God calls it my perfection;
I call it God's God-Compassion.

8. WHY DO YOU QUARREL?

Why do you quarrel with your
    indolence?
Who created it, after all?
You and your own stupidity-life.

Why do you quarrel with your
    failure?
Who created it, after all?
You and your own
    insincerity-mind.

9. WHEN HE WAS A BABY GOD

When he was a baby God
Everybody loved him.

When he was a grown-up God
Everybody needed him.

When he was an old God
Everybody claimed him,
Even the real God Himself.

10. THE ROAD FROM DREAM TO REALITY

All his nights are dreams,
All his days are realities.
His aspiring life
And
His surrendering heart
Have built the road
That leads from the dream-sky
To the reality-land.

11. LORD, SAVE ME

Lord, save me.
I talk too much.

Lord, save me.
I know so little.

12. YOU SAY

You say
You are a God-lover.
I do not know
Why or how you can afford
To hesitate so much.

You say
You are a God-fulfiller.
I do not know
Why or how you can afford
To sleep so much.

13. WHEN I THINK

When I think,
God shouts at me from a distance:
"Stop thinking."

When I concentrate,
God runs to me and says:
"Continue, continue, My son."

When I meditate,
God says:
"I am so happy that you know
   the supreme secret."

When I contemplate,
God says:
"For both of us nothing can ever
   remain undone."

14. MY LORD SUPREME BLESSED ME

My Lord Supreme blessed me
Not once, not twice
But thrice.
His first blessing gave me
   the power
To forget the hurting past.
His second blessing gave me
   the power
To face the challenging present.
His third blessing gave me
   the power
To welcome the fast-approaching
   future.

15. A MANTRA IS A SEED

A mantra is a seed.
It develops into a plant.
The plant grows into a tree.
The tree bears fruits.
But who can eat them?
Only he who is sincerity's delight
And
Intensity's height.

16. CAPACITY AND NECESSITY

God, You have the capacity
And I have the necessity.
Let us try to become one.
I tell You,
Once we are fulfilled,
You will be proud of Your capacity
And I shall be proud of my
   necessity.

17. I AM SURE

I am sure of only three things:
My love
Is my God-application,
My service
Is my God-consecration,
My surrender
Is my God-perfection.

18. WHAT CAN YOU DO FOR ME?

Inspiration, what can you do for me?
"I can tell you how near God is."

Aspiration, what can you do for me?
"I can tell you how great and good
   God is."

Realisation, what can you do for me?
"I can tell you how sincerely
   and desperately
God needs you."

19. GOD RESPECTED MY INDIVIDUALITY

God respected my individuality.
He never acted like an intruder.
He waited and waited
Until I finally invited Him.
Since God was so nice to me,
Let me also try to be nice to Him.
Let me unreservedly
Respect, honour and adore
His individuality's
Universality.

20. THE ILLUMINING VISION

What is intuition?
The illumining vision of the seer.

What is realisation?
The perfection-sun of the Yogi.

21. I LOVE PATIENCE

I love patience
Because
It is mild.

I love patience
Because
It is sweet.

I love patience
Because
It is subtle.

I love patience
Because
It is enduring.

I love patience
Because
It overcomes all the buffets of
   my life.

22. ALAS, WHAT CAN I DO?

I worship God.
The world does not care even to
   believe it.
Alas, what can I do?

I love the world.
God does not say that He at least
   believes it.
Alas, what can I do?

23. I AM FLEXIBLE

O earth, I am flexible.
I can be what you want me to be.
Just tell me what I should do.

O Heaven, I am alive.
I am eagerly waiting
To hear from you
How to please you
In your own way.

24. REALITY AND TOTALITY

What is love?
Love is the reality
Of the life-force.

What is oneness?
Oneness is the totality
Of Eternity's creation vast.

25. GOD-LIFE

God-life is not the mere control
Of the physical breath.
God-life is the perfect regulation
Of the life-energy
In the soul's inimitable way.

26. REVERE AND LOVE

The difference between
Religion and Yoga is this:
Religion reveres God
Openly and loudly.
Yoga loves God
Soulfully and unreservedly,
Constantly and unconditionally.

27. MY TEACHERS' LESSONS

My desire-teacher taught me:
"Life is matter-enveloped."
I believed him.
I really did.

My aspiration-teacher is teaching
 me:
"Life is soul-enclosed."
I believe him.
I really do.
I shall always believe him.

28. HELPERS

Helpers invisible
All-where to be found.
Helpers visible
Nowhere to be found.
This is my unmistakable discovery.
I share it with you
Soulfully and unconditionally.

29. ANOTHER NAME FOR JUSTICE

Another name
For God's Justice
Is constant Forgiveness-light.

Another name
For man's justice
Is continuous forgetfulness-night.

30. LEISURE

Leisure is not relaxation.
Leisure is not recreation.
Leisure is the continuous flying
 of our fulfilling
 and fulfilled
 attention.

31. DON'T DENY IT!

Vital, don't deny it!
I saw you with your
  friend pression
This morning.

Mind, don't deny it!
I saw you with your
  friend suspicion
Last night.

Heart, don't deny it!
I saw you with your
  friend insecurity
Only yesterday.

You three are the least
  reliable friends.

32. THREE SWEET DISCOVERIES

I am the discoverer
Of three sweet discoveries:
God likes me.
God has real concern for me.
God considers me
A faithful instrument
Of His Vision-Will.

33. A THING TO BE

Aspiration
Is a thing to learn.
Illumination
Is a thing to feel.
Realisation
Is a thing to be.

34. HIS SMILE, HIS CRY

His soul-smile immortalises
The mortal part in me.
His heart-cry feeds
The flame divine in me.

35. THE SEER-POET

The seer-poet smiles in the
  morning
At the rising sun
And cries in the evening
For the illumining moon.

The Yogi-poet glows
In realisation-day
And lives
In perfection-light.

36. ON THEIR WAY

A liberated man
Is on his way to silence-soul.
A realised man
Is on his way to perfection-goal.

37. TWO INVENTORS

God invented heart.
Man invented fear.
Why do we say that
Man is inferior to God?
God invented mind.
Man invented doubt.
Why do we say that
God is superior to man?
God created life.
Man created death.
Why do we not say that
Both are equal?

38. IN THE EMPTINESS OF THOUGHT

In the blackness of thought
I saw my failure-night.

In the whiteness of thought
I saw my success-day.

In the emptiness of thought
I saw my progress-sun.

39. DIG, PLOUGH AND SOW

Don't dig the past, don't dig.
The past is a painful experience.

Don't plough the barren field of
   the mind, don't plough.
The mind is a division-frustration.

Don't sow the dissatisfaction-seed
   in the heart, don't sow.
The heart is a satisfaction-light.

40. MIND AND HEART SPEAK

My mind says to my heart:
Heart, I have capacity.
But I want your ability, too.

My heart says to my mind:
Mind, I have no capacity of
   my own.
My capacity is all God-capacity.
How I wish
To share with you my
God-given
Capacity!

41. I DID NOT BELIEVE

The God of Creation
I saw,
But I did not believe my eyes.

The God of Illumination
I felt,
But I did not believe my heart.

The God of Perfection
I became,
But I did not believe my life.

42. THE RENUNCIATE, I

He had his head
Clean-shaven.
God showed him
A smiling face
But
Suffered a bleeding heart.

43. THE RENUNCIATE, II

He had his alms-bag
Hanging from his shoulder.
God said,
"Son, you
Can do something better."

44. THE RENUNCIATE, III

He was clad
In a saffron robe.
God's Eye gave God
A painful experience.

45. THE RENUNCIATE, IV

He had a staff
In his hand.
God was searching
For His Satisfaction-Smile.

46. THE RENUNCIATE, V

Normal and natural
He stood soulfully facing God.
God in no time embraced him,
His whole earth-existence.

47. WHY I AM SO HAPPY TODAY

You want to know
Why I am so happy today.
I am telling you why:
My inner urge
To capture and embrace
The hiding inner man
Has become insistent, irresistible.

48. IN THE WILD CONFUSION-MARKET

Suddenly he slipped away
From home
To embrace the life of solitude
And see the Face of God.
He saw God.
Where?
In the wild confusion-market
Of village-ignorance.

49. EVERYTHING IS PREORDAINED

No such thing as chance
In God's world.
In God's scheme of things
Everything is divinely and
    supremely
Preordained.
God wanted me to realise Him
And I have fulfilled
His Eternity's Desire.

50. ARE YOU A MASTER?

Are you a Master?
Then earth loves you.

Are you a path-finder?
Then Heaven loves you.

Are you a lover?
Then God not only loves you
But needs you, too.

PART VII

SOUND BECOMES, SILENCE IS

1. LOSE AND CHOOSE

To lose everything
Is to need God, God alone.
To choose God
Is to lose nothing, absolutely nothing.

2. OUR POWER OF REALISATION-LOVE

When the son grows old,
His parents' love does not diminish.
When the sun disappears
Behind the screen of evening-night,
Our love does not diminish.
Absence of beauty's light
And
Light's beauty
Can never take away
Our power of realisation-love.

3. JOURNEY

Simplicity-boat I have.
Sincerity-boatman I am.
Purity-passenger I accept.
Divinity-shore we reach.

4. HIS DREAMS

His infant dream:
He will see the Face of God.
His adolescent dream:
He will become
The best instrument of God.
His adult dream:
He will please God
In God's own Way.

5. LET ME TELL YOU THE DIFFERENCE

Let me tell you
The difference
Between
My God-realisation
And
My God-manifestation.
When I think of my God-realisation,
I think of a wrestler
Fighting a weakling.
When I think of my God-manifestation.
I think of a weakling
Fighting a wrestler.

6. HE LOVED HIS FLATTERERS

He loved his flatterers.
He loves his fault-finders.
He will love
Without fail
His consciousness-transformer.

7. WE SHALL NEVER KNOW

Not because I want to
But because I have to
I teach the world.
Why?
God alone knows.
I shall never know.
Not because I have to
But because I want to
I learn from the world.
Why?
I alone know.
The world will never know.

8. WE ARE FOOLS

You are a superlative fool.
You think
God-realisation is not meant
   for you.
He is a superlative fool.
He feels
God-realisation is nothing but
   self-deception.
I am a superlative fool.
I tell the world
That God-realisation
Is not enough to make me smile.

9. GREAT AND GOOD

You wanted to become great.
Therefore
God's endless Compassion
Has made you great.
I wanted to become good.
Therefore
God's breathless Necessity
Has made me good.

10. KILLED AND REVIVED

Everybody knows
That his sweeping ambitions
Killed him.
But nobody knows
That his surrendering love of God
Has revived him
And immortalised him.

11. THEREFORE HE NEEDED GOD

Wounded he was.
Therefore
He needed God the Compassion.
Helpless he was.
Therefore
He needed God the Power.
Dying he was.
Therefore
He needed God the Smile.

12. LOOK, LOOK!

Look, look!
Something is waiting for you.
Subordinate your
Own interest.
God-profit is all yours.

13. I WORK, I LOVE

I work always.
For whom?
For my lower self.
I love always.
Whom?
My higher Self.

14. I NEED YOU

O earth-success,
I need you
Unmistakably.
O Heaven-progress,
I need you
Desperately
Immediately
Eternally.

15. WHEN YOU ARE CRYING

When you are smiling
I see how beautiful you are.
When you are crying
I see how meaningful you are.

16. WHEN I REALLY *AM*

My body dances
When I *do*.
My heart dances
When I *become*.
My soul dances
When I really *am*.

17. LIFE AND DEATH FOLLOW ME

Both life and death follow me.
Life follows me
To hear
My success-story.
Death follows me
To see
My progress-smile.

18. I LOVE EVERYTHING

I have nobody to love me,
Not even God.
But
I love everyone and everything,
Including myself,
Including my undying
Ignorance-life.

19. LETHARGY-NIGHT, ENERGY-DAY

Forgive and forget
Lethargy-night.
Remember and prosper
In energy-day.

20. O FAITH, HELP ME!

No more, no more doubt.
Faith, help me!
I want to conquer my enemy.
Today I shall turn
My shameless enemy
Into a helpless slave.
O Faith, help me, help me!

21. FOR A MOMENT ONLY

Lord, can You not come for a
   moment only,
To see how grateful I am to You?
Lord, can You not come for a
   moment only,
To see how proud I am of You?
Lord, do come.
You do not have to spend
Much time with me.
Come for a moment only.

22. INDIAN DEVOTION, AMERICAN LOVE

Indian devotion
Has made his heart pure.
American love
Has made his life sure.

23. CLIMB UP WITH ME

Climb up with me,
O earth-sorrows.
Climb down with me,
O Heaven-smiles.
Stay with me
Wherever I am,
O God-concern.

24. AN UNFINISHED GOD, AN UNFINISHED MAN

You are an unfinished God.
You need my dedication-moon.
I am an unfinished man.
I need Your Compassion-Sun.

25. GOD AND I TALK

In silence-room
God talks to me
About His complete
    Manifestation.
In sound-room
I talk to God
About my constant realisation.

26. THE ONLY WAY TO PLEASE THEM

Let me weep.
This is the only way
I can please Mother Earth.
Let me smile.
This is the only way
I can please Father Heaven.
Let me become.
This is the only way
I can please
Both
My Father's Head
And
My Mother's Heart.

27. WHEN GOD SPEAKS TO YOU

Open your eyes
When God speaks to you.
He wants to share His greatness
   with you.
Open your heart
When God speaks to you.
He wants you to claim
   His goodness
As your very own.

28. DO YOU KNOW?

Do you know what makes
   you smile?
It is your aspiration-flame.
Do you know what makes
   God smile?
It is His Compassion-moon.

29. PERFECTION-FRUIT LASTS

Aspiration-tree grows.
I knew it. I knew it.
Realisation-flower blossoms.
I know it. I know it.
Perfection-fruit lasts.
I shall know it. I shall know it.

30. I AM SURE YOU MUST KNOW

Earth-ignorance, you are
   something
Far from what I love.
I am sure you must know it
By this time.
Heaven-compassion, you are
   something
Far from what I shall ever deserve.
I am sure you must know it
By this time.

31. THE FACE OF HAPPINESS

The face of happiness
I have.
The happiness of face
I do not have.
Nobody can have it
Except the all-loving
And all-forgiving God.

32. STAY ALWAYS IN A BIG WORLD

Your mind is a small world.
Do you not know that?
Your heart is a big world.
Do you not know that?
Don't be a fool.
Stay always in a big world
To manifest God powerfully,
Convincingly and universally.

33. NO PATIENCE

Life has no patience.
Death has no patience.
Heaven has no patience.
Only earth-surrender
Has patience
To offer to animal-man
And
God-man alike.

34. OUR ENERGY-LIVES

Your life was repulsive energy.
His life was expressive energy.
My life is progressive energy.
Just believe me, don't doubt me
If you really want to know
   the truth.

35. TWO CONQUERORS

Tear-drops
I have discovered
To conquer Heaven.
Smile-sea
I have invented
To conquer earth.

36. IF NOT TODAY

Lord, if not today,
Sometime You can show me
Your Compassion-Beauty.
Lord, if not today,
Sometime I can show You
My perfection-necessity.

37. WHO IS THE ULTIMATE JUDGE?

Who is the ultimate Judge,
God or I?
If it is I,
Then God has to surrender
To my ignorance-sea.
If it is God,
Then I have to surrender
To God's Compassion-moon.
Lord, let us enter into a friendly
   competition.

38. TWO QUESTIONS

Two questions I always have
   asked:
God has everything;
Why does He need me?
I have nothing;
Yet why do I not need God?

39. DO YOU KNOW THE DIFFERENCE?

Do you know the difference
Between you and me?
When I think of you
I live in an inferior universe.
When you meditate on me
You live in a superior universe.

40. I WANT TO AVOID MYSELF

I have done many things in this
　　life.
Now I want to do only one thing.
I want to avoid myself.
I want to avoid myself,
My real reality-existence.

41. FLOAT WITH THE CURRENT

Float with the current
If you have nothing to give.
Float with the current
If you have only to dance aimlessly.
Float not with the current
If you have something to give.
Float not with the current
If you have something to give
　　unreservedly.

42. WORLD-ADMIRATION

You want world-admiration
Although
You do not deserve it.
He needs world-admiration
But
He does not want it.
I want world-admiration
But
I do not need it.

43. OLD HABITS, NEW HOBBIES

God loves me.
This is one of His old habits.
I love God.
This is one of my new hobbies.

44. TRY NOT TO PROVE

Try not to prove.
Try to improve.
Try not to grow.
Try to glow.

45. PREACH AND PRACTISE

In the inner world
My Lord preaches the necessity
Of sound-life
And I practise it
In the outer world.

In the outer world
I preach the necessity
Of perfection-life
And my Lord practises it
In the inner world.

46. TRUTH ULTIMATELY TRIUMPHS

Prowess eventually fails.
Justice eventually fails.
Truth ultimately triumphs,
Eternally and universally lives.

47. WEALTH AND STRENGTH

Material wealth
And
Physical strength
Have made him unbearably
    vainglorious.
One day
Spiritual wealth
And
Psychic strength
Will make him unreservedly
    prosperous.

48. TRY A LITTLE MORE

Lord, I do not want to live
    on earth.
I have tried;
I have failed.
"Son, try a little more.
Who knows,
You may succeed.
And then I can afford to smile."

49. A PERFECT GENTLEMAN

Death, I don't need your presence.
"Man, it is not because you need
But because you deserve my
    presence
That I arrive at your door.
I always want to act
Like a perfect gentleman."

50. LORD, WHY DO I TALK?

Lord, why do I talk?
When shall I realise
That my talking
Invariably brings disgrace
To my soul-light on earth?

51. DUTY BEFORE PLEASURE

Duty before pleasure:
If we do that
We can achieve and
Treasure God-Light.
Pleasure before duty:
If we do that
We shall dance death-dance
With death
Before
We sing life-song
With life.

52. WHO SHALL DECIDE?

Who shall decide
When Masters disagree?
When Masters disagree
The disciples must decide.
They must go to the
Supremely superior Master,
The only real Master, God.

53. DO I BELIEVE IT?

God's Will
Leads me to God
To make me another world-saviour.
Do I believe it?
Perhaps.
Do I appreciate it?
Perhaps.

54. HASTE MAKES WASTE

Haste makes waste.
Therefore
I do not haste.
I do not want to waste
My love of God.
Waste makes haste.
Therefore
I do not waste.
I do not want to haste
My proud judgement of
    the world.

55. IT IS NEVER TOO LATE

It is never too late
To aspire.
My heart feels it.
It is never too early
To realise.
My soul knows it.

56. TOMORROW NEVER COMES

Tomorrow never comes.
Therefore
I am appreciating
My earth-beauty
Today
And
God is demanding
My Heaven-duty
Today.

57. WE LOVE BECAUSE

I love God
Because
I need Him.
God loves me
Because
He has to love
His Self-extension-reality.

58. PURE AND SURE

God is pure.
Therefore
He touches my heart.
I am sure.
Therefore
I teach myself
And God, too,
How to regulate our lives.

59. THEY TELL ME

My sight tells me
Where God is.
Therefore, I am lucky.
My faith tells me
How God is.
Therefore, I am happy.
My love tells me
Who God is.
Therefore, I am peaceful.

60. YOU ARE DEFINITELY AS GOOD AS GOD

You may or may not be
As great as the world thinks
But you are definitely
As good as God
Eternally is.
Who has made you so good?
God.
Why?
Because He desperately needs
Another God
To play with Him.

61. I AM TRYING

As a doctor
I am trying to cure myself,
    my ailments.
As a lover
I am trying to love myself,
    my ignorance.
As a server
I am trying to serve myself,
    my reality.

62. MY IGNORANCE-FRIEND

He who will not be always
  with me
Is definitely against me.
Who is he?
My present ignorance-friend.
But I am not a bad man, after all.
I shall unmistakably
Do something for my
  ignorance-friend —
When I am illumined,
When I am perfect.

63. TO SEE THE FACE OF GOD

To see the Face of God
I enter into you.
To see the Heart of God
You enter into me.

64. SEEK AND FIND

I have sought.
God asks me to remain silent.
I have found.
God asks me to remain silent.
What did I seek?
My perfection.
What did I find?
God-perfection.

65. WHEN YOU ARE PURE

When you are pure
God-Joy is with you.
When you are sure
You are all alone.
No, not even your best friend,
Earth-pleasure, is with you.

66. THE DANCER

Yesterday
I danced with Life.
Life does not know how to
  dance well.
Today
I am dancing with Death.
Death is a hopeless dancer.
Tomorrow
I shall dance with God.
We both will be able
To teach each other.

67. WHAT SHALL I BE?

Yesterday
What was I?
God's Love-touch.
Today
What am I?
God's Oneness-light.
Tomorrow
What shall I be?
God's Perfection-height.

68. I AM ANGRY

My earth is not aspiring.
Therefore
I am angry with my earth.
My Heaven is not smiling.
Therefore
I am angry with my Heaven.
My God is not descending.
Therefore
I am angry with my God.

69. I TALK

In the morning
I talk and thus empty
My ignorance-vessel.
In the evening
I talk and thus feed
My aspiration-plant.

70. LIKE IT OR NOT

Like it or not,
Think of God.
Like it or not,
Think more of God
Than of yourself.
Like it or not,
Think only of God.

71. SILENCE, PLEASE!

Silence, please!
God is coming.
I hear His Voice.
Silence, please!
God is come.
I see His Face.
Silence, please!
God needs you,
You alone,
Desperately.

72. IF YOU DO NOT ABIDE BY THE LAW

If you do not abide by the law
You will be at the feet of the law.
If you abide by the law
You can not only sit
On the top of the law
But also far transcend
The law
Easily.

73. THE PATIENT ONES

Patient seed,
I admire your aspiration-duty.
Patient flower,
I admire your illumination-beauty.
Patient fruit,
I admire your perfection-reality.

74. HE IS LOST

He is lost, totally lost.
Because of his stupidity
He is unfit for earth;
Because of his impurity
He is unfit for Heaven.
He is lost, totally lost.

75. HE OFFERED TO GOD

In his first year
He offered to God
His promise-smile.
In his hundredth year
He offered to God
His failure-tears.

76. THE FOOL

Life's courtesy
He ignored.
Indeed, he was a fool.
Death's discourtesy
He challenged.
Indeed, he was a fool.

77. THE PRACTICAL DESIRE

To see the Face of God
Is a theoretical desire.
To become the Heart of God
Is a practical desire.
God cares for the practical desire
Infinitely more than for the
  theoretical desire.

78. YOU ARE MORE THAN WORTHY

Lord, I am unworthy of You.
"Son, you are and you are not.
If you look behind,
You are unworthy of Me.
If you look forward,
You are more than worthy of Me,
My Love, Joy and Pride."

79. FAMILY DIVINE

Mother Mary's feet were pure.
Father Joseph's eyes were sure.
Their son Jesus' heart was both
Pure and sure.

80. TRUTH'S TRUE ECSTASY

There was a time
When falsehood's false ecstasy
He enjoyed.
But now
Truth's true ecstasy
Enjoys him triumphantly.

81. LET ME DARE AND DARE

Let me dare and dare;
One day ignorance will surrender.
Let me dare and dare;
One day ignorance will aspire
And then in peace
I shall retire.

82. I AM THE ROAD

When I think of God
I am the road to nowhere.
When I love God
I am not only the road
But also the goal
Here,
There,
Everywhere.

83. AM I NOT SUPERIOR TO GOD?

Once in a thousand days
I pray to God,
Yet God is satisfied.
Once in a thousand years
God appreciates me,
Yet I am satisfied.
Therefore
Am I not superior to God?
My Lord God says I certainly am.

84. TRY TO SATISFY

Try to satisfy humanity.
You certainly can.
Try to satisfy yourself.
Indeed, this is an impossible task.
Try to satisfy God.
Lo, you have already done it
And you have done it quite well.

85. TWO SUPREME SECRETS

I have explored
Two supreme secrets:
I do not need myself
As much as God needs me.
God not only says
But He actually feels
That I am as perfect
As He is.

86. THE ONLY PERFECT SOLUTION

Him to obey
Is unhappiness.
To Him to surrender
Is torture.
Him to love
Is the only
Perfect solution.

87. A GIFT

God-realisation
Is not a chance.
God-realisation
Is a gift
To satisfy
My necessity-hunger.

88. BEFORE AND AFTER

Before God-realisation
I was allowed to act
Only inside the Heart of God.
After God-realisation
I am allowed to act
Not only inside the Heart of God
But also inside the body of
   ignorance.

89. I PREFER

I prefer glowing faith
To mere belief.
Therefore
I am happy.
I prefer fulfilling surrender
To mere glowing faith.
Therefore
I am complete.

90. THE ONE WITHOUT EQUAL

For God-realisation
There was none to equal his zeal.
For God-manifestation
There was none to equal his
   frustration.

91. SILENCE SPEAKS, SILENCE LEADS

Silence is not silent.
Silence speaks.
It speaks most eloquently.
Silence is not still.
Silence leads.
It leads most perfectly.

92. I HATE MY LIFE

I hate my dream-life
Because
It is not true.
I hate my reality-life
Because
It is not false.

93. THEY SURPRISE YOU

Your ignorance
Surprises you.
His recognition
Surprises you.
My acceptance
Surprises you.
God's Compassion-Illumination
Surprises you.

94. HUNGER HE CONQUERED

Earth-hunger he conquered
To please and fulfil God.
Heaven-hunger he conquered
To please and reveal man.

95. THEY DO NOT DESERVE

Earth does not deserve
My obedience.
It deserves my acceptance.
Heaven does not deserve
My obedience.
It deserves my co-operation.

96. FATE APPROACHES US

Fate approaches us.
It shows us its supremacy.
We show our supremacy,
Not by reproaching fate
But by transforming it
Totally
And
Perfectly.

97. THREE HEARTS TO LOVE ME

Three hearts to love me:
Simplicity-heart,
Sincerity-heart,
Purity-heart.
One soul to illumine me:
Perfection-soul.

98. REMEMBER HIM

Remember him.
He served you
With breakfast-light.
Remember him.
He served you
With luncheon-delight.
Remember him.
He served you
With dinner-height.

99. I REALLY FEEL SORRY FOR YOU!

I really feel sorry for you!
When I look at you during
  the night
I see in you the eye of tired day.
When I look at you during the day
I see in you the surrendered heart
  of night.

100. WHEN

Beauty glows
When love expands.
Divinity triumphs
When sincerity flows.

101. I CHOSE TIME

I chose time.
Therefore
I saved time.
Because
I have time
I shall pray and meditate
To stay only in God's Life
Of Silence-sound.

102. EXCHANGE

He has exchanged
His existence-cry
For God's Compassion-Light.
God has exchanged
His Existence-Delight
For his hope-sea.

103. FREEDOM AND CONSCIENCE

Freedom of conscience:
Perfection-choice.
Conscience of freedom:
Satisfaction-silence.

104. IN THEIR EYES

In the eyes of humanity
I am a forgotten man.
In the eye of divinity
I am a forgotten God.
In my own eye
I am a forgotten nothingness-sound.

105. GENERALLY HE PRAYS

Generally he prays.
Therefore
God-Compassion descends.
Generally he meditates
Therefore
God-Pride smiles.

106. MY LIVES

My earth-life
Is a bondage-slave.
My Heaven-life
Is a freedom-voice.
My God-life
Is the fulfilment of my
   perfection-choice.

107. EMOTION

Emotion of the inferior man:
It breaks before it builds.
Emotion of the superior man:
It just builds and builds.
Emotion of the God-man:
It just appreciates, claims
   and owns.

108. MY EARTH-LIFE

My earth-life
Was a chain of obligation-
   frustration.
My earth-life
Is a road of division-separation.
My earth-life
Shall be perfection-destruction.

109. O CURIOSITY-INSPECTION

O curiosity-inspection,
Start looking within.
You have the same God-goal,
The same God-love,
The same God-perfection
As I have.
Only one thing:
You care not to know
What you have.
But
You care to know
Whether what I have is real
　or
A false fascination-light.

110. PERFECTION-SUN

The human in him does not know
That there is a limit
To his imperfection-night.
The divine in him eternally knows
That there is no end
To his perfection-day,
　perfection-light,
　perfection-sun.

111. NO DIFFERENCE

No difference
Between
Ignorance-conqueror
And
God-lover.
No difference
Between
My earth-height
And
My Heaven-light.

112. TO BREAK THE LAWS

My life wanted to break
Earth-laws.
It failed to break;
Therefore
It badly suffers.
My life wanted to break
Heaven-laws.
It succeeded in breaking;
Therefore
God-Compassion cares not
For my heart-arbour.

113. LORD, I MARVEL

Lord, I marvel at Your
Compassion-shower.
"Son, I marvel at your
Ignorance-power.
I marvel at your
Ingratitude-tower."

114. NOTHING DIES, NOTHING LIVES

Nothing dies,
Not even your little stupidity.
Nothing lives,
Not even your stupendous
　sincerity.

115. O PROCRASTINATION-KING

O doubt, O procrastination-king
Give up role, give up art.
Become
Earth's ever-loving Light
And
Heaven's ever-transcending
　Dream.

116. TWO DWELLING PLACES

Live in the mind.
You do not know
Who you are.
Live in the heart.
You will know
Not only who you are
But also
What God has for you
And
What God is to you.

117. MY TWO WORLDS

Truth, where are you
In my vast world?
Falsehood, where are you not
In my tiny world?
Desire, how long will you remain
The bridge between
My tiny world
　and
My vast world?

118. NO MAN

No man
Is wise enough
To see
God-height in man.
No man
Is pure enough
To live always
In God's Height of
   Self-transcendence.

119. NO MATTER WHAT

A desire-man
Is bound to complain
No matter what he has
And
What he is.
An aspiration-man
Is bound to smile
His satisfaction-smile
No matter what he has not
And
What he is not.

120. SMILE WITH GOD-SATISFACTION

Cry for life-perfection.
You will enter into the world
Of incessant expectation.
Smile with God-satisfaction.
Lo, you have entered into
   the world
Of God-realisation
To enter into the world
Of God-manifestation.

121. DON'T CRY!

Don't cry!
Your heart will one day love the
   God-face.
Don't cry!
Your eye will one day win the
   God-race.

122. DO YOU HAVE FAITH?

Do you have faith in God?
"Yes, I have."
Then you will climb up to
   God-height.
Do you have faith in yourself?
"Yes, I have."
Then soon you are bound to be
Another God.

123. ASCEND, DESCEND

Ascend, ascend!
At the end of your
 Heaven-bound journey
You will grow into
God the Eternal Lover.
Descend, descend!
At the end of your
 earth-bound journey
You will grow into
God the Eternal Beloved.

124. NEITHER CAN TRULY LIVE

No disciple can truly live
Without some sincerity within.
No Master can truly live
Without some divinity within.

125. MY BEAUTIFUL BODY

God played His role:
He created my beautiful body.
I am now playing my role:
I am contributing ugly impurity
To my body.

126. MY HELPLESS BODY

I played my role:
I created my helpless body.
God is now playing His role:
He is contributing
 perfection-strength
To my body.

127. MY EXPANDING VITAL

God played His role:
He created my expanding vital.
I am now playing my role:
I am contributing dark frustration
To my vital.

128. MY DEPRESSION-VITAL

I played my role:
I created my depression-vital.
God is now playing His role:
He is contributing giant
 determination
To my vital.

129. MY SEARCHING MIND

God played His role:
He created my searching mind.
I am now playing my role:
I am contributing poison-doubt
To my mind.

130. MY RESTLESS MIND

I played my role:
I created my restless mind.
God is now playing His role:
He is contributing climbing
   aspiration
To my mind.

131. MY LOVE-HEART

God played His role:
He created my love-heart.
I am now playing my role:
I am contributing destruction-fear
To my heart.

132. MY INSECURITY-HEART

I played my role:
I created my insecurity-heart.
God is now playing His role:
He is contributing
   satisfaction-oneness
To my heart.

133. MY IMMORTAL SOUL

God played His role:
He created my immortal soul.
I am now playing my role:
I am contributing taut bondage
To my soul.

134. MY HELPLESS SOUL

I played my role:
I created my helpless soul.
God is now playing His role:
He is contributing
   perfection-fulfilment
To my soul.

135. HUMAN LOVE, DIVINE LOVE

Human love is a ready tongue.
God's Compassion-light forgives
Its ceaseless flow.
Divine love is a ready hand.
The human mind suspects
Its unconditional offer.

136. YOU CAN NEVER MEASURE

Pray to God.
You can never
Overestimate your necessity-cry.
Meditate on God.
You can never
Measure your opportunity-train.

137. STRANGER-FOES

Objection is a stranger-foe
To the searching mind.
Rejection is a stranger-foe
To the loving heart.
Indifference is a stranger-foe
To the aspiring soul.

138. GOD IS MINE

God is mine.
I know it. I know it.
This is my mind's absolutely
   honest opinion.
I am God's.
I feel it. I feel it.
This is my heart's absolutely
   firm conviction.

139. OPPORTUNITY AND SUCCESS

Opportunity is not success
But success
Is the recognised or unrecognised
Fulfilment of opportunity.

140. A SUPREME SECRET

I tell you a supreme secret:
The invocation divine of
   aspiration-flames
Every human being
With no exception
Must accept
Either in the immediacy of today
Or
In Eternity's future.

141. MY SELF-TRANSCENDENCE

Yesterday
I was the realisation
Of imperfection-night.
Today
I am the revelation
Of perfection-light.
Tomorrow
I shall be the manifestation
Of satisfaction-height.

142. O GOD-NECESSITY

O God-necessity in me,
I am ready.
Do accept me.
If I fail,
You can reject me.
But now do give me
A chance, at least.

143. ABSENCE OF PAIN, ABSENCE OF JOY

The absence of pain
Is not the presence of joy.
The absence of joy
Is not the presence of pain.
The absence of pain
Is the presence of our love for
  God.
The absence of joy
Is the presence of our love for
  ourselves only.

144. I HAVE TWO WORLDS

I have two worlds:
Human and divine.
My human world is too small
And it always wants to remain
  small.
My divine world is larger than the
  largest,
And yet it always longs
For its self-enlargement.

145. MY POOR FRIEND GOD

Unlike my human friends,
My poor friend God has
  completely
Run out of His Advice-drops.
What now He has
Is His Compassion-sea.

146. MY TWO FRIENDS

Regularity, my friend,
You think of me
With your concern-shower.
Punctuality, my friend,
I think of you
With my surrender-power.

147. I TREASURE

Somnolence-world my body
　treasures.
Aggression-world my vital treasures.
Desire-world my mind treasures.
Love-world my heart treasures.
Delight-world my soul treasures.

148. DESIRE, WILL AND SURRENDER

Desire feels
It can eventually create a
　new world.
Will knows
It can immediately create a
　new world.
Surrender reveals the mystery
　supreme
That God has already created
　for it
A new world.

149. I HAVE YET TO DISCOVER

My soul-essence is God:
That I have already discovered.
My life-substance is God:
That I have yet to discover.
God alone knows
When I shall succeed
Or
Whether I shall ever succeed at all.

150. HIDE-AND-SEEK

My faith and doubt
Played hide-and-seek.
Finally my faith realised
That it wanted to play a new
　game: God-game.
Doubt admitted it was an
　unhealthy game
And gave up the game altogether.
It did not care for any other game.

151. HE WILL WIN IN THE END

He will win in the end.
Although he is failing
In loving the world
In God's own way,
He will win in the end.

He will win in the end.
Although he is failing
In becoming supremely divine
In God's own Way,
He will win in the end.

152. GOD'S SATISFACTION-FOOD

I am of God.
Therefore
My gratitude-plant
Loves God.
I am for God.
Therefore
God's Satisfaction-food
Immortalises me.

153. DO NOT LET THEM WORRY YOU

Do not let them worry you.
After all,
Fear is a tiny ball,
Doubt is a tiny plant
And
Impurity is a tiny pond.
You can throw the fear-ball away,
Far away.
You can uproot the doubt-plant,
You easily can.
You can stop swimming in the
　　impurity-pond;
Immediately you can.

154. WITH SUCH SPEED

With speed faster than a thought
I have cast aside
My earth-experience.
With speed slower than a tortoise
I have embraced
My Heaven-realisation.

155. SPEND SOME TIME

Spend some time in feeling.
Heaven is not as indifferent
As you feel.
Spend some time in seeing.
Earth is not as stupid
As you see.

156. HIS IS THE SMILE

His is the smile
That knows how to forget
His incessant earth-pains.
His is the cry
That knows how to multiply
His infinite Heaven-gains.

157. PLEASE ACCEPT ME

Please accept me
As your disciple.
I shall not disappoint you.
I was born with sincerity.
Please accept me
As your Master.
I shall not deceive you.
I shall die with sincerity.

158. YOU WANT PROGRESS

You want success.
Lo, success has come to you.
You want progress.
Then you must go to progress.
Where is it?
It is inside the heart
Of God's Satisfaction-smile.

159. YOUR MEMORY IS FAILING YOU

Your memory is failing you.
You did love God.
Your memory is failing you.
You did consider God
Your best Friend,
Your only Friend.

160. MY WILL-LIFE

My thought-life
Chases humanity-fox away.
My will-life
Embraces divinity-dog
    unconditionally.

161. HE IS BUSY

His heart is busy
With his past follies.
Let us illumine him.
His mind is busy
With his future glories.
Let us warn him.

162. THEREFORE, I AM

I am on God's side.
Therefore,
I dare to become,
And I will become.
God is on my side.
Therefore,
I am,
I eternally am.

163. HE IS PREPARED

He is prepared
To abandon even Mother Earth
Because
She is too slow.
He is prepared
To abandon even Father Heaven
Because
He is too fast.

164. I AM PROUD

I am proud of my mind
Because
It is powerful enough
To lessen my earth-pangs.
I am proud of my heart
Because
It is powerful enough
To hasten the Hour of God.

165. A SACRED SMILE

My earth-life
Is a secret sorrow
Of my dying heart.
My Heaven-life
Is a sacred smile
Of my challenging soul.

166. TWO DECLARATIONS

I look at God and declare:
Truth is all.
God looks at me and declares:
All is truth.

167. I DO NOT NEED ANY OTHER

I do not need
Any other weapon
To conquer my frustration-night.
My dedication-weapon
Is enough.
I do not need
Any other path
To reach my realisation-goal.
My meditation-path of
    surrender-light
Is more than enough.

168. THE BEGINNING AND THE END

The end is important,
And not the beginning.
Look at your totally transformed
Vital life.
The beginning is as important
As the end.
Look at your soul-promise
To Mother Earth
For God-manifestation.

169. NEWS TRAVELS

Sad news travels fast:
I forget to feed humanity.
Good news travels slowly:
I love to serve humanity.

170. WHAT WE ASK IS IMPOSSIBLE!

What you ask is impossible!
I cannot give you my duty's smile.
What I ask is impossible!
You cannot give me your
    heart's cry.

171. NO TIME LEFT

No time left.
Please forgive me, Lord,
Immediately.
No time left.
I have accepted you, Lord,
Unreservedly.

172. WHEN THEY DIE

When my success dies,
Forgetfulness deletes it.
When my progress dies,
God revives it
Immediately
And
Cheerfully.

173. THEY WERE HAPPY

Earth was happy
When I heard
About the Goal-seed.
Heaven was happy
When I saw the face
Of the Goal-plant.
God was happy
When I became
The Goal-Tree.

174. SWEET DREAMS, HARD REALITIES

Sweet dreams, my sweet dreams,
Are you really real?
I think you are.
Hard realities, my hard realities,
Are you not always false?
I know you are.

175. GOD HAS NOT SAID A WORD

God has not said a word.
It is I who have told you
That God does not care for you.
I hate myself for this
    inconsiderate lie!
God has not said a word.
It is you who have told me
That God does not need me.
I hate you for this deliberate lie!

176. ALAS!

My body sees no door.
Alas!
My mind sees no shore.
Alas!
My vital wants to roar.
Alas!
My heart fails to soar.
Alas!

177. THE LIFE OF FAILURE

Yours is the life
Of bombastic failure.
I feel sorry for you.
Mine is the life
Of soundless failure.
You may not feel sorry for me,
But God does.
He always feels sorry for me.

178. WHAT HAS THE COURAGE?

What has the patient courage?
My life-seed.
What has the immediate courage?
My life-tree.
What has the eternal courage?
My life-fruit.

179. MY HEAVEN-LIFE, MY EARTH-LIFE

My Heaven-life
Was a birthless and
   deathless dream.
I enjoyed it.
My earth-life
Is an uncharted fruitless waste.
I am trying to enjoy it.

180. BELIEVE IT OR NOT

Believe it or not,
I have seen God, the real God,
Inside you, inside
Your purity-body.
Believe it or not,
I have seen God, the real God,
Inside you, inside
Your beauty-eye.

181. ESSENCE AND SUBSTANCE

My soul-essence
Is the perfection-seed.
My life-substance
Is the determination-soil.

SOUND BECOMES, SILENCE IS

182. MY RAINBOW-LIFE

My animal life
Is a rainbow of binding ropes.
My human life
Is a rainbow of encouraging hopes.
My divine life
Is a rainbow of fulfilling scope.

183. ONE IN EACH

One God-realised man
In every self-sacrifice!
One God-manifested man
In each perfection-flame!

184. YOU SAW THE LIGHT OF DAY

Not to swerve from the
   path of truth
You saw the light of day.
To serve man and become perfect
You saw the light of day.
To become the Satisfaction-silence
   of God
You saw the light of day.

185. THREE TORTURES

Fear, what is it?
A self-imposed torture.
Doubt, what is it?
A self-betrayed torture.
Impurity, what is it?
A self-ridiculed torture.

186. THE TREE OF TIME

Silence, what is it?
The root of time.
Sound, what is it?
The trunk of time.
Perfection, what is it?
The tree of time.

187. NO DOOM

No doom, no doom,
I want you to bloom.
No sigh, no sigh,
I want you to fly.
No satisfaction, no satisfaction,
I want you to be all perfection.

188. THEY ARE STRONG

Faith is strong
In God-Assurance.
Aspiration is strong
In God-Compassion.
Love is strong
In itself.

189. WHAT KIND OF MASTER?

What kind of Master are you?
My own Master never told me
That I was a hopeless case.
What kind of disciple are you?
My own disciples always
   worship me
As God, the only God.

190. THREE NEW DREAMS

I have three new dreams.
I wish to share them with you
If I may:
God wants me to accept you;
God wants me to teach you;
God wants me to perfect you.

191. ONE DAY THEY WILL LEARN

One day
They will learn
To love her.
Her ignorance-disciples
Will love her.
One day
They will learn
To value her.
Her aspiration-disciples
Will value her.

192. WHAT ARE YOU DOING, MASTER?

What are you doing, Master?
"I am thinking of you."
Is that so? Thank you, Master.
What were you doing
Before I came, Master?
"I was thinking of you."
Is that so? Thank you, Master.
What will you be doing, Master,
After I leave you?
"I will be thinking of you."
Is that so? Thank you, Master.

193. MY THREE TEACHERS

Necessity taught me
How to become a Yogi.
Integrity has taught me
How to become a poet.
Curiosity is teaching me
How to become an artist.

194. A THOUGHTLESS YOGI

He was a thoughtless youth.
He needed compassion-flood
From the world at large.
He is now a thoughtless Yogi.
The world is now at his feet
For the illumination-sea.

195. IN YOUR BABY-HEART

Not in your giant mind
But in your baby-heart
I see not only the Heart of God
But also His whole Body
And His real Soul.

196. GOD-NEWS

Where is God?
Where you are.
How is God?
It entirely depends
On your mental state.
Who is God?
Undoubtedly the life-loving
Self in you.

197. YOU WILL SAVE AND ILLUMINE

If you want to live
Only for yourself,
You will die
Before you close your eyes.
If you want to live
For God and God alone,
You will save and illumine
Not only your little world,
But God's entire world.

198. HOW CAN I, WHY SHOULD I?

How can I put up
With the world
When I know perfectly well
That the world is doing
  everything wrong?
How can I?
How can I?
Why should I shut up
When God is asking me
To teach the world constantly
And
Unconditionally?
Why should I?
Why should I?

199. LORD, I AM SICK

Lord, I am physically sick,
Vitally sick, mentally sick.
When are You going to cure me?
"Son, you do not have to remind
  Me
Of My Duty.
And I am telling you,
As long as you are not spiritually
  sick,
I do not worry about you."

200. I FIX MY EYES

I fix my soulful eyes
On my Master's feet
For compassion.
I fix my soulful eyes
On my Master's heart
For liberation.
I fix my soulful eyes
On my Master's eyes
For perfection.

PART VIII

THE SILENCE-SONG

THE SILENCE-SONG

1. FROM HEAVEN HE CAME

From Heaven
He came into the world
With an unconscious headache.

From earth
He will return to Heaven
With a conscious fever.

2. DEVOTION

My devotion is sweet
When I touch your beauty's feet.

My devotion is sweeter
When I feel your beauty's eyes.

My devotion is sweetest
When I clasp your beauty's heart.

3. GRACE

I do not know what
   God's Grace looks like.
I do not know what
   God's Face looks like.
But I do know that my
   God's Grace
Is all for me,
That my God's Face
Is all within me.

4. SINCERITY

God told me that it was
   my insincerity
That spoke when I said that
I had not seen the Face of God
And had not felt the Love of God.

God told me that it was
   my sincerity
That spoke when I said that
God-realisation I have,
God-revelation I am working on,
God-manifestation I badly need.

5. CONSCIOUSNESS

Concentrate
To lengthen your
   consciousness-realm.

Meditate
To heighten your
   consciousness-sky.

Contemplate
To deepen your
   consciousness-sea.

6. LIGHT

"Light,
Where are you?
What are you?
Who are you?"

Where am I?
I am in your revelation-smile.
What am I?
I am your earth-teacher and
  Heaven-friend.
Who am I?
I am your Eternity's soul
And
I am your Infinity's goal.

7. BEAUTY AND LUSTRE

God's Beauty tells me that my
  outer world
Is pure.
God's Lustre tells me that my
  inner world
Is sweet.

My outer world's beauty tells God
That it is all for Him.
My inner world's lustre tells God
That it is all of Him.

8. POWER

Physical power I used
To see how indispensable I was.
Vital power I used
To see how great I was.
Mental power I used
To see how vast I was.
Psychic power I used
To see how kind I was.
My own power I used
To see how unconditional I was.
God-Power I used
To cry with earth's heart
And
Smile with Heaven's soul.

9. LOVE

In the outer world
Love is duty's might.
In the inner world
Love is duty's height.
In God's world
Love is God's unhorizoned Vision,
God's growing and glowing
  Reality.

10. INNER POISE

God gave him inner poise
But now he has replaced it
By outer voice.
In the future,
God will replace his outer voice
By His yet unknown Choice.

11. REVELATION

When you are in the body-life
You conceal and conceal.
When you are in the soul-life
You reveal and reveal,
You fulfil and transcend
And transcend and fulfil.

12. INNER SURETY

Inner surety
God's fulfilling Promise in me,
God's glowing Reality in me,
My own inner Immortality
   for God.

13. PROGRESS

"My Lord, have I made any
   progress in my
Inner life and my outer life?"
Yes, My child, you have made
   progress in both
Your inner life and your
   outer life.
I see the progress of your
   inner life
In the increasing depth
Of your silence-life.
I see the progress of your
   outer life
In the expanding smile
Of your sound-revelation.

14. SWIFT PROGRESS

Swift is your progress
When you discover your soul's
   colour.
Swifter is your progress
When you discover your soul's
   mission on earth.
Swiftest is your progress
When you discover that your soul
Is your earth-child and
   Heaven-Father.

15. SATISFACTION

My mind was satisfied
When it saw the satisfaction-seed.

My heart was satisfied
When it became the
　satisfaction-tree.

My soul was satisfied
When it ate the satisfaction-fruit.

I was satisfied
When I became the
　surrender-flower
For God-satisfaction.

16. WHAT IS LIFE?

What is life?
Body's life is possession-smile.
Vital's life is destruction-frown.
Mind's life is suspicion-might.
Heart's life is dedication-light.

17. ILLUMINATION

I had my God-illumination
In yesterday's ignorance-night.
I have my psychic illumination
In today's ignorance-pride.
I shall have my
　mental illumination
In tomorrow's ignorance-failure.

18. TRIALS

Trials and tribulations are
　for those
Who have forgotten
The might of surrender divine.
Success and progress are for those
Who claim and treasure God's
Love-experience on earth
And God's Light-experience in
Heaven
As their own, very own.

19. GROWTH

Cry if you want to see your
　inner growth.
Smile if you want to see your
　outer growth.
Dance before your failure-night
And your success day;
You will see the growth
Of the Absolute Supreme.

20. GOD-PERFECTION

Involution is God-Perfection
In inconscience-night.
Evolution is God-Perfection
In man's Heaven-bound flight.

21. INSECURITY

Insecurity is not
My helplessness-beauty.
Insecurity is
My stupidity-sterility.
Insecurity is
My God's undying sigh.

22. EACH BIRTHDAY

Each birthday
Of an unaspiring man
Is the destruction-dance of death.

Each birthday
Of an aspiring man
Is the ever-increasing
   Satisfaction-Smile of God
In His Vision's self-transcendence
   height.

23. DEATH, WILL YOU COME TO ME?

Death, if I don't speak to God
Will you come to me?
"No!"

Death, if I don't love God
Will you come to me?
"No!"

Death, if I feel a sincere need
   for you
Will you come to me?
"No!"

Then when will you come to me?
"I shall come to you
Only when God asks me to feed
   you,
Embrace you and immortalise
   you."

24. SANCTITY

Sanctity, sanctity,
You are my darkening body's
   necessity.
Sanctity, sanctity,
You are my blossoming soul's
   divinity.
You are my perfecting God's
   Reality.

25. HIM I WORSHIP

Him I worship
Because he told me
That I need God-Love.
Him I worship
Because he told me
That God does need me
Sleeplessly,
Compassionately
And
Unconditionally.

26. I AM AFRAID OF BEAUTY

I am afraid of earth-beauty.
It is nothing but ugliness.

I am afraid of Heaven-beauty.
It seems it is all-devouring power.

I am afraid of God-Beauty.
It tells me that it will eclipse
My long-treasured individuality.

27. DO YOU WANT TO BIND YOUR CONSCIOUSNESS?

Do you want to bind your
   consciousness?
Easy, just feed your jealousy-sister.
Do you want to blind your
   consciousness?
Easy, just feed your
   impurity-brother.

Do you want to liberate
   your consciousness?
Easy, just feed your
   Compassion-mother.
Do you want to immortalise
   your consciousness?
Easy, just feed your
   Salvation-father.

28. COMPASSION

Compassion, compassion.
My earth-compassion
Feeds my sacrifice-flames.

Compassion, compassion.
My Heaven-compassion
Feeds my satisfaction-sun.

Compassion, compassion.
My God-Compassion
Feeds my perfection-goal.

29. THE SILENCE-SONG OF SELF-TRANSCENDENCE

I love you
Not because you are exceptionally
  great.
I love you
Not because you are exceptionally
  good.
I love you
Because you constantly sing
The silence-song of
  self-transcendence.

30. YOU GAVE ME ONLY ONE HEART

Lord, You gave me only one heart.
I use it constantly
Only for You.
How then can You ask me
To use it for Your creation as well?
Lord, either give me one more
  heart,
One totally separate heart
To love Your creation with,
Or
Allow me to do
What I have always been doing
Cheerfully and devotedly,
Although You are so nasty to me
  at times.

31. A BIG PERHAPS

"I really do not know
Why I love you still.
I really do not know
Why I need you still."

My child, I do not know either.
A big perhaps:
In the inner world
We love each other unreservedly.
A bigger perhaps:
In the outer world
We need each other constantly.

32. A DELIBERATE LIE

At last I have realised
That I am telling a deliberate lie
When I say that I really and truly
  love God.
If I really and truly loved God,
I could not have blamed
His vast body, creation,
Constantly and bluntly.

33. WHY AM I SO FOND OF YOU?

"Lord, is it because You are great
That I am so fond of You?
Lord, is it because You are good
That I am so fond of You?"

No, your reasons are incorrect.
You are fond of Me for another
  reason.
You are fond of Me
Because in Me you see
Your own fulfilled capacity.

34. LORD, OPEN YOUR EYES

"Lord, You always ask me
To keep my eyes open.
How is it that You never
Keep Your Eyes open?
Just open Your Eyes and see
How I am suffering.
I really want to die.
Your world does not want me,
Your world does not need me.
It only knows how to torture me
Mercilessly and constantly."
My child, world-despair has
  possessed you,
But I always claim you
As my Eternity's own.

35. MY BODY TELLS YOU

My body tells You, Lord
Not to scold me.
My body feels that I need
A little more rest.
I tell You, Lord,
That if I am allowed
To get up at my own time
I shall love You,
I shall serve You,
I shall even glorify You.

36. SCOLDING IS NOT A HEALTHY EXPERIENCE

My mind tells You, Lord,
To scold me in private
If You really have to.
I need not tell You, Lord,
That scolding is not a healthy
  experience
For the one who scolds
Nor for the one who is being
  scolded.

37. SCOLDING DOES NO GOOD

My vital tells You, Lord,
Not to scold me.
I know I always do something
    wrong,
But when You scold me
It does me no good.
After all, who has changed his life
By being scolded?
No one!
Therefore, love me, Lord,
Love me even more,
Especially when You are tempted
    to scold me.

38. MY HEART TELLS YOU TO SCOLD ME

My heart tells You, Lord,
To scold me when I do anything
    wrong.
What both of us want from
    my life
Is perfection-delight;
Therefore, Lord, scold me.
I deserve it; I need it.
My sense of perfection
Badly needs it.

39. HIS ENVY-LIFE

His envy-life never dies!
There was a time
When he envied the
    world-champion athletes.
There was a time
When he envied the
    world-philosophers
    and saints.
And now whom does he envy?
He envies his soul in its purest
    beauty.
He envies his God in His absolute
    Perfection.

40. REMINDERS

Each flower reminds me
Of what I can eventually become.
Each fruit reminds me
Of what I eternally am.

41. FRIEND

Yesterday I desired
To be earth's friend.
I knew I deserved it.

Today I am desiring
To be Heaven's friend.
I think I deserve it.

Tomorrow I shall prove
To be my own friend,
My real friend.
I hope I deserve it.

42. UNNEEDED

Despair, I do not need you.
You are too weak.
Sadness, I do not need you.
You are long-dead.

43. EARTH-NECESSITY, HEAVEN-REALITY

Achieve and become:
Indeed, this is the earth-necessity.
Become and achieve:
Indeed, this is the Heaven-reality.

44. SINNERS

Earth, you have sinned
By hiding my God-realisation.

Heaven, you have sinned
By ignoring my God-realisation.

God, you have sinned
By not allowing me
To equal You.

45. TWO PURE EYES

Two pure eyes:
One eye silently tells me
I am of God's Eternity.
Another eye loudly tells me
I am for God's Infinity.

46. OFFERINGS

A sunless day offers me
Heaven's helpless tears.
A lifeless night offers me
Earth's hopeless hopes.

47. ENJOYING GOD-LOVE

He enjoyed God-love
To ascend and transcend.
He enjoys God-love
To build and shelter.
He shall enjoy God-love
To serve humanity's
Heart-pangs
And Divinity's
Soul-smile.

48. WHEN I JUDGED

When I judged God,
God smiled at me.

When I judged Heaven,
Heaven warned me.

When I judged earth,
Earth devoured me.

49. SILENCE I NEED

Earth-silence I need
To see the inner man in me.

Heaven-silence I need
To love the inner man in me.

God-silence I need
To become the inner man in me.

50. FOR MY SAKE

Earth, for God's sake, ascend.
Heaven, for God's sake, descend.
God, for my sake, condescend
To give earth the needed capacity
And Heaven the needed
   responsibility.

PART IX

SILENCE-SEED AND SOUND-FRUIT

SILENCE-SEED AND SOUND-FRUIT

1. INNER STRENGTH

Either I shall have to
Cry like a child
Or I shall have to
Smile like a child.
These are the only ways
To constantly gain inner strength.
There are no other ways.
When I cry like a child
Or smile like a child,
Lo, inner strength becomes mine.

2. JOY

A human life of joy
Is a life of and for
God's Satisfaction-Toy
In humanity,
In His Universal Reality.

3. ONENESS

Oneness with the past
Is our oneness with
   frustration-night.

Oneness with the present
Is our oneness with
   hesitation-night.

Oneness with the
   fast-approaching tomorrow
Is our oneness with
   God-preparation
For a new dawn.

4. SPONTANEITY

Spontaneity
Is God-transcending
Reality,
Divinity
And Immortality
In our life of
   ever-mounting oneness
With the Absolute.

5. AVATAR

An Avatar is he who is
Heaven's unrecognised infinite
   capacity
For
Humanity's immortal perfection.

6. MOTHER

The human mother tells the child,
"Look up! There is the truth."

The divine Mother tells the child,
"Look within! There alone
Is the beauty of truth."

7. GRATITUDE

Gratitude
Is self-expansion
And
God-manifestation
In the life of the sincere seeker's
Ever-mounting aspiration.

8. PUNCTUALITY

The seeker's regularity
Makes God
Smile.

The seeker's punctuality
Makes God
Dance.

9. THE GURU'S LOVE

If ever a disciple realises,
Even for a fleeting second,
What the Guru's love is,
Then God-realisation for him
Can no longer remain a far cry.
God-realisation then becomes
As easy as drinking water.

10. SUPREME

As long as the animal in us
Plays the role of our Supreme,
We cannot become a
 genuine seeker.

As long as the human in us
Plays the role of our Supreme,
We cannot become a real seeker.

But
The day the Divine in us
Plays the role of our Supreme,
That day not only will we
Have the Supreme as our guide,
But we will ourselves become the
Supreme —
Our only Goal.

11. LIGHT

Give light;
You will receive more.

Become light;
You will receive much more.

Ask God
Whether to give light or become
  light;
You will become boundless light.

12. DEVOTION

Devotion
To the inner reality
Is liberation
From the shackles
Of temptation and frustration.

13. CRY

Cry for name and fame;
God will not allow you
To participate in His
  cosmic Game.

Cry for surrender-participation
In His cosmic Game;
God not only will allow you
To play with Him,
But also will share with you
His infinite Delight.

14. CHILD

A human child
Cries for possession.
A divine child
Cries for perfection-progress on
  earth
And
Perfection-progress in Heaven.

15. SALVATION

If you think of sin,
Then you need salvation.

If you think of ignorance,
Then you need liberation.

If you think of oneness,
Then you need God-realisation,
Self-realisation.

16. SELF-GIVING

The self-giving life-tree
Becomes slowly,
Steadily
And unerringly
The God-nourishing,
God-immortalising
Fruit.

17. CREATION

Creation is
God-preparation
In silence,
God-transcendence
In silence.

18. MARRIAGE

A God-ordained marriage
Leads to
Heaven's door.

A man-made marriage
Is the door to
Hell itself.

19. ACCEPTANCE

A surrendered life
Is God-satisfaction acceptance-light
In the heart
Of a genuine seeker.

20. PEACE

Peace is not in seeing,
Peace is not in receiving,
Peace is not in feeling,
Peace is not in giving;
Peace is in praying to God
For peace-role
In the seeker's aspiring life.

21. EDUCATION

The best education
In the human life
Is self-giving.

The best education
In the divine life
Is unconditional surrender
To God's Will.

22. VISION

With our outer vision
We see the world
The way we want to see
　the world.

With our inner vision
We see the world
The way God wants us to see
　the world.
How does God want us to see
　the world?
He wants us to see the world
As God-preparing perfection.

23. CAPACITY

God never asks us
To do something beyond our
   capacity.
He always grants us
Infinitely more than the
   necessary capacity
When He asks us to do
   something for Him.

24. BEYOND

The Beyond
Is in my heart's cry
For my nature's transformation
And
For the constant Satisfaction
Of my Beloved Supreme.

25. SACRED

A sacred life is needed
To receive God.

A sacred life is needed
To reveal the divine in us.

A sacred life is needed
For the real in us
To become universally real.

But a supreme life is needed
To carry the message of God.

26. IMMORTALITY

Immortality
Is not a vague word;
It is a reality.
And this reality dawns
Only when the seeker becomes
A conscious and constant cry
For God-satisfaction in himself.

27. SPIRITUALITY

Spirituality
Is the only reality
That grows in our inner life,
That glows in our outer life
And
That flows in God's
   ever-transcending
Silence-Life.

28. HOPE

Real hope is not mere wishful
   thinking.
Real hope is the seed of reality
   in us
Which is bound to manifest itself
In God-satisfaction
Reality-tree,
Reality-flower,
Reality-fruit.

29. IGNORANCE

When I consciously do not mix
With ignorance-night,
Delight spontaneously mixes
　with me
And promises me
That light will always mix
　with me.

30. INSTRUMENT

Lord Supreme,
Make me a hallowed instrument,
A flute,
So that you can play on me
With Your all-illumining,
All-liberating,
All-immortalising
Delight.

31. SOUL

The soul not only tells us about
The existence of the
　supreme Goal,
But also shows us
Where the Goal is
And
What the Goal is.

32. BECOMING

Lord Supreme,
I am becoming
A surrendered instrument of
　Yours
Precisely because
That is what You want
For Your constant and continuous
Satisfaction in me.

33. ENERGY

The divine in me grows
Only when I devotedly allow
The supreme Energy to flow.
What is the supreme Energy?
The supreme Energy is
　my constant
Offering of my gratitude-heart
To the Supreme.

34. SILENCE AND SOUND

God's Silence-Life
Is God's perfect Love-Life
In God.

God's Sound-Life
Is God's constant Satisfaction-Life
In man.

35. SOULFULNESS

Man's soulfulness
Is God's all-fulfilling Oneness
With the seeker's promise
To the Absolute Supreme
For God-manifestation.

36. REALITY

Earth-bound reality tells me
That I am of ignorance-night
And for ignorance-night.

Heaven-free reality tells me
That I am eternally
What God wants me to be:
His constant and conscious
　instrument.

37. DIVINE JOURNEY

The divine journey
Is the continuous, eternal journey
That is not only nearing
　God-Reality
But is actually bringing
　God-Reality
To itself.
And this journey is not only
　the soul's
Continuous preparation
In us,
But also the soul's full blossoming
For us.

38. CHILD

A human child
Eventually becomes
God-Perfection.

A divine child
Eternally remains
In God-Satisfaction.

39. ETERNITY

Eternity
Is the God-height in man.

Infinity
Is the God-length in man.

Immortality
Is the God-depth in man.

40. CLARITY

Clarity is the greatest wealth
That a human mind can achieve.

Purity is the best wealth
That a human heart can achieve.

Surrender is the best treasure
That a human life can achieve.

41. PRAYER

When I pray,
I pray to God to make me perfect.
When I meditate,
God tells me that
I have all along been perfect,
But I have only to realise it.

42. WILL

Human will is nothing more
Than disheartening hesitation.
Divine Will is nothing short of
God-preparation in us,
God-Perfection for us
And
God-Satisfaction in and
  through us.

43. FAITH

Inner obedience
Immediately increases our
  outer faith.
Outer obedience to the
  spiritual Master
Immediately increases our
  inner faith.
And when our inner faith is
  increased,
Our outer ignorance is not only
  decreased
But immediately and
  totally diminished.
At that time we become
Perfect instruments of
  God-manifestation.

44. ENLIGHTENMENT

Salvation
Is the first enlightenment
In our inner eternal journey.

Liberation
Is the second enlightenment
In our heavenward eternal journey.

Realisation
Is the third and last
All-illumining and all-fulfilling
Enlightenment
In our eternal journey
Towards ever-transcending
Existence, Consciousness and Bliss.

45. BLISS

Bliss
Is divine intensity-height.
Bliss
Is God-intensity
For
Universal Reality.

46. CREATIVITY

Creativity
Is a God-loving reality in us.
Creativity
Is constant God-embodiment,
God-revelation and
   God-manifestation
In the seeker's evolving life
Of God-Satisfaction.

47. EVERLASTING

There is only one everlasting
   reality
In the human heart
And that everlasting reality is
   man's
Constant, increasing and
   expanding
Gratitude.

48. SERVICE

Sow the unconditional love-seed.
Lo, God grants you
The God-service-tree,
The tree that bears
Nectar-fruit
And
Nectar-satisfaction.

49. GOD-DREAM

God-Dream
Is unrecognised
Reality in us.

God-Reality
Is unmanifested
Divinity for us,
Only for us.

50. SURRENDER

I surrender my outer existence to
   God
Not because He is very great,
Infinitely great,
But because He is the only Reality
That loves me sincerely,
Truly,
Eternally.
Even I do not love myself
The way God loves me.
To Him alone I surrender.

PART X

THIS IS GOD'S HOME

THIS IS GOD'S HOME

1. THIS IS GOD'S HOME

This is not my home
But
This is God's Home.
Here there are no demands
To pay the rent.
To pay rent is to insult
God's Compassion-Sea.
No rent! Just stay
And enjoy yourself.

2. YOU KNOW NOT HOW

You know not how to add;
Therefore
You can never be glad.

You know not how to subtract;
Therefore
You shall never attract.

You know not how to multiply;
Therefore
You shall fail to fly.

You know not how to divide;
Therefore
Your face is doomed to hide.

3. TWO SAGES

Just because
You are an ancient sage
You like to live in a cage.

Just because
I am a modern sage
I enjoy nothing save the
    world-stage.

Since I do not have the heart
To ridicule you,
You must not have the mouth
To underestimate me.

4. HIS HEART WILL SAIL

I tell you,
Although his body is frail
His will will not fail.
Although his mind is in jail
His heart
And its cry
Will continue to sail.

5. I BLAME THEM NOT

I blame not God
Although
My wild vital feels
That God must embody more
Compassion.

I blame not man
Although
My wise mind feels
That man is a fathomless
Ignorance-sea.

I blame not the cosmic gods
Although
My soulful heart feels
That the cosmic gods no longer play
Their cosmic game well.

I blame not myself
Although
I know perfectly well that
In the world of imperfection-night
Nobody can transcend
My ignorance-height.

6. TWO FLAMES

A heavenly flame
Has kindled the life
Of my earthly fame.

An earthly flame
Has destroyed the heart
Of my earthly game.

7. BONDAGE-SEA, FREEDOM-SKY

Bondage-sea
Within, without,
My unlit vital enjoys.

Freedom-sky
Within, without,
My illumined soul employs.

8. YOU CANNOT CONTAIN GOD

Because
You were vain
You did not contain God.

Because
You complain against the
   Heavens
You do not contain God.

Because
You will disdain earth
You will not contain God.

9. WE ARE INSANE

You are insane
Because you have lost
Your head-power.

He is insane
Because he has lost
His heart-power.

I am insane
Because I have forgotten
My God-Hour.

10. DON'T WASTE YOUR TIME

Don't waste your time
In comparing your earth-capacities
With God's Heaven-capacities.
God does not need an equal.
He desperately needs you,
Your heart-beauty's lustre-smile.

11. DO YOU WANT TO BE FRUITFUL?

Lord, do You want to be fruitful?
Then make me grateful.

Lord, do You want me to be
   fruitful?
Then make Your
   Compassion-Life
More thoughtful.

I tell You, Lord,
There is no other way,
There can be no other way.

12. YOU HAVE NO FAITH IN GOD

You have no faith in God.
No harm, just run speedily
With faith in yourself.
You will reach your goal.

I have faith in God.
Although I went slowly
With my faith in God,
I have already reached my Goal.

13. WHERE ARE YOU?

Beloved, my Beloved,
Where are You?
"Love Me in the tears of your
    silence.
I shall come to you."

Beloved, my Beloved,
Where are You?
"Love Me in the smiles of your
    sound.
Only then can you come to Me."

14. TWO DISCOVERIES

Twice I was right.
Once when I discovered
That the death of love human
Is joy.
Once when I discovered
That the birth of joy
Is love divine.

15. I NEED FIVE FAVOURS

Lord, I need five favours
    from You:
Educate my mind,
Elevate my heart,
Dominate my vital,
Tolerate my body,
Inundate my soul.

16. I NEED FOUR FAVOURS

Son, I need four favours
    from you:
Investigate Me,
Communicate with Me,
Frequent My gate,
Terminate your dance
With the prince of gloom.

17. I WARN YOU

I warn you,
Don't ridicule my aspiration.

I warn you,
Don't undervalue my dedication.

I warn you,
Don't belittle my God-Vision.

I warn you,
Don't imitate my
    God-Manifestation.

18. ASK US

Ask God who knows —
You or I?
God will tell you the truth.

Ask me who loves —
God or I?
I shall tell you the truth.

19. BECOME GOD'S SERVICE-TREE

Smile!
You will become
The lustre of God's service-tree.

Cry!
You will become
The heights of God's service-tree.

20. THREE INDESCRIBABLE THINGS

Three things I fail to describe:
Earth's bondage-night
Heaven's freedom-sky
God's Compassion-Light.

21. MY WISDOM WHISPERS

My ignorance thunders:
You are nothing,
I am everything.

My knowledge declares:
You know something,
But I know much more.

My wisdom whispers:
You and I know nothing of
  everything
On earth,
And everything of nothing
In Heaven.

22. GREAT AND GOOD

Father, You always love me;
Therefore
You are great.

"Daughter, you always need Me;
Therefore
You are good."

Father, You always forgive me;
Therefore
You are good.

"Daughter, you always remember
  Me;
Therefore
You are great."

23. MY TWO DISCOVERIES

My two discoveries:
Apart from God
I have no existence-light;
Apart from man
I have no aspiration-might.

24. MY PLAN

This is my plan:
I shall serve God
Unconditionally.

This is my plan:
I shall love man
Untiringly.

This is my plan:
I shall perfect my life
Unimaginably.

25. MY EARTHLY AND HEAVENLY TASKS

On earth
I have only one task:
I have to unmask
God in my gratitude-heart.

In Heaven
I have only one task:
I have to constantly bask
In the supernal pride
Of God's Satisfaction-Sun.

26. ONLY ONE FLAW

Unlike me, O my mind, you have
Only one flaw:
You do not know
How to withdraw
From the hustle and bustle of life.

Unlike me, O my heart, you have
Only one flaw:
You house deathless and
 breathless fear.

27. WHEN I PRAY, WHEN I MEDITATE

When I pray
My Lord tells me,
"Daughter, come up
And see what I have for you."

When I meditate
My Lord tells me,
"Daughter, I am coming down
To see what you have for Me."

28. GOD'S DIFFERENT ROLES

In my outer world
God is Power.

In my inner world
God is Love.

In God's own world
God is the Transcendence-Delight
Of Perfection-Source.

29. O GREAT BEYOND

O great Beyond,
Because I sleep
You weep.

O great Beyond,
Because you play
I pray.

30. LORD, COME TO ME

Lord, come to me and play.
"Son, come to Me and stay."

Lord, come to me and see.
"Son, come to Me and be."

Lord, come to me and fly.
"Son, come to Me and cry."

Lord, come to me and grow.
"Son, come to Me and glow."

Lord, come to me and stand.
"Son, come to Me and expand."

31. WITHOUT YOU

Without seeing You
How can I serve You
O Lord of Duty?

Without seeing You
How can I love You
O Lord of Beauty?

Without seeing You
How can I live,
O Lord of Reality?

32. HOW STRANGE!

The pain of Heaven-separation
I soulfully endured.

The pain of ignorance-separation
I fail to brook.

How strange!
How strange!
How strange!

33. WHO FORGIVES ME?

Who forgives me?
Not you,
But God.

Who tolerates me?
Not you,
But God.

Who has accepted me?
Not you,
But God.

Then how do you expect me
To be with you,
To be for you,
To be in you,
You stark, impossible fool!

34. NO OTHER PATH

No other path
But the path of expanding love.

No other soul
But the soul of illumining peace.

No other goal
But the goal of fulfilling
    perfection.

35. THE CHASE

I chase God
Because
I see not His Face.

God chases me
Because
I fear His Embrace.

36. A FOOL AND A ROGUE

He was such a fool.
Not saying a word to
    Father-Heaven
He left for Mother-Earth.

He is such a rogue.
Not saying a word to
    Mother-Earth
He is leaving for Father-Heaven.

37. LOVE-TEARS

Love-seed
Cries for dedication.

Love-tree
Cries for perfection.

Love-fruit
Cries for satisfaction.

38. FIVE CATEGORIES OF HUMAN BEINGS

There are four categories
Of human beings.
The first category only gives.
The second category
   only receives.
The third category gives
   and receives.
The fourth category neither gives
   nor receives.
I wish to form a new category.
My category
Will love and admire
All the other categories.

39. A DISGRACE

I must say,
It is a disgrace
That I have not yet seen
The Face of God.

It is a disgrace
That I have not claimed God
As my very own.

It is a disgrace
That even now
I have not become another God.

40. LET NOTHING DISTURB YOU

Let nothing disturb you
And your soul's glorious poise.

Let nothing disturb you
And your life's dedication-choice.

41. HOW CAN I BE HAPPY?

How can I be happy?
I am torn between
A misunderstanding mind
And
A misunderstood heart.

How can I be happy?
I am torn between
An ignoring Heaven
And
An ignored earth.

42. LEARN SILENCE!

Learn silence!
You will become
The illumining Vision of God.

Learn obedience!
You will become
The manifesting Mission of God.

43. LET ME TRY AGAIN

Let me try again.
This time I must please God
In God's own Way.

Let me try again.
This time I must become another
    God
To play with Him
For all Eternity.

44. YOU KNOW HOW BUSY I AM

You know how busy I am.
Why do you have to tell me
Who God is?

You know how busy I am.
Why do you have to tell me
About man's countless
    imperfections?

You know how busy I am.
Why do you have to tell me
That the world does not need me?

45. IS IT BECAUSE I AM PERFECT?

Why don't You scold me,
   my Lord?
Is it because I am perfect?
"Either you are perfect or
You are going to be perfect."

Why do You love me most,
   my Lord?
Is it because I am perfect?
"Either you are perfect or
You are going to be perfect."

Why do I think of You all the
   time, my Lord,
Is it because I am perfect?
"You think of Me all the time
Not because you are perfect,
Not because you are one day
   going to be perfect,
But because I think of you all
   the time."

46. TO SEE YOU

To see you
Is to feel your ceaseless love.

To see you
Is to discover that I am not alone
In my undivine self.

To see you
Is to enjoy
The most auspicious birthday
   of life.

47. INCREASE MY COURAGE, LORD

Increase my outer courage, Lord.
I shall dispel the shades
Of ignorance-night.

Increase my inner courage, Lord.
I shall drink deep
Of Perfection-Light.

48. GIFTS

Lord, longing is my future gift
   to You.
Forgiveness is Your constant gift
   to me.

Self-giving is my future gift
   to You.
Satisfaction is Your constant gift
   to me.

49. MIND AND HEART

Mind, what man has:
A battlefield to conquer.
Heart, what God is:
A peaceful home to prosper.

50. PRAYER AND MEDITATION

Prayer is man's
Purity's beauty.
Meditation is man's
Beauty's necessity.

PART XI

DEDICATION-DROPS

DEDICATION-DROPS

1. DEDICATION

Dedication
Is God's Satisfaction
In Heaven's soul
And
In earth's heart.

2. SURRENDER

The finite surrenders
To the Infinite
Not because the Infinite
Is all-powerful,
But because the Infinite
Is all-love;
Plus the Infinite
Is the yet unrecognised reality
Of the finite itself.

3. CONSCIOUSNESS

Consciousness
Is the bridge between
Earth's aspiration-cry
And
Heaven's satisfaction-smile.

4. PURITY

Purity
Is the supreme necessity
To grow into
Divinity's
Immortality.

5. LIGHT

Light
Is oneness-perfection
In Eternity's Height,
Infinity's Length
And
Immortality's Depth.

6. COSMOS

The divine in us
Is not only conscious of
    everything
That exists in the cosmos,
But also embodies everything
That is inside the cosmos.
Something more,
The divine in us
Is the cosmos,
The entire cosmos,
Itself.

7. CONSISTENCY

Consistency
For a divine purpose
Is a continuous forward
  movement
Along Eternity's road toward
Self-perfection
And
God-satisfaction.

8. COURAGE

The human courage
Wants to break.
The divine courage
Wants to sail.
The supreme Courage
Wants Perfection-manifestation
Here on earth.

9. PEACE

Peace
Is in minimising and diminishing
The desire-life
And
Increasing and fulfilling
The aspiration-life,
The life divine.

10. LIFE

The animal life
Finds satisfaction
In destruction-night.
The human life
Finds satisfaction
In temptation-day.
The divine life
Finds satisfaction
In the aspiration-moon,
The liberation-sky
And
The reality-sun.

11. WORSHIP

We worship Someone
Who is not high above our heads,
But who is inside the very depth
  of our hearts,
And who loves us infinitely more
Than we love ourselves.
Not only that,
He alone loves us
Really,
Truly,
Divinely
And
Unconditionally,
And nobody else,
Not even we ourselves.

12. DEVOTION

Devotion
Is the magnet
That pulls us towards the
  ecstasy-height,
The height that makes us see
  and feel
What we truly are:
Unmanifested divinity.

13. DETACHMENT

Detachment
Does not mean negligence.
Detachment
Does not mean lack of concern
  for humanity.
True detachment means
Not to try to influence the world,
Convince the world
Or guide the world
In one's own way,
But to allow the world to grow
In God's way,
For in each individual
There is a spark of divinity.
Let divinity act
In and through each individual —
Seeker or non-seeker —
For the Inner Pilot knows best
How to operate
In and through each human being.

14. HUMILITY

Humility
Is the mental clarity in us,
The vital reality in us
And
The physical divinity in us.
Humility
Is the most fruitful
Consciousness-reality in us.

15. UNION

Union
Is God-Vision in us.
Oneness
Is God-Reality in us.
Perfection
Is God-Satisfaction in us.

16. SIMPLICITY

In the divine ladder
Simplicity
Is the first rung,
Sincerity
Is the second,
Humility
Is the third,
Purity
Is the fourth and highest.

17. TRANSFORMATION

Transformation
Of the body-consciousness
Has been a dream of the Supreme
For millennia.
This transformation
Of the body-consciousness
Will be the real Reality,
The perfect Perfection-Reality
On earth.

18. WORK

To work under compulsion
Is to eventually revolt.
To work because that is the
　only thing
That can give us satisfaction
Or bring about our perfection
Is to become conscious and
　constant friends
Of our eternal Pilot Supreme.

19. LOVE

We love God
Because He is great:
This is what our desire-life
Has taught us.
We love God
Because He is good:
This is what our aspiration-life
Has taught us.
As long as we remain in the
　desire-world,
We shall love God
Because He is all-powerful.
The moment we enter into the
　aspiration-world,
We love God
Because He is all Goodness,
All Kindness,
All Compassion
For us.

20. DELIGHT

Delight is our source,
Delight is our course
And
Delight is the all-illumining,
All-fulfilling force
In us,
With us
And
For us.

21. SINCERITY

Sincerity
Is not the seed.
Sincerity
Is the fruit
Of God-action
In us,
Through us
And
For us.

22. PATIENCE

Patience
Is not helpless surrender
To one's fate.

Patience
Is one's secret and sacred
Undying cry
To see the face of satisfaction-light.

23. MANIFESTATION

Sincere aspiration itself
Is God-manifestation
For God-revelation
And
God-satisfaction in us.
Manifestation-divinity
Is Perfection supreme
And
Perfection supreme
Is Reality absolute.

24. SILENCE AND SOUND

In silence
We grow and glow;
In sound
We love and serve.
Silence-life
Is the tree.
Sound-life
Is the fruit.
If there is no tree,
There can be no fruit
And if there is no fruit,
There is no need for a tree.
Silence and sound both
Are of paramount importance.

25. DYNAMISM

Dynamism of the soul
Is the illumining discovery
Of the seeker in us.
Dynamism is not aggression.
Aggression is the precursor of
 destruction.
Dynamism is God-enthusiasm
 in us
For God-realisation,
God-revelation,
God-manifestation
And
God satisfaction.

26. JOY

Joy is our progress.
Progress is God's Choice.
God's Choice is our inner
 Immortality's
All-illumining,
All-fulfilling
And
All-liberating
Voice.

27. SOULFUL INVOCATION

A soulful invocation
Of God's Presence
Brings God's immediate
 Satisfaction-Smile
To the seeker's promise-heart.

28. GOD'S FEET

God's Feet do not kick us.
God's Feet only shelter us,
And show us the goal.
Furthermore,
God's Feet walk on our behalf
And reach the goal for us,
And bring the infinite Light,
Peace and Bliss
To offer to us,
For our own use.

29. PATIENCE

Patience
Is not forced surrender
Or helpless surrender
To the reality-existence.

Patience
Is the secret of secrets
That allows God's Hour to dawn
According to God's own Will.

Patience
Means allowing God to arrive
Before our heart's door
At His own time.

30. FAMILY

In a human family
We quarrel and struggle
Because we feel that each one
Has to survive
For his own earth-satisfaction.

In a divine family
We strive devotedly and soulfully
Because we feel that each individual
Is responsible for the collective satisfaction
And collective perfection.

In a divine family
God plays the preparation-role,
The perfection-role,
The satisfaction-role.

The divine family
Is the only thing
That God desperately needs
Here on earth.

31. GRATITUDE-FLOWER

Lord Supreme,
Make my heart gratitude-flower
Not for my satisfaction,
But for Your Satisfaction
In and through me.

Lord Supreme,
Make my heart gratitude-flower
So that You can grow and glow
   and flow
In my universal Reality
Inside Your Dream-Boat —
The Dream-Boat You have made
   of me
And, at the same time, for me.

32. GOD-REALISATION

My desire-life tells me
That I do not need God;
What I need is God's creation.

My aspiration-life tells me
That I do not need
   God's creation;
What I need is God alone.

My surrender-life tells me
That I need only the thing
That God wants me to have,
For His constant Satisfaction.

33. SUPREME'S JUSTICE

The human in us will never know
What the Supreme's supreme
   Justice is.
The divine in us always knows
What the Supreme's supreme
   Justice is.
The Supreme's supreme Justice
Is Forgiveness-Light
In order to prove the Supreme's
Oneness-Might
In His eternal Perfection-Height.

34. LOVE

The animal love in us
Is the dance of destruction.
The human love in us
Is the song of temptation.
The divine love in us
Is the game of perfection.
The supreme Love in us
Is the satisfaction of constantly
Self-transcending heights
Of Delight.

35. SURRENDER

There was a time
When I surrendered out of fear,
But that surrender only made me feel
How useless, hopeless, worthless
I was.
But now I surrender to whom?
To the real in me,
To the Supreme in me,
To the Inner Pilot in me,
To the divine Lover
And
To the divine Beloved in me.
Now my surrender is not imposed.
Now my surrender is my expansion.
Now my surrender is the song
Of self-illumination,
Self-perfection
And
God-satisfaction
In me.

36. DELIGHT

There are two oceans in front of me:
The ocean of night
And
The ocean of delight.
The ocean of night tells me,
"Child, I shall give you
What you need.
Come and take it from me."
The ocean of delight tells me,
"Child, I shall give you
What I am.
Even if you do not care for
What I am,
I care for you.
I shall always care for you
And wait for you,
For your God-Hour,
For it is I who have to make you feel
That you are of the Source
Which is Delight
And
You are for the Goal
Which is equally Delight."

37. TRUTH

A painful truth
Is worse than a lie.
Truth that hurts,
Truth that destroys,
Is no truth.
Truth that illumines,
Truth that reveals,
Truth that perfects,
Truth that transforms the animal
   in us
And
Satisfies the human in us
And
Fulfils the divine in us
Is the only Truth.

38. DISCIPLINE

The discipline of the body
Culminates in glorious awareness.
The discipline of the vital
Culminates in glorious dynamism.
The discipline of the mind
Culminates in glorious clarity.
The discipline of the heart
Culminates in glorious oneness,
Inseparable oneness
With the world of
   inner aspiration
And
With the world of
   outer dedication.

39. SONG

The song that carries me
To the world of
   depression-frustration
Is the song of my desire-life.
The song that carries me
To the world of
   salvation-liberation
Is the song of my aspiration-life.
The song that carries me
To the world of God-satisfaction
Is the song of my self-giving,
Constant self-giving.

40. BLISS

Sweet is bliss
When I see the Face of
   my Beloved
The way I want to see it.
Sweeter is bliss
When I feel the Heart of
   my Beloved Supreme
The way I want to feel it.
Sweetest is bliss
When I see His Face
And
Feel His Heart
The way my Beloved Supreme
Wants me to.

41. COURAGE

The supreme courage lies
In demanding and commanding
 the mind
To live in the oneness-love of
 the heart.
The supreme courage lies
In demanding and commanding
 the vital
To live in the heart of the
 illumining mind.
The supreme courage lies
In demanding and commanding
 the body
To live in the vast receptivity of
 the dynamic vital.

42. SACRIFICE

When I sing the song of duality—
You as an individual,
I as an individual—
The song of sacrifice I sing.

When I sing the song of
 oneness-reality,
There is no sacrifice,
For in the realisation of
 oneness-light,
There can be no sacrifice,
Only the song of transformation,
Constant transformation.

The lower and the higher
Fulfil each other.
The lower in me fulfils the higher
By serving the higher.
The higher in me fulfils the lower
By transforming the lower.
In the real fulfilment of one's
 total existence
There is no sacrifice;
It is only the game of
Oneness-song
And
Oneness-dance.

43. FAITH

With personal effort we start.
With personal faith we continue.
With divine faith we complete
 the game.
With supreme awareness of
 constant God-faith
In us and for us,
We eternally remain the chosen
 instruments
Of the Absolute Supreme
In His Heart of Divinity
And
In His Life of Infinity
And
In His Dream of Eternity.

44. HUMILITY

Humility
Is the purity-eye in us.
Humility
Is the beauty-heart in us.
Humility
Is the reality-soul in us.

With purity-eye we measure
 the distance
To our Goal.
With beauty-heart we run
 the fastest
Towards our Goal.
With reality-soul we eventually
 become
The Goal itself.

45. GRATITUDE

In the life of aspiration and
 dedication
The gratitude-deer always runs
 the fastest,
Always achieves the most,
Always becomes the
 perfection-satisfaction
Of the highest
And
Most fulfilling and fulfilled
Supreme in us.
Gratitude is not a human
 achievement.
Gratitude is a divine treasure
Granted to us
By the Inner Pilot within us,
The Absolute Supreme.

46. ONENESS

When I aspire,
I know my oneness-role
With aspiring humanity.
When I serve,
I know my oneness-soul
With smiling Divinity.
When I become
 gratitude-perfection,
I become the oneness-goal
Of the Divine within
And
The Divine without.

47. WILL-POWER

Will-power
Is the soul's light within us.
Will-power
Is the hero divine within us.
Will-power
Is the self-giving love in us
For the Reality in us.
And the Reality in us
Is the Inner Pilot,
The Supreme.

48. ONENESS

What we call consecrated oneness
In the morning,
We call that very thing
Inseparable oneness
In the afternoon.
What we call inseparable oneness
In the afternoon,
We call that very thing
Perfection-oneness
In the evening.

49. PERFECTION

Perfection
Smiles at justice-light.
Perfection
Laughs at injustice-might.
Perfection
Fulfils itself in
    compassion-delight.

50. INDEPENDENCE-DAY

Independence-day
Is not the day of equality
But the day of
Human life's equanimity
And
Human heart's beauty.

PART XII

UNION AND ONENESS

UNION AND ONENESS

1. UNION AND ONENESS

A happy union reigns supreme
When beauty's light
And duty's delight
Meet together.

A happy oneness reigns supreme
When earth's cry
And Heaven's smile
To each other lose.

2. UNION

Union with God
Is not and cannot be total
    satisfaction.
But oneness with God
Is total and constant satisfaction.
Union is not oneness.
Union can be withdrawn.
Union is not and cannot be
    always safe;
It cannot be eternal.
But oneness can never be
    withdrawn.
Once oneness is established,
No matter on which plane,
Everything is established.
Then abiding satisfaction
    takes place
In the aspiring heart.

3. ONENESS

Oneness with our role
Makes us feel
That we can eventually become
    great.
Oneness with our soul
Makes us feel
That we can eventually become
    good.
Oneness with our goal
Makes us feel
That the goal,
The soul
And
The role
Are of us,
In us
And
For us.
Why?
Because the Source is for us
And
The flow is also for us.

4. SINCERITY

Real sincerity
Is the sincerity
That sees reality
The way reality wants to be seen,
And that becomes
　the reality itself.
Real sincerity
Does not see reality
With its own eye.
Real sincerity
Sees reality
With the eye of reality itself.

5. SIMPLICITY

Simplicity
Is the most
Striking
And
Challenging
Speed
When we run along the road
Of Eternity's
Fulfilling
Achievement-light.

6. SURRENDER

Let us surrender to God
Not only what we have
But also what we are.
What we have
Is a real inner cry for God.
What we are
Is our conscious or
　unconscious oneness
With ignorance.
Let us offer both
To the Pilot within.

7. COMPASSION

Write down how many things
　you want.
Meditate on how many things
　you need.
When you write them down
You will see
That you want millions of things.
When you meditate
You will notice
That you need only one thing
And that is God the Compassion,
God the eternal Compassion.

8. LIGHT

The human in us
Does not want light.
The animal in us
Knows not the existence of light.
The divine in us
Knows that it is nothing but light itself.

9. THE FUTURE OF THE WORLD

Your life of perfection
Is the future of the world.
Your life of satisfaction
Is the future for the world.
Your life of
    unconditional surrender
Is the future in the world.

10. SMILE

When my inner cry is pure
God's outer Smile is sure.
My ascending cry
And
God's descending Smile
Inseparable
Ever shall remain.

11. TRUTH

When I make a promise
I make friends
With truth.
But when I keep a promise
My existence becomes
Another name for truth.

12. SELFLESSNESS

Selflessness is:
I am of God,
I am for God,
Him to please,
Him to serve
In His own Way
At every moment
Is my heart's selflessness.

Selflessness is
Heart-giving,
Life-giving.
What we call selflessness today
Becomes God-awareness
    tomorrow,
And
The day after, that very thing
Becomes God-oneness,
Eternity's God-oneness.

13. DEVOTION

Devotion in the heart
Is the expansion
Of our Divinity's real life.
Devotion in our entire life
Is the fastest speed
To reach our destined Goal.
Devotion is the strongest magnet
That pulls us to our
   Eternity's source:
Delight.

14. GRATITUDE

Gratitude
Is life's ever-climbing tree
That enjoys God's
Ever-transcending Height,
His Infinity's Delight,
His Immortality's Life
And
His Perfection's Smile.

15. ASPIRATION

Imagination was aspiration.
Inspiration was aspiration.
Now aspiration is inspiration.

When imagination was aspiration
I felt that I was of my Inner Pilot
And
I was for my inner Pilot.

When inspiration was aspiration
I felt that I could fly
To my Eternity's Beloved
   Supreme.

When aspiration is inspiration,
When the real becomes conscious
Of its existence in us,
God the unmanifested Reality
Becomes not only the manifested
   Reality
But the only Reality
In the world of glowing hope,
In the world of flowing reality.

16. CONSCIOUSNESS

The human in us
Cries and climbs
And climbs and cries.
The divine in us
Smiles and descends
And descends and smiles.
Consciousness
Is the connecting link,
The golden thread that unites
Our heart's climbing cry
With
Heaven's descending smile.

17. TO BE FREE

Why do I want to be free?
If I want to be free
Because the rest of the world is bad,
Then God will ask me
To create another world of my own
Since His creation has failed me.

But if I want to be free
So that I can be of greater service
To my sisters and brothers,
To God's entire creation,
Then God in me selects the hour,
And at that choice hour
The aspiring human in me achieves
Freedom from life's
    ignorance-night.

If I want to be free
To love the world,
To be part and parcel of the world,
Then God is all eagerness
To grant me freedom.
But if I want to be free
Because the world is full of
    ignorance,
The world is nothing but a
    devouring tiger,
Then God feels that I am not the
    right person
For Him to grant freedom to.
He will grant me freedom
Only when He sees that this
    freedom
Is for dedicated service,
For the transformation of the
    human race.

18. GRATITUDE

Earth's gratitude
And
Heaven's plenitude
Are one and inseparable.

Human heart's gratitude
And
Divine soul's plenitude
Are one and inseparable.

19. TRANSFORMATION

Transformation of the mind
Is all we need.
Once the oldest member of
   our family
Is transformed,
The younger members of
   the family,
Will automatically and
   spontaneously
Be transformed;
Therefore
The transformation of the mind
Is of paramount importance.

20. ASPIRATION

Yesterday
What we called aspiration
Today
We call that very thing
   realisation.
And tomorrow
We shall call that very thing
God-satisfaction
In
God-manifestation.

21. EXPANSION

The expansion
Of human consciousness
Is the beginning
Of divine revelation
In and through
The seeker.

22. CERTITUDE

Remain in the heart always,
Soulfully and unconditionally.
Then the soul's certitude
Will become
Your constant and eternal Friend.

UNION AND ONENESS

23. ETERNAL

To be an eternal cry
Of the heart,
In the heart,
For the heart,
Is to grow into
The eternal satisfaction-life
Of the ever-transcending Beyond.

24. ENTHUSIASM

Enthusiasm is a divine gift,
And this divine gift
We get from higher worlds.
Enthusiasm lost,
Life-satisfaction is lost;
God-perfection in man
Remains a far cry.

25. ONENESS

Oneness with the silence-light
And oneness with the
   sound-might
Can make the real seeker
An eternally perfect instrument
In the Heart of the Supreme.

26. COURAGE

To speak ill of the world
Needs courage,
But fortunately or unfortunately
Everybody has that courage.

To love the world
As one's own,
Very own,
Needs courage.
Unfortunately, most of us are
   wanting
In that courage.

The courage of the heart,
The courage of the soul
We badly need,
And not the courage
Of the unruly,
Aggressive,
Impure,
Demanding vital.

27. DISCIPLINE

If you discipline your life,
God not only will play with you,
But also will teach you how
   to play
Most soulfully and most
   satisfactorily
The way He Himself plays
In His cosmic Game.

28. COMPASSION

God's Compassion
Is the magnet
That pulls us up
High,
Higher,
Highest,
To His Silence-Height
And
His Perfection-Light.

29. PURITY

Purity
Is man's conscious and constant
Surety
In his life of aspiration-cry
And
In his life of satisfaction-smile.

30. SERVICE

Service is the illumining light
That fulfils the divine,
Perfects the human
And
Transforms the animal
In the seeker.

31. CAPACITY

When capacity is of real necessity,
Capacity knocks at our door
To enter into our life.
When capacity is not of real
   necessity,
Capacity likes to remain
A perfect stranger.

32. PATIENCE

Patience is the divine friendship
That we enjoy with divine Time,
The ever-lasting Time,
That has far transcended
   the snares of death
And the frustration of bitter
   failure.

33. LIGHT

The real light
Is within
And not without.
The real light
Is self-giving
And God-becoming.

34. VICTORY

The animal victory
Lies in utter destruction.
The human victory
Lies in tremendous hesitation
Or
In total suspicion.
The divine victory
Lies in constant and conscious
Self-expansion and
　God-manifestation
In the seeker's ever-aspiring heart.

35. DETERMINATION

Determination is in our
　dynamic vital,
In our challenging vital,
In our transforming vital.

Will power is in our
　immortalising soul,
In our God-fulfilling dream,
In our God-satisfying divinity.

36. SINCERITY

Sincerity is the first step
　towards purity.
Purity is the first step
　towards self-discovery.
Self-discovery is the first step
　towards God-revelation.
God-revelation is the first step
　towards God-satisfaction and
　man-satisfaction
All at once.

37. SALVATION

Salvation is the foot
Of God the Satisfaction-Tree.
Liberation is the middle
Of God the Satisfaction-Tree.
Realisation is the top
Of God the Satisfaction-Tree.

38. SOULFUL

Live in the heart.
All the soulful qualities,
Capacities,
Realities
Of the ever-lasting,
　ever-illumining Real
Will beckon you,
Will claim you
As their own,
Very own.

39. FREEDOM

What is real freedom?
Real freedom is not to strike
     someone
At one's sweet will.
Real freedom is one's mastery
Over the attachment-world,
Over the temptation-world,
Over the uncompromising,
Unaspiring human world.
Real freedom lies in acceptance
     of reality
And in perfection of reality.
Accept, transform, perfect:
That is the real freedom.

40. PURITY

Cry for purity
The way a child cries for its
     mother.
Cry and cry,
For there is no other way
     to invoke purity,
No other way to inundate our
     earthly existence
With purity.
Cry and cry.
Inside the soulful cry
Purity-seed germinates.
This seed will one day grow into
     a tiny plant,
And then into a banyan tree.
Cry and try, try and cry.
There is no other way
To sow the purity-seed
And to see it grow into
The purity-banyan tree.

41. SELF-OFFERING

The self-offering of the lower self
Is the self-offering
Of what we have temporarily
   accepted
As our own.
The self-offering of
   the higher self
Is the self-offering
Of something which we
   eternally are
But unfortunately
Are not aware of.
Our false life we are claiming as
   our own.
Our true life, natural life,
We are not claiming as our own.
The higher life is our true life.

42. OBEDIENCE

Obedience
Is not blind self-giving
To another individual.
Obedience
Is not the play of compulsion.
Obedience
Has to be full of inner recognition
Of our high, higher, highest part
Playing its role
In different human beings.
Obedience
Is the acceptance of our
   higher life,
Of which we are not yet conscious.

43. REALISATION

First we have to know
What our ignorance-realisation
Has given us.
When we are frustrated
With our ignorance-realisation,
We shall cry for
   nectar-realisation.
And that nectar-realisation lies in
   our
Conscious, constant self-giving
To our own Source,
Which is the ever-transcending
Delight
Of the Beyond.

44. NECTAR

If we give what we have,
If we give what we are
To our Source,
Then it is not only possible
   and practicable,
But inevitable
For us to drink nectar.
What do we have to give?
We have to give what we see,
We have to give what we feel,
We have to give what we claim,
We have to give what we are
In the outer world
To the Source.
This moment we are
   ignorance-prince;
Next moment we are
   aspiration-prince.
This moment we represent
   darkness and ignorance;
Next moment we represent
   light and delight.
Whatever we represent at any
   moment
Should be offered to the
   Lord Supreme.
If this moment we represent
   ignorance,
Then we must offer it.
If the next moment we represent
   wisdom-light,
Then we must offer it.
Then at every moment
We can drink from the fount
Of divine nectar-delight.

45. HUMILITY

Humility
Is the expansion of one's
   real reality
In a sweet, illumining and
   fulfilling way.
Humility
Is not the helpless surrender
To something or someone else.
Humility
Is not a frightened child.
Humility
Is real receptivity in us.
If we receive with devoted
   humility,
Then immediately our
   receptivity-vessel increases.
Humility
Is the secret of secrets
For self-expansion,
For world-inspiration
And
For world-transformation.

46. TRANSFORMATION

The transformation of the body
Comes last.
The transformation of the heart
Comes first.
How does the transformation of
   the heart
Take place?
The transformation of the heart
   takes place
When a seeker can consciously
   feel
That he is not the body
And
He is not of the body,
But
He is for the body.
To be for the body does not mean
To be satisfied with the animal
   propensities,
To wallow in the pleasures of
   ignorance.
But if the seeker cries
For the transformation of
   the body
And the body-consciousness,
Then the seeker becomes perfect.
Once we transform the body,
This body can then be utilised
For God-manifestation on earth.

47. PURIFY

How can I purify my mind?
I can purify my mind
Only by looking at a flower
And praying to God
To make me as pure as the flower.
How can I purify my mind?
I can purify my mind
Only by looking at the moon
And praying to God
To make my mind as peaceful as
   the moon.
How can I purify my mind?
I can purify my mind
Only by looking at a candle flame
And praying to God
To make my mind as one-pointed
As the flame.
By looking at a flower,
By looking at the moon
And
By looking at the candle flame
I can purify my mind.
Once purification takes place in
   the mind,
Slowly and steadily
The body and vital become pure.
Mental purity comes first
For the illumination
Of the entire body-consciousness.

48. RESPONSIBILITY

Our first responsibility
Is to please the omnipresent God,
The Source, the Inner Pilot.
First we have to please God
Who is our Heaven-Friend
Earth-Friend,
Hell-Friend,
Everywhere-Friend.
Our second responsibility
Is to please our nearest and
    dearest ones
On earth,
Those whom God wants us to
    claim as our own.
Our third responsibility
Is to please ourselves.

49. PURITY

Purity
Is the real divinity
In the heart of a human soul.
This divinity
Ultimately makes us feel
That the Absolute
Is not only the Absolute
But also
The Supreme Beloved
In us,
For us.

50. LIGHT

In our life of aspiration
With the outer light
We see,
With the inner light
We become
And
With the Light of the Supreme
We know what we eternally are:
God's Dream-Boat
And
God's Reality-Shore.

Notes to *Union and Oneness*

15. In the original first edition, the third line read "Now aspiration is aspiration."

PART XIII

THREE SOULFUL PRAYERS

THREE SOULFUL PRAYERS

1. THREE SOULFUL PRAYERS

Lord, three soulful prayers
I have all along treasured.
Today I place them at Your Feet.
May I always remain awake
To see Your Face.
May I always remain conscious
To feel Your Grace.
May I always remain
A descendant of Your Grace.

2. MOVEMENT

Doubt moves not forward.
Faith runs not backward.
Fears crawls not forward.
Courage marches not backward.
Love runs forward, upward
   and inward,
And never backward.

3. OUR EARTH-BIRTH EVOLVES

Our earth-birth evolves
When our animal ego
Is dissolved.

Our divine life begins
When we love
Inner Reality's lustre-moon.

4. HIS LIFE COVERED

His truth-life covered
Below, above.
His love-life covered
Within, without.
His bliss-life covered
All-where.

5. ONE ACCEPTED SECOND

Countless rejected hours
Have taken me away
From God-Heart.
One accepted second
Will bring me back
To God's Feet,
My Haven-Home.

6. JUST YESTERDAY

The night that greedily devours,
Just yesterday he saw.
The day that devotedly aspires,
Just today he is seeing.
The sun that eternally illumines,
Just tomorrow he will become.

7. FRUITLESS AND HOPELESS

Fruitless,
Fruitless is my
　hesitation-ignorance.
Hopeless,
Hopeless is my
　determination-somnolence.
Lifeless,
Lifeless is my action-dullness.
Godless,
Godless is my darkness-oneness.

8. GOOD-BYE

Good-bye, my sad earth,
I shall always remember
Your sacrifice-sea.

Good-bye, my strong Heaven,
I shall always remember
Your illumination-flood.

9. YOU CALL IT, I CALL IT

You call it dedication,
But
I call it the length of aspiration.

You call it aspiration,
But
I call it the height of dedication.

Dedication becomes,
　aspiration becomes.
Dedication becomes
God the Body;
Aspiration becomes
God the Soul.

10. CHINMOY-REALITY

In Heaven
Chinmoy-reality:
Illumination-role.

On earth
Chinmoy-reality:
Aspiration-soul.

In the Supreme
Chinmoy-reality:
Oneness-goal.

11. I AM HELPLESS

True, my body is not submissive,
But what can I do?
I am helpless.

True, my vital is impulsive,
But what can I do?
I am helpless.

True, my mind is not pure,
But what can I do?
I am helpless.

True, my heart is not sure,
But what can I do?
I am helpless.

12. DO NOT IMAGINE

Do not imagine!
The animal in you
Becomes jealous
If you imagine.
Do not think!
The divine in you feels sad
That you are a hopeless case
If you think.
Just act and become,
And become and act.

13. I SEE, I FEEL

I see Divinity the Doer.
I feel Eternity the Knower.
I like Infinity the Seer.
I love Immortality the Lover.

14. ABANDON THEM!

Abandon your worries!
Confidence is your divine
    birthright.
Abandon your sense of
    worthlessness!
You are God-Eternity's
    Satisfaction-Light.

15. ALL KNOW NOT

Greatness knows not
The weakness of its incapacity.

Goodness knows not
The strength of its capacity.

I know not
The usefulness of my sincerity.

16. HOW PURE IS THE EYE

How pure is the eye of
 Mother earth.
How cheerful is the eye of
 Father Heaven.
How soulful is the eye of my
 earth-peace.
How fruitful is the eye of my
 Heaven-Love.

17. A REGULAR ASPIRATION-HEART

A regular aspiration-heart
Is bright like a used key
To open up God's Door.
And once you are in,
God-Peace blesses you,
God-Love treasures you
And God-Joy embraces you.

18. THREE THINGS HAVE CONFUSED HIM

Three things have really
 confused him
And his life:
The tears of God's World,
The fears of the higher world,
The cheers of the lower world.

19. AN ATTENTIVE EYE

An attentive eye
Does not make a mistake.

A sympathetic eye
Does the right thing.

An illumining eye
Is the right thing.

20. SCOLDING IS A FOOLISH THING

Scolding is a foolish thing,
But if it is done well,
It may transform someone's
 nature.
I may remain foolish,
But if my foolishness
Unconsciously elevates
Somebody's consciousness,
I am more than prepared
To scold.

21. IN THE MORNING

In the morning
My Lord has only two names:
Compassion and Love.

In the afternoon
My Lord has only one name:
Justice.

In the evening
My Lord has no name:
I shall have to give Him
A suitable name.

22. MY NEEDS

My Indian heart
Needs more compassion.

My American body
Needs more vitality.

My African legs
Need more speed.

My Chinese head
Needs more wisdom.

My European mind
Needs more nobility.

My German vital
Needs more determination.

23. A FAVOUR

My Lord, I have all along
Championed Your Cause:
Complete and perfect
    manifestation on earth.

In return can You not
Do me a favour?
Can You not give me
A fraction of Your
    Satisfaction-Smile?

24. NO HOPE

Earth has no hope.
Heaven has no hope.
Why, why?
Because
God has decided that He will not
Care any more
For Heaven's
    consciousness-aloofness
And
Earth's constant silliness.

25. I CRY, I TRY

I cry in the depth
Of despair.
I try in the depth
Of doubt.
I surrender in the depth
Of fear.

26. LORD, I LOVE YOU

Lord, I love You
Because You are great;
I love You
Because You are good.
Your greatness inspires me
To be great like You.
Your goodness elevates me
To be good like You.

27. YET HE IS NOT AFRAID

Doubt strikes him
Like a thunderbolt,
Yet he is not afraid of doubt.
He invokes faith.
In faith he sees Divinity's Face.

28. A TERRIBLE OATH

Don't You know
What a terrible oath I have taken?
I shall not leave You
No matter what You do,
No matter what You say,
No matter what becomes of me.
Lord, I cannot leave You;
And You cannot ignore me.

29. HER TRAGEDY

When he heard about her tragedy
He smiled and said to her:
"You deserve it!"
When she heard about his tragedy
She cried and said to him:
"Not you, but I who needed it!"

30. HATE ME IF YOU HAVE TO

Hate me if You have to.
Scold me and insult me
If You want to.
Punish me if that is what
   You want.
But, for God's sake, O Lord,
Don't leave me.
That will be too much!

31. SACRED JOY, SECRET SORROW

My God-realisation
Was a sacred joy.
My God-manifestation
Is a secret sorrow.

THREE SOULFUL PRAYERS

32. I AM HAPPY

I am happy
Because
I have smiled
At the Beauty
Of
The Universal God.

I am happy
Because
I have cried
For the Reality
Of
The Transcendental God.

33. MIND-ROAD AND HEART-ROAD

Do you know
Why
You are so unhappy?
You are unhappy
Because
Your mind-road is dangerously
   overcrowded
By notorious travellers.
Try your heart-road.
Your own luck will travel
With very few fortunate
   travellers.

34. YOUR NEW SONG

Your life does not
Have to be so dull.
Just sing a new song
To replace your frustration-song.
Your new song is:
"God is all for me."

35. WHO WILL REMEMBER?

Will anyone remember me
When I am gone?
Yes,
My untiringly expecting,
My sleeplessly demanding
And
My constantly frustrated
Children-friends.

36. OUT OF MY ELEMENT

How long can I remain
In ignorance-night?
Not for long.
Why?
Because there I am out of
   my place-element.

37. WHAT IS PROGRESS?

What is success?
Money-power.
What is success?
Fame-tower.

What is progress?
Oneness-height.
What is progress?
Perfection-delight.

38. SONG AND DANCE

Mine is one joyful song.
God's is one thankful Song.

Mine is one perfection-dance.
God's is one Satisfaction-Dance.

39. TWO SONGS

Compassion: God's Life-Song.
Gratitude: My life-song.
From this very moment
I shall be singing these two songs
In God's own Way.

40. HE WILL BE ONLY TOO HAPPY

You do not have to use your eyes;
You can use God's Eyes.
He will be only too happy
To grant you His Eyes.

You do not have to use your ears;
You can use God's Ears.
He will be only too happy
To grant you His Ears.

You do not have to use even your
    own heart.
You can use God's Heart.
God will be only too happy
To grant you
    His Heart Universal.
He will without fail,
He will.

41. I AM NOT LIKE THAT

I am not like that.
I am not as bad as you think.
I do pray in the morning.

I am not like that.
I am not as bad as you think.
I do meditate in the evening.

I am not like that.
I am not as bad as you think.
I do offer my gratitude-heart
To my Beloved Supreme
At midnight.

THREE SOULFUL PRAYERS

42. THEY DO NOT LOVE

What are the three main reasons
Why people are not happy?
People are not happy
Because they do not love.
People are not happy
Because they do not love God.
People are not happy
Because they do not love God
In God's own Way.

43. ENOUGH

You say:
Seeing is not enough.
I say:
Feeling is enough.
And our common Lord God says:
Becoming and nothing else
Is more than enough.

44. FAILURE INCARNATE

I am sorry that you cannot trust
    the Bible.
Do one thing:
Try to trust God.
If even that you cannot do,
Then you must dare
To trust yourself.
Here, too, if you fail,
(I definitely hope you won't),
I will have no other choice but
    to call you
"Failure incarnate".

45. I LOOKED

I looked at the morning dew.
Humility captured my heart.

I looked at the ocean.
Immensity captured my heart.

I looked at the sky.
Infinity captured my heart.

46. WHEN LOVE SUFFERS

When love suffers
It is surprisingly meaningful.

When the lover suffers
It is singularly soulful.

When the Beloved suffers
It is supremely powerful.

47. BLESSINGS

An unbelievable blessing:
Obedience.
An unimaginable blessing:
Faith.
An incomparable blessing:
Gratitude.
An unbelievable,
    unimaginable,
    incomparable,
Ever-illumining
And
Ever-fulfilling blessing:
Complete and constant oneness
With the Will of our
    Beloved Supreme.

48. WHEN CALAMITY COMES

When calamity comes
God becomes real.
Until then
God seems to be seemingly real.

49. BE PREPARED

Be prepared.
The Supreme will soon come
And knock at your door.
Be prepared.
He will then touch your heart.
Be prepared.
Then He will examine your life.
Be prepared.
Finally He will feed your
    aspiration-breath
And help you don your
    dedication-uniform.

50. DO YOU NOT REMEMBER?

God once secretly told you that
He loves you.
Do you not remember it?

God once openly told you that
He needs you.
Do you not remember it?

PART XIV

MY FIFTY GRATITUDE-SUMMERS

MY FIFTY GRATITUDE-SUMMERS

1

Aspiration begins.
Surrender continues.
Gratitude concludes.

2

Enthusiasm is
God's God-Beauty
In His seeker-children.

3

Sincerity is my heart's
Silver dawn.
Purity is my soul's
Golden sunrise.

4

We know and we do not know.
We know how to roam,
But we do not know
How to return Home.

5

My Beloved Supreme,
I prayed to You to make me
A realised soul.
Alas! Instead of making me
A realised soul,
You have made me
A mechanised human body.

6

Aspiration
Is my heart's beauty.
Illumination
Is my soul's beauty.
Satisfaction
Is my Lord's Beauty.

7

Forget what God has
Already forgotten:
Your insincerity-mind,
Your impurity-heart
And
Your ingratitude-life.

8

How can I have
A new king: my God,
In my heart-kingdom
If I do not dethrone
The present king: my ego?

9

My psychic gladness
And
My vital madness
Never live together.

10

Be
A God-dreamer.
All your fear-tortures
Will leave you.

11

When
I am sincere,
My Beloved Supreme
Is pleased with me.
When
I am pure,
I am satisfied
With my Beloved Supreme.

12

God
Is for
My aspiring heart.
Spirituality
Is for
My searching mind.

13

I pray to God
For His Absolute Vision
And not for
His Possession-Universe.

14

My mind's discovery:
God has given me
Heavy burdens.
My heart's discovery:
God has given me
Strong shoulders.

15

The gift of my outer life
To my inner life
Is my constantly soulful
Service.
The gift of my inner life
To my outer life
Is my sleeplessly fruitful
Love.

16

Yesterday
My mind was
An uneducated and ignorant fool.
Today
My mind is
An educated and learned fool.
Tomorrow
My mind shall be
A sleepless ignorance-hunter.

17

Am I ready to scold
My impurity-mind?
Am I?
Am I ready to warn
My insecurity-heart?
Am I?

18

Because
You are a childlike believer,
Your God is a constant
Giver.

19

He had to enter into
His own spiritual grave.
Why? Because he was
Sleeplessly fond of his
Confusion-mind.

20

I may not know
The beginning. But
I shall definitely know
The end.

21

Simplicity
Is and will forever remain
A perfect stranger
To the modern mind.

22

A purity-life
And
A gratitude-heart
Are immediate neighbours.

23

The most glorious beginning
Of my miracle-life: I have
Started loving God, my Beloved
Supreme, in His own Way.

24

God is ready to give me
Another chance.
Alas, am I ready?
Will I ever be ready
To accept it?

25

Each aspiring life
Is a prolonged and
Extensive Dream
Of God.

26

My past was completely
Destroyed on the day
I employed my surrendering
Thoughts to help me
Reach my God.

27

O my vital, do not complain;
You may be totally wrong.
O my mind, do not assert;
You too may be
Totally wrong.

28

Be not afraid of God,
Be not afraid.
Your sweet reunion
Need not be delayed.

29

Reveal constantly
What you are: a supremely
Chosen instrument of God.
Conceal powerfully
What you are not:
A giant prince of
Ignorance-dream.

30

An uninspiring thought,
Short or long, is spiritually
Wrong.
An unaspiring life,
Short or long, is spiritually
Wrong.

31

My wisdom-flames
Pray to God.
My stupidity-seas
Pray for God.

32

Self-perfection:
Yes!
Self-annihilation:
No!

33

I export
Aspiration-flames
From earth to Heaven.
I import
Satisfaction-suns
From Heaven to earth.

34

Each time
You have a chance,
Hurl your wisdom-lance
At ignorance-tiger.

35

The divine
Will definitely conquer
The human, the way
The human
Has conquered the animal.

36

If you accept
Fantasies,
Ecstasy will not
Receive you.

37

O my mind,
You have talked enough.
Now begin to listen.
I have got a superb teacher
For you. You will simply
Love your new teacher: heart.

38

Confusion
Cannot last.
Just change
Your direction.

39

When told that all human beings
Are by nature ungrateful,
Everybody thinks that
He is an exception.

40

I see you
As an ordinary man.
You see yourself
As a demigod.
God sees you
As another God.

41

Do you want to be
The real winner,
Do you?
Then lose to Truth,
Lose!

42

It is not enough
To love God
In the God-lover.
We must also love God
In the God-hater.

43

The illumining soul
Uncovers,
And
The aspiring heart
Discovers.

44

Success
Is an incident.
Progress
Is an experience.

45

Make your choice:
Do you want to be
The servant of a book
Or
A good student
Of your soul?

46

God-seekers
Feast
On God's great
Silence.

47

There is only
One perfect road
And
That road is ahead of
You,
Always ahead of
You.

48

Only
The God-centred souls
Can spread
Their victory-trophies
At God's Feet.

49

His mind lives
Inside the secret
Sorrow-cave.
His heart lives
Inside the sacred
Sorrow-home.

50

His life's late-evening discovery:
God's Forgiveness-Power
Has smashed
God's Justice-Tower.

PART XV

THE LOSER AND THE WINNER

THE LOSER AND THE WINNER

1

The Loser
Does not want to remember
If and when he has blamed others
For his own sad losses.

2

The Winner
Wants to know
When and where he has
Deeply appreciated his
   well-wishers.

3

The Loser
Wants to hear only
His own opinion of himself.

4

The Winner
Wants to hear
Others' opinions of him.

5

The Loser
Secretly admires the winner
And openly hates the winner.

6

The Winner
Openly encourages the loser
And secretly belittles the loser.

7

The Loser
Breathlessly desires admiration.

8

The Winner
Sleeplessly desires satisfaction.

9

The Loser
Is hesitation-mind.

10

The Winner
Is determination-soul.

11

The Loser
Professes his future perfection.

12

The Winner
Confesses his present limitation.

13

The Loser
Cries for the celestial Bliss
But is willing to be satisfied
With the terrestrial joys.

14

The Winner
Cries for the celestial Bliss
And nothing else will ever satisfy
His sleepless hunger.

15

The Loser
Thinks that victory
Is something amazingly great.

16

The Winner
Knows that victory
Is wanting in permanent
   satisfaction.

17

The Loser
Thinks that his fate is
   unchangeable.

18

The Winner
Knows that he is his own
   fate-maker.

THE LOSER AND THE WINNER

19

The Loser
Thinks that he has to bravely face
World-injustice,
His enemy number one.

20

The Winner
Knows that he has to
   sleeplessly love
Determination,
His friend number one.

21

The Loser
Thinks that he deserves
Genuine appreciation from the
   winner.

22

The Winner
Also realises that
Only if somebody else is the loser
Can he become the winner.

23

The Loser
Has a deathless hunger
For appreciation-ocean
But shamelessly fails
To acknowledge its limitations.

24

The Winner
Is fond of world-appreciation,
But is painfully conscious
Of its limitations.

25

The Loser
Is ready to kill himself.

26

The Winner
Is eager to better himself.

27

The Loser
Thinks that merit can be
 discarded.

28

The Winner
Knows that merit has to be
 rewarded.

29

The Loser
Knows what to say.

30

The Winner
Knows what to do
And also how to do.

31

The Loser
Tells the world that
Shameless partiality
Is the order of the day.

32

The Winner
Tells the world that
Blameless impartiality
Is the order of the day.

33

The Loser
Loves the ecstasy of success.

34

The Winner
Enjoys the confidence of success.

35

The Loser
Becomes a mad elephant
After the defeat.

36

The Winner
Remains a swift deer
After his victory.

THE LOSER AND THE WINNER

37

The Loser
Thinks that he has lost
The most perfect world.

38

The Winner
Thinks that there can be
An infinitely better world.

39

The Loser
Wants to become great
By dint of his exasperation.

40

The Winner
Wants to become perfect
By virtue of his dedication.

41

The Loser
Thinks that the entire world
Is ruthlessly against him.

42

The Winner
Surprisingly feels
That the entire world
Is for him.

43

Sound teaches
The Loser
The art of endless talking.

44

Silence teaches
The Winner
The art of growing peace.

45

The Loser,
At the end of his journey's close
Unwillingly dies.

46

The Winner,
At the end of his journey's close
Smilingly embraces death.

47

The Loser
Is confusion-frustration.

48

The Winner
Is concentration-penetration.

49

The Loser
Feels that God is NOT
Compassion-Light.

50

The Winner
Knows that God IS
Justice-Light.

PART XVI

I MEDITATE SO THAT

I MEDITATE SO THAT

1

I meditate
So that when
"The Hour of God"
Strikes I shall not
Be late in my
Unconditional
Surrender-examination.

2

I meditate
So that my mind
Cannot complicate
My life.

3

I meditate
So that I can
One-pointedly concentrate
On the things that I
Desperately need.

4

I meditate
So that I can easily
Obliterate my past mistakes
That are still haunting me.

5

I meditate
So that I can accelerate
My progress while I am
Running forward,
Flying upward
And
Diving inward.

6

I meditate
So that I can
Bravely terminate
My long-standing friendship
With ignorance.

7

I meditate
So that I can liberate
My earth-bound life
And
Place it inside
My Heaven-free life.

8

I meditate
So that I can celebrate
The Transcendental Victory
Of my Beloved Supreme,
Not only in my own life,
But also in the life of
His entire creation.

9

I meditate
So that I can inundate
My entire being
With the omnipotent
Power of peace.

10

I meditate
So that at every moment
I can elevate
My thought-life
To God's Will-Power-Life.

11

I meditate
So that the animal in me
Cannot humiliate the
Human in me.

12

I meditate
So that I can perpetuate
My eternity's God-hunger
And
God-love.

13

I meditate
So that Heaven's golden Gate
I can open up
With my heart's aspiration-key.

14

I meditate
So that I can most perfectly
Elucidate the Satisfaction-Reality
Of God's Perfection-Dream.

I MEDITATE SO THAT

15

I meditate
So that my clever and
Tricky mind cannot
Instigate me, even for
A fleeting second,
To speak ill of my Lord's
Beautiful creation.

16

I meditate
So that nothing on earth
Can intimidate me
On my way to God-discovery.

17

I meditate
So that I can easily
Differentiate the vital feelings
Of the lower worlds
And
The psychic feelings
Of the higher worlds.

18

I meditate
So that I can facilitate
All the complexities
Of the world
While I am succeeding in
 the outer life
And proceeding in my inner life.

19

I meditate
So that I can cheerfully
And
Perfectly communicate
With
God the Compassion-Delight
Before
God the Justice-Light
Appears before me.

20

I meditate
So that every morning
And
Every evening I can
Soulfully accommodate
The presence of the cosmic
Gods and Goddesses
Inside my aspiration-heart.

21

I meditate
So that every day
I can donate
Freely and unconditionally
My heart's purity-breath
And
My soul's divinity-life
To humanity.

22

I meditate
So that I can separate
The thorns of my desire-life
From
The roses of my aspiration-life.

23

I meditate
So that I can always feel
That I have only one
Intimate Friend,
And that Friend
Is my Lord's
Ever-increasing
Forgiveness-Light.

24

I meditate
So that my Lord's
Blessingful Messages
Can constantly
Reverberate in the inmost
Recesses of my heart.

25

I meditate
So that my vital does not
Care to fascinate the
World with its charm
But to strengthen the
World with its dynamism.

26

I meditate
So that I can confidently
State my Lord's Views
And never, never my views.

27

I meditate
So that I can become
Earth's sleeplessly
Crying delegate
To Heaven's constantly
Consoling Oneness-Home.

28

I meditate
So that I can graduate
From the University
Of God's Transcendental
Delight.

29

I meditate
So that nothing remains
Obdurate in my life
To please God cheerfully
And
Constantly in His own Way.

30

I meditate
So that every day I can
Cultivate a new
   Aspiration-dedication-field
Inside my heart's soulful purity
And my soul's fruitful
Divinity.

31

I meditate
So that my mind
Cannot hallucinate
In this world of illusion
And
Delusion.

32

I meditate
So that I do not underestimate
My divine potential
Which will unmistakably
And
Triumphantly lead me
To the Destination —
The Golden Shore.

33

I meditate
So that I do not allow
My fertile mind
To fabricate any
God-intoxicated story
To gain world-attention.

34

I meditate
So that I never procrastinate
In my self-giving duty,
My only duty.

35

I meditate
So that my life can be
Constantly affectionate
To God's Heart.

36

I meditate
So that I can soulfully
Propagate my Lord's Messages
In the fields of my
　aspiration-purity
And my dedication-beauty.

37

I meditate
So that someday
I can originate
A new hope for the sorrowful
And
Pitiful world.

38

I meditate
So that the impurity-mind
Of my outer life
Cannot assassinate
The purity-heart
Of my inner life.

39

I meditate
So that I can be ready
Every day for the immediate
Acceptance of God's
Transcendental Smile
And
The immediate rejection
Of Satan's universal frown.

40

I meditate
So that I can decorate
My heart's purity-temple
According to God's
Express Choice.

41

I meditate
So that God's blue Light
Of Infinity permeates
My entire being.

42

I meditate
So that I can associate
Myself with God's Beauty
In the Angels' World.

43

I meditate
So that I do not speculate
Anything with my mind-power
But envision the future
Realities with my heart-power.

44

I meditate
So that
I can consecrate
Each breath of mine
To better human life.

45

I meditate
So that the divine in me
Can tolerate the human in me
And
The human in me can illumine
The animal in me.

46

I meditate
So that I can abdicate
My Ignorance-Throne
Once and for all
In this incarnation.

47

I meditate
So that I can participate
In the Beauty-Contest
With the Angels
And
In the Compassion-Contest
With the Cosmic Gods.

PART XVII

I PRAY SO THAT

I PRAY SO THAT

1

I pray
So that I can play
With my Lord's Compassion-Eye
Every day at least for an hour.

2

I pray
So that I can become
An illumining ray
Of my Lord Supreme
In His Task
Of world-transformation.

3

I pray
So that I do not remain
An unaspiring, meaningless
And useless
Lump of clay.

4

I pray
So that every day
I can celebrate
As God's Victory-Day
Inside my gratitude-heart.

5

I pray
So that my Lord's Way
Becomes my way,
My only way.

6

I pray
So that I can realise
That God-Compassion
And God-Forgiveness
Pay my wages
For my aspiration and dedication
Infinitely more than I deserve.

7

I pray
So that I do not have to delay
When the final hour strikes
For the complete transformation
Of my human nature.

8

I pray
So that I do not allow
The sword of my impurity-mind
To slay my purity-heart.

9

I pray
So that my mind of complexity
Can stay
Inside my heart of simplicity
Which is nothing other
Than visible divinity on earth.

10

I pray
So that I never betray
My ever-indulgent
Compassion-Lord Supreme.

11

I pray
So that every day I can feel
The same joy
As I feel on my birthday.
Then every day
I can make a soulful promise
To become a choice instrument
Of my Lord Supreme,
As I do on my birthday.

12

I pray
So that I never
Become disheartened
While I essay to bring about
The complete transformation
Of my nature.

13

I pray
So that I can compel
My earth-bound mind
To obey
My Heaven-free soul.

14

I pray
So that I do not
Give up working
On my nature's transformation
Only halfway
As many ill-fated seekers do.

15

I pray
So that I do not doubt
When my heart is eager
To convey
Blessingful messages to me
From my Beloved Supreme.

16

I pray
So that my Lord examines me
Every day with His X-ray
To see if my mind is assailed
By dark doubts.

17

I pray
So that my heart's
Aspiration-tree
And my soul's
Manifestation-plant
Never decay.

18

I pray
So that I do not become a prey
To ignorance-sea
Even in my unconscious moments
And unconscious movements.

19

I pray
So that I do not disobey
My sweet Lord
Even when my impure vital,
My dark mind
And my insecure heart
Torture me ruthlessly.

20

I pray
So that every day I can offer
A new surrender-heart
And a new gratitude-life
To my Beloved Supreme.

21

I pray
So that my heart's faith-sword
Can easily slay
The haughty heads
Of my shameless doubts.

22

I pray
So that my aspiration-heart
And my dedication-life
Can weigh measureless weights.

23

I pray
So that every day
I can relay the message
Of my Lord's Victory-Day.

24

I pray
So that I do not lose
The fragrance of my heart's
Security-perfume.

25

I pray
So that every day
I can enjoy the feast
Of God-manifesting possibilities.

26

I pray
So that I can
Completely erase
The failure-life of centuries.

27

I pray
So that every seeker's faith
May return
From its mind-exile.

28

I pray
So that every day
I can tell the world
That the taste
Of God's Compassion-Biscuit
Is by far the best.

29

I pray
So that every day
I can see a hope-bud
Blossoming inside my heart.

30

I pray
So that every day
My inner life
Remains alarmed
And my outer life
Remains unharmed.

31

I pray
So that like God, I too
Will never remain
Unemployed.

32

I pray
So that I remember
That a life of relaxation
Can never escape the torture
Of unmistakable taxation.

33

I pray
So that God
Does not give me
An undeserved inner promotion.

34

I pray
So that the perfection
Of my dream-world
And the aspiration
Of my reality-world
Do not collide.

35

I pray
So that every day
I can see my Beloved Supreme
Watering my heart's faith-plant
With His Infinity's
   Compassion-Eye.

36

I pray
So that every day
I can confide in my soul,
My confidence-counsellor.

37

I pray
So that I can forget
Even the very existence
Of my former employer:
Ignorance.

38

I pray
So that every day
The seeker-traveller in me
Walks only on truth-trail.

39

I pray
So that every day
The vision-musician in me
And the perfection-music in me
Remain extremely fond
Of each other.

40

I pray
So that my Beloved Supreme
Keeps my doubting mind
Out of service,
Even temporarily.

41

I pray
So that every day
I can see and feel
The oneness
Between my aspiration
And my Lord's Satisfaction.

42

I pray
So that I can synchronise
My heart's inner choice
With my life's outer voice.

43

I pray
So that I can soon see
The complete collapse
Of my unbearably tall
Self-image.

44

I pray
So that my doubtful mind
Does not dare to forge
My faithful heart's signature.

45

I pray
So that my invisible soul
Can secretly make
My visible heart invincible.

46

I pray
So that I can learn
That my self-reproach
Is by no means God-approach.

47

I pray
So that my Beloved Supreme
And I together
Whistle our sweet and fond
Oneness-song.

PART XVIII

I AM READY

1. Dedication

14 April 1982

My dear Father,

On the occasion of your most auspicious centenary, I am offering you my five hundredth rose, "I am Ready," from my crying and smiling heart-garden.

May you remain in Heavenly Peace, Light and Delight until I come and join you.

Yours in the Eternal Father Supreme,

Madal

2

My Lord, break me,
My vital is ready.

My Lord, melt me,
My heart is ready.

My Lord, mould me,
My mind is ready.

My Lord, make me,
I am fully ready.

3

God's Compassion-Heart
　melts me,
My aspiration-heart.
God's Concern-Eye moulds me,
My dedication-life.
God's Love Arms make me,
My surrender-breath.

4

Even the most adequate answer
To the question "Who am I?"
Does not satisfy my heart.

Only the accurate answer
To the question "Whose am I?"
Satisfies me completely.

5

Self-examination quickly
　precedes
Self-realisation.

Self-realisation devotedly
　precedes
God-manifestation.

6

Purity is self-evident;
My aspiration-heart knows it.

Satisfaction is God-Fulfilment;
My dedication-life knows it.

7

A pure mind blossoms in peace.
A pure heart blossoms in bliss.
A pure life blossoms in oneness,
God-Oneness.

8

What I wanted
Was a flicker of hope.
But my Lord came
And stood before me
To give me
His Infinity's All.

9

A spiritual Master is
An eternal student.
He soulfully learns
Wisdom from God;
He ungrudgingly and
　compassionately
Learns ignorance from his
　disciples.

10

My Lord, kick me, kick me.
That is the only way
I can move forward.

My Lord, bless me, bless me.
That is the only way
I can rise upward.

My Lord, love me, love me.
That is the only way
I can dive inward.

11

I shall love the world
More soulfully today.
Do you know why?
Because
God has given me
One of His richest Treasures:
He has sown His
Confidence-Seed
In me.

12

Because
Of your restless mind,
You have lost.
Because
Of your faithless heart,
You have lost.
Because
Of your cheerless life,
You have lost.

13

Three things I daily do:
I dream
With my cheerful eyes,
I cry
With my tearful heart,
I fly
With my powerful soul.

14

My mind
Was born to grow divinely.
My heart
Was born to glow supremely.
My life
Was born to flow perpetually.

15

Soulfulness has given me
What it embodies: God's Heart.
Selflessness has given me
What it embodies: God's Life.
Finally,
God has given me
What He has and what He is:
Satisfaction-Smile.

16

My desire-life, are you blind?
Can you not see
That I am running fast,
Very fast,
Away from you?

My aspiration-life, look!
At long last
I have the soul-urge
To run towards you.

17

An enquiring mind must oscillate
Between
Victory-satisfaction
And
Defeat-frustration.

A self-giving heart will never oscillate.
It lives in God
And
Lives for God.

18

The heart feels that it can never be
Too early to realise God.

The soul knows that it can never be
Too late to manifest God.

19

I love, I love, I love.
I love the silver process of seeing.
I love the golden progress of the seen.
I love the diamond fulness of the Seer.

20

I shall not add anything
To my heart's hunger for God.
I shall not remove anything
From my soul's feast with God.

21

Be not alone,
Man's ignorance-tiger
Will come and devour you.
Be not alone,
Go and learn the secret of
    sacrifice-delight
From God's Sacrifice-Horse.

22

Steadily
Each and every thought
Sculptures its own life.
Ultimately
Each and every life
Sculptures its own God.

23

Be not enamoured
Of what you see outwardly.

Be not indifferent
To what you feel inwardly.

24

Your mind's selfishness
Is your all-exclusive individuality.

Your heart's selflessness
Is your all-inclusive universality.

25

My sweet Lord Supreme,
Even if I happen to be
The most unaspiring
Seeker-child of Yours,
Do you not agree with me
That I have no protection-shelter
Other than You?

26

As a human being can
Easily and effectively discard
His discouraging and
   disheartening dreams,
Even so he can renounce
Cheerfully and permanently
His unaspiring animal life.

27

My Lord, if I have
Your Forgiveness-Sun,
Then who can hurt me?
And if I do not have
Your Forgiveness-Sun,
Then who can console me?

28

The seeker-watcher sees
The God-Day.
The lover-smiler knows
Not only the God-Hour
But also the God-Moment.

29

O my truth-searching mind,
God is more than greatness.
O my God-loving heart,
God is more than goodness.
God is His Eternity's own
   Perfection-cry.
God is His Immortality's own
   Satisfaction-Smile.

30

O my Pilot Supreme,
Your outer Name is Concern-Sky,
Your inner Name is
   Forgiveness-Sun.
You cry every day at my
   heart's door
To gain a new entry
So that cheerfully and proudly
You can steer my life-boat.

31

God through man
Reveals His Eternity's
Beauty-cry.
God for man
Reveals His Immortality's
Prosperity-Smile.

32

One great consoling message
From your Master
Can totally stop the withering
Of your God-realising realities
And God-manifesting
   inevitabilities.

33

Happy are my eyes to see You,
My Lord!
Happy is my heart to feel You,
My Lord!
Happy is my life to claim You,
My Lord,
As my own, very own!

34

If you want to enjoy the death-cry
Of your poverty-stricken ego,
Then you must at once
Check the escalating growth
Of your desire-night.

35

I see the growth
Of my happy consciousness
Only inside my full obedience
To my soul's wisdom-height.

36

Yesterday
I lived inside
My mind's disastrous
   uncertainty-sea.
Today
I am living inside
My heart's rapturous
   divinity-ocean.
This is what my Lord's
Unconditional Grace
Has done for me.

37

Celestial intimacies
Are bound to suffocate
In the narrow grasp
Of petty alternatives:
Possession-greed
And
Rejection-seed.

38

Every flower-heart
Has a soul.
Every flower-soul
Has a special
God-ordained role.

39

Since my Lord's infinite Smile
Has not changed,
I must not change my heart's
Eternal cry.

40

If my outer smile is mighty,
Then my inner cry is almighty.

If my self-giving is strong,
Then my God's Satisfaction
Is stronger
Than the strongest.

41

Do not
Expect anything from this world.
You will be sadly disappointed
And
Badly frustrated.

Do not
Surrender to this world.
Yours will be the unmistakable
And
Ultimate victory.

PART XIX

MY HEART'S THIRTY-ONE
SACRED SECRETS

MY HEART'S THIRTY-ONE SACRED SECRETS

1

My heart needs only one freedom:
The freedom to dream.

2

A depressed heart
Means a confessed failure.

3

Because you are always depressed,
God has secretly told His choice
   children
That you are not a member
Of His inner Family.

4

The Hour of God
Mercilessly threatens
   the doubting mind
And
Measurelessly enlightens
   the aspiring heart.

5

O man of eloquence,
My mind sincerely admires you.

O man of silence,
My heart soulfully loves you.

6

The farther away I am from
   my inner hunger,
The greater is my outer
   insecurity.

7

Before you declare
That you have realised God,
Can you not tell the whole world
That God has truly and
   unconditionally
Loved your teeming ignorance?
Try it.
It may not be an easy task.

8

You tell God:
"My Lord, will You accept what
    I have for You —
My eternity's hunger-cry?"

God tells you:
"My child, will you accept what
    I have for you —
My Immortality's Feast-Smile?"

9

You live for yourself alone.
How do you then expect God
    to live with you
And any human being
    to die for you?

10

Alas,
My mind, the silly talker,
Has taken away all the
    wisdom-light
That I received from my Lord's
Silence-Eye.

11

Two souls
Meet to promise.

Two hearts
Meet to love.

Two minds
Meet to challenge.

12

The quicker
I unlearn,
The wiser
I become,
The better
I love
My Beloved Supreme.

13

An aspiring heart
Is the only secret-sharer
Of my sacred soul.

14

My Lord,
I do not want to carry the
   heavy burden
Of knowledge any more.
I wish to carry the tiny briefcase
Of wisdom-delight
Which You have given me
As a blessingful gift.

15

Yesterday for the first time
I loved my searching mind.

Today for the first time
I am loving my crying heart.

Tomorrow for the first time
I shall love my smiling soul.

16

During the night
I stay with my old and
   mature friends:
Dreams.

During the day
I stay with my young and
   immature friends:
Realities.

17

A sacred heart-flower
Is a secret treasure-fruit
Of God.

18

A purity-heart
Never allows the waves of life
To become wild.

19

A surrender-heart
Is the safest island
In an unknown life-sea.

20

Secretly
My soul creates purity.

Openly
My heart enjoys it.

Secretly
My heart creates beauty.

Openly
My mind enjoys it.

21

A surrender-life
Means a continuous illumination.

A gratitude-heart
Means a spontaneous perfection.

22

The outer world thinks
That I am a devouring tiger.

The inner world knows
That I am a roaring lion.

23

Man thinks
That I am in no way superior
To any wild animal.

God knows
That I am in no way inferior
To any cosmic god.

24

Self-awareness
And
Conscious oneness with God
Are not
Two different things.

25

My heart's inner examination
Determines
My life's outer perfection.

26

Self-giving
Means a glorious success.

God-becoming
Means a stupendous progress.

27

My own gratitude-heart
Is all that matters.

28

Detachment
Is man's never-failing smile.

29

If you want your soul
To be truly proud of you,
Then every day challenge
The giant pride
Of impossibility.

30

I do not want to know
What has made your mind
Exceptionally great.
But I do want to know
What has made your heart
Soulfully pure.

31

Look,
The entire world is in favour
Of your becoming another God.

PART XX

MY GOD-HUNGER-DREAMS

MY GOD-HUNGER-DREAMS

1

God
Needs a special assistant.
My heart's budding gratitude
Is applying for the post.

2

God
Needs a perfect partner.
My life's blossoming surrender
Is applying for the post.

3

If
You cannot change your mind,
Then change the subject.
Try
A new subject:
God-Realisation.

4

No God,
No God.
Openly and proudly
He says.
God lives.
God is.
Secretly and sacredly
He feels.

5

Go forward,
If your aspiration-heart
Is pure.
Go backward,
If your suspicion-mind
Is impure.

6

God the Justice
Unconditionally
Surrenders to
God the Compassion
Almost
ALWAYS.

7

Can we not adore
God's Forgiveness-Feet
Exactly
The same way He admires
Our sincerity-hearts?

8

Deception
Is not something
New to the mind.
Aspiration
Is not something
New to the heart.
Illumination
Is not something
New to the soul.
Compassion
Is not something
New to the God.

9

To buy one single
Satisfaction-smile from my heart
God is ready to spend
His astronomical
Compassion-Tears.

10

Who
Cared for me?
God the Forgiveness-Heart.
Who
Cares for me?
God the Compassion-Eye.
Who
Will care for me?
God the Transformation-Hand.

11

Jesus,
Do show me
The God-seeker
Who is crying for You.
Christ,
Do show me
The God-lover
Who is smiling at You.

12

What
Have I to call my own
Since
I have disowned
God's Compassion-Eye
And
His Forgiveness-Heart?

13

My Lord,
May I borrow Your Vision-Eye?
My child,
I am not in the habit of
Lending anything to anyone.
But
You can have My Vision-Eye
Permanently
For the asking.

14

My
Aspiration-life
Is still alive
Because
Every morning and
Every evening it bathes
In my Lord's
Compassion-Forgiveness-Sea.

15

The mind calls Him
"Absolute Supreme."
The heart calls Him
"Oneness-Fulness-Love."

16

Confidence-explorers
Are destined to be
Promise-fulfillers.

17

If
You can love your
Today's newness-dawn,
Then
God will grant you
His Tomorrow's
Fulness-Day.

18

God
Does not want your mind
To enjoy any more
Hesitation-hobby.
God
Does not want your vital
To loiter any more
In your aspiration-heart-lobby.

19

A God-realised soul
Is a service-searchlight
Of God's Dream-Manifestation-
   Reality.

20

I shall
NEVER, NEVER
FORGIVE
My unforgiving mind.

21

Your road
Is an unending series
Of red lights
Precisely because
You do not care for
The green lights'
Welcome-heart.

22

Man asks God
Every day
One question:
"Why is life so hard?"
God answers the question
With His Infinite
   Compassion-Heart.
Alas!
The acceptance
Of God's Answer-Light
Is not in the very nature
Of man.

23

A self-seeking man
Unconsciously
Makes friends with
Eternity's
Frustration-clown-frowns.

24

My
Love of purity's call
Is the Headmaster
Of my heart-school.

25

Man
Is his long-promised
Surrender-flame.
God
Is His long-promised
Satisfaction-Sun.

26

What
I have for myself
Is a self-smitten mind.
What
God has for me
Is His Divinity-flooded Heart.

27

Morning
Is the time when I become
The Heaven-ascent-resolution.
Evening
Is the time when my
Surrender-life becomes
The God-Descent-Solution.

28

The aspiration-heart
Has always room
For one more creation of God.
The doubting mind
Has no room even for God.
NEVER.

29

How
Do you tell me that you have
Nothing to do?
Have
You taught your mind
Its departure-song?
Have
You taught your heart
Its arrival-dance?

30

God
Is equally proud of my outer
  mind's
Disappearance-jungle
And
My inner heart's
Appearance-garden.

31

My Lord
Does not want
My surrender-life
From my suffering heart-tears.
My Lord
Wants my surrender-life
From my flying heart-smiles.

32

If you are doing
The right thing
God is not going
To ask you
When you started it
And
When you are going
To end it.
He is all happiness
In what you are doing.

33

Just to dream
Of the Ultimate Goal,
The God-seeker has to be
An exceptionally brave soul.

34

Without God's
Compassion-Approval
My self-reliance
Is a most expensive joke.

35

The aspiration-flames
Of a God-seeker
Are God's own
Future-Capacity-
 Fulfilment-Dreams.

36

You
Are not indispensable.
Just believe it.
Lo, your mind is flooded
With peace.

37

Be not an ascetic.
At the end of your journey's close,
Even God the constant
 Satisfaction
Will not be able
To recognise you.

38

When I concentrate,
I concentrate on my
Perfection only.
When I meditate,
I meditate on God's
Satisfaction only.

39

Direct knowledge-light
I want.
Interpretation is
Interruption.

40

The more my outer mind-dog
Barks,
The more my inner God-Lion
Sleeps.

41

God wants from me
Only one thing:
My constant concern
For His Compassion-Liberation-Boat.

42

Your mind wants to be
A world-destroyer.
Do you know what God wants
From your mind?
He wants your mind to be
A peace-pioneer.

43

My mind
Has given me its peerless wealth:
Inspiration-Dawn.
My heart
Has given me its peerless wealth:
Aspiration-day.
My soul
Has given me its peerless wealth:
Realisation-Sun.

44

Only when
Your mind becomes
A God-dreamer,
You can have peace.
Only when
Your heart becomes
A God-lover,
You can have perfection.

45

May my mind become
A fast-running aspiration-river.
May my heart become
A fast-increasing realisation-sea.
May my soul become
A fast-blossoming
  perfection-shore.

46

If
You want to cash in
God's Love-Check,
Then
You must go to
His Compassion-Bank.

47

What
Is hesitation,
If not a thorn
In your
God-Promise-Garden?

48

True,
God is His Eternity's
Patience-Light.
But He wants me to have
His own Infinity
Sooner than at once.

49

If
You forget
To feed your aspiration-flames,
Then
God will forget
To read your life-book.

50

God trusts me.
Therefore He has put
His Divine Life
In my human hands.
Can I not likewise trust God
And put my human life
In His Divine Hands?

MY GOD-HUNGER-DREAMS

51

If
I want to ring
God's Delight-Bell,
Then I must live
Inside my life's
Gratitude-breath.

52

God's Compassion
And
My life's perfection
Someday, somewhere, somehow
Are bound to meet.

53

Let us cry together.
God will soon come.
Let us smile together.
Lo, God has just arrived.

54

God
Is not a Visitor
Of my fearful sleep.
God
Is an Admirer
Of my soulful dreams.

55

My Lord Supreme,
My soul-reality's All,
Countless times
I have withdrawn from You.
I have withdrawn
My promise-oneness.
I have withdrawn
My willingness-oneness.
I have withdrawn
My soulfulness-oneness.
I have withdrawn
My surrender-oneness-bliss.
Still You have not
Withdrawn from me.
You remain
Your Eternity's Compassion-Eye.
You remain
Your Infinity's Forgiveness-Heart.
You remain
Your Immortality's
   Vision-Fulfilment-Cry.

PART XXI

THE GOD OF THE MIND

THE GOD OF THE MIND

1

The God
Of the mind
Has a very short life.

2

The love of the mind
Fails to reach
The supreme Destination.

3

A real God-lover
Does not have to borrow
Anything
From yesterday and tomorrow.

4

Each
Breathing moment
Is
A miracle.

5

Divine feelings
Are
Supreme realities.

6

In your inner life
Never
Be sparing in crying.

In your outer life
Never
Be sparing in smiling.

7

I am determined
To make God extremely
FAMOUS
Here on earth.

8

Each
Aspiration-flame
Is
A God-representative.

9

Patience
Is at once
God and man's
Sacred victory-secret.

10

Forgiveness
Means transformation
Of a human heart
Into a divine life.

11

May my life
Every morning grow into
A new
Flower-fragrance-prayer.

12

Today
I am not alone.
The fragrance of my
Heart-flower-garden
Will stay with me.

13

Uniqueness I see in others.
That means
God has already blessed me
With His Fulness.

14

Doubt openly blows out
The candle of the mind.
Impurity secretly blows out
The lamp of the heart.

15

God's inner Message to me:
Self-transcendence.
God's outer Message to me:
Heart-vigilance.

16

Do not
Blame the world.
Find
A solution.

THE GOD OF THE MIND

17

Today
I am determined
To give space
To the unloved ones.

18

Make
Healthy choices.
Perfection
Will be yours.

19

God's
Protection appears unseen.
We see it
Only when it disappears.

20

Surprise God!
Breathlessly tell Him
That you love Him
Only, only, only.

21

Receptivity-inability
Is a universal
Experience-disease.

22

Perfect happiness is
Enthusiasm minus
Expectation.

23

God tells me
That He likes to remain
Permanently
The Landlord of my heart-house.

24

How long do you want
To keep your heart-book
Out of print?
How long?

25

A true peace-lover
Feels that he can
Never be overworked.

26

A purity-heart
Is always a champion
Of universal oneness-delight.

27

I have two teachers.
My heart-teacher teaches me
Reliance.
My mind-teacher teaches me
Defiance.

28

Humanity's
Real and only poverty:
Unwillingness.

29

Every morning and every evening
God gives me the same
Advice:
Never leave your heart
    unguarded.

30

Is there any human being
Who is not the embodiment
Of opposing realities?

31

Now, this very moment,
Is the best time
For me to retire
From ignorance-army.

32

My Lord, my Lord,
I beg of You
Not to allow my unworthiness
To lead me astray.

THE GOD OF THE MIND

33

If you allow your mind to be
Paralysed by uncertainty,
Then your heart will automatically
Be paralysed by unwillingness.

34

Self-giving means
The unmasking of the
Golden Face of the future.

35

Who is the real loser?
He who enjoys
The superiority-inferiority-game.

36

Oneness-bravery
Means
Freedom from self-slavery.

37

My eyes weep tears
Only when my heart enjoys
Ecstasy's flood.

38

God is desperately looking for
　　you
To get from you
A copy of your heart-key.

39

It is impossible to believe
That you never get any call
From Above
On your aspiration-line.

40

Is there any human being
Who does not enjoy
The flickering of optimism-lamp?

41

There are only three roads
That do not have speed limits:
Heart's aspiration-road,
Life's dedication-road and
God's Satisfaction-Road.

42

A gratitude-heart
Can smilingly illumine
A doubting mind.

43

Who serves the server?
God the Satisfaction Infinite.

44

God's Compassion-Eye
Cries and cries
When I count my defeats
On the battlefield of life.

45

Unconditionally you love God.
That means you never allow
Your aspiration to take a break.

46

A God-seeker
Can never retire.

47

Your sterling faith in God
Can easily brave
Numberless buffets.

48

The mind cannot speak to God.
But it can overhear
When God and the heart talk.

49

My morning aspiration
Is my best
Heart-satisfaction-song.

50

God
Wants every human being
To pass the heart-fitness test.

51

First
Be an illumined individual;
Then you can become
The creator of a fulfilled world.

52

Love God sleeplessly.
He will grant you your heart's
Rainbow-choices.

53

God
Is supremely proud of you,
Because you have tamed
Your earthquake-emotion-life.

54

I cannot believe that
You do not have the number
Of our Beloved Supreme
In your heart-directory.

55

What I call a pure thought,
God calls it His Heart's
Flower-Smile-Song.

56

O God-lover,
How can you dare to imagine
A pain-flooded future?

57

On principle,
I never allow my mind
Even to touch
My soul's throne.

58

God's
Compassion-Eye
Pays
All my ignorance-bills.

PART XXII

O MY HEART

O MY HEART

1

O my heart,
I love you and I need you.
I love your earthly purity-cry
And I need your
　Heavenly divinity-smile.

2

O my heart,
Our Lord Beloved Supreme
　has told me
That He will supply your
　every need
Born and yet unborn.

3

O my heart,
Do tell me if I am not the person
　you want me to be.
I shall always have the time,
And I shall always have the
　eagerness
To perfect myself so that I can be
　claimed by you as your own,
　very own.

4

O my heart,
Because you choose to live
　compassionately,
My life and I hope to live happily.

5

O my heart,
Do not allow my undisciplined
　vital to befriend you.
That friendship will be the
　greatest waste
Of your unhorizoned potential.

6

O my heart,
Today you have made me
　unimaginably happy
By launching your aspiration-boat
On my life's dedication-river.

7

O my heart,
Sleeplessly you are teaching me
How to anchor my human love
In God's divine Love.

8

O my heart,
You expect permanent happiness
 on earth.
And in every way you deserve it,
 too.
But alas, alas, alas.
Will it ever happen?
Will you ever be flooded with
 happiness?
I shall pray and pray and pray to
God for you.

9

O my heart,
Every day you lovingly teach
 my mind
How to climb up the mountain
 of awareness
And every day my soul fondly
 teaches you
How to fly in the sky of
 selflessness.

10

O my heart,
You are desperately trying to
 discipline my mind.
Do you not know
That it is as useless
As trying to tame the wind?

11

O my heart,
Your will is your own
 oneness-satisfaction-friend.
Therefore, I am so proud of you.
Alas, my mind's will is its own
 division-destruction-enemy.

12

O my heart,
When I am not with you
And when I am not for you
I am forced to move
From unhappiness-death to
 fruitlessness-death.

13

O my heart,
I am exceedingly happy today.
Do you know why?
Today I have completely passed
 through the longest dry desert
 of my doubting mind,
And now I am being blessed
By the beauty of your
God-fragrance-garden.

14

O my heart,
I am exceedingly happy
To see every day
New and charming leaves
On your God-revealing life-plant.

15

O my heart,
Like you I wish to be a student
   of divine love.
Like you I shall never want to
   finish my schooling.

16

O my heart,
I am so sorry to have kept
   you waiting
For my life's perfection-marks
So that you can give me proudly
Your satisfaction-award.

17

O my heart,
Like you I wish to be sleeplessly
   and intimately personal
   with God.
O my heart, do be my private
   wisdom-light-tutor.

18

O my heart,
Time and again God has told me
That your part in His sweet
Dream-Play is extremely
   significant.
Therefore, my pride in you
   knows no bounds.

19

O my heart,
When I am not with you
I live in yesterday's
   falsehood-doubt-cave.
When I am with you
I live in tomorrow's
   truth-conviction-palace.

20

O my heart,
Just because I am for you
I am enjoying the slow, steady
    and unerring progress
Of God-revealing and
    God-manifesting faith
In my entire being.

21

O my heart,
I am secretly telling you that
    every day
I plead with my undivine mind
To come and study at your faith
    boarding school.
Alas, my mind is nothing other
    than shameless unwillingness.

22

O my heart,
When I soulfully pray to God,
He sends you to me with the
    message:
"Nothing is too much."
And when I unconditionally
    meditate on God,
He sends you to me with the
    message:
"Nothing is too soon."

23

O my heart,
You are constantly telling me
That my life's gratitude-telegrams
    can and will reach God
Sooner than the soonest
From anywhere in the world.

24

O my heart,
I shall never be able to enjoy
    energising rest
Unless and until I see my mind
Under your
    wisdom-illumination-arrest.

25

O my heart,
If I had only known
How much you cared for me,
I would not have stayed with my
    doubt-poison-mind,
Even for a fleeting second.

26

O my heart,
You are your mounting
    aspiration-flames
To reach the highest
    illumination-heights.
Therefore, I am divinely and
    supremely proud of you.
Look at my utterly stupid mind:
It is dying for death-desire-drugs.

27

O my heart,
You are always ready with your
    aspiration-candles.
Alas, will my mind ever be ready
    with its inspiration-matches?

28

O my heart,
When I do not live in your
    illumination-province,
A doubt-volcano forces me
    to move
From the frustration-town to the
    failure-village.

29

O my heart,
Your daily
    surrender-gratitude-life
Is saving me from the undying
    undercurrent of expectation.

30

O my heart,
I am all gratitude to you
For teaching me to say goodbye
To my very, very old partner:
    doubt.

31

O my heart,
Every day I am learning from you
Two most significant lessons:
A soulful receptivity and a
    prayerful readiness
To surrender to God's Will.

32

O my heart,
How kind of you to share with
    me unconditionally
The sweet, sweeter, sweetest
    taste of gratitude.

33

O my heart,
I am sleeplessly grateful to you,
For you have asked me
To call God my Beloved,
My only Beloved Supreme.

34

O my heart,
I am extremely fond of you
For many divine things you
  embody,
But especially for the
  snow-white innocence
Of your childlike smile.

35

O my heart,
You simply do not know what
  negativity is.
Therefore, to my greatest joy,
You are a perfect stranger
To unfriendliness-disaster-crime.

36

O my heart,
Your tremendous and momentous
  receptivity-capacity
Is pleasing me far beyond your
  imagination.
And I do hope that my most
  sincere appreciation-capacity
Is pleasing you in a small
  measure.

37

O my heart,
When I am inside you
Do you know what
  I deeply enjoy?
I enjoy a sea of silence-delight
That can never be attacked
  and bitten
By thought-mosquitoes.

38

O my heart,
Your fondest dream is constant
God-satisfaction.
And my bravest promise is
God-manifestation here and now.

O MY HEART

39

O my heart,
You are asking me to look at
The beauty of your moon-light
And the prosperity of your
    sun-power.
I am at once all obedience and
    all ecstasy.

40

O my heart,
You are my delight-sea within,
You are my delight-mountain
    without.
Like you, my only oneness-friend,
I shall start my day with a soulful
    surrender-song
And end my day with a
    beautiful gratitude-dance.

41

O my heart,
Your great and good
    encouragement-strength
Has rescued me countless times
From drowning in a sea of
    self-pity-tears.

42

O my heart,
When I breathe in your
    fragrance-light,
How easily I surrender to God
My heavy
    world-resentment-burden.

43

O my heart,
I am all gratitude to you,
For your breathless willingness
To serve God in God's own Way
Is permeating my entire being.

44

O my heart,
My superiority-giants and
    my inferiority-ghosts
Simply disappear the moment
    they see me
Swing with you in your
    oneness-cradle.

45

O my heart,
Selfish actions have imprisoned
   the world.
You are desperately trying to
   liberate the world.
God the Compassion is crying
   through you.
I know, someday God the Victory
Will, without fail, smile
   through you.

46

O my heart,
I need no credentials
To arrive at God's Door
Only when I accompany you.

47

O my heart,
You always get the first preference
When you dial God's
Emergency-Heart-Number.
And when you call,
   unlike other callers,
God Himself answers
   immediately.

48

O my heart,
Every day you are feeding me with
God's Nectar-Delight.
I need no more useless
   God-explanation from my
   scholar-friend.
I need no more useless
   God-understanding from my
   philosopher-friend.

49

O my heart,
Yesterday I saw you in your
   aspiration-career.
Today I am seeing you with a
   perfection-crown on your head.
And whose perfection-crown?
God's, definitely God's.

50

O my heart,
It is you who have taught me
How to write every day
Most soulful love-letters to God.

My prayer-life and my
   meditation-life
From this moment on
Will cheerfully, sleeplessly
   and unconditionally be at
   your service.

PART XXIII

O MY MIND

O MY MIND

1

O my mind,
Do not tell others
That they are suffering
Because they have done
    something wrong.
For God's sake,
Do not add insult to injury!

2

O my mind,
Stop advising others.
It is high time for you
To be a better creation of God's
Than what you think you are.

3

O my mind,
You will soon be dominated
By ruthless guilt.
For you are using guilt
To manipulate your dear ones.

4

O my mind,
You need not be doomed
To disappointment!
God does know
That you need purity
More than anything else.
Lo, God is giving you
    another chance
To sincerely and soulfully pray.

5

O my mind,
As a self-giving player,
My heart is infinitely better
    than you.
Play with the better competition.
Your capacity for self-giving
Will quickly and considerably
    improve.

6

O my mind,
Do you know
Why you are good for nothing?
You are good for nothing
Because you daydream too much
About the uncertain future.

7

O my mind,
Your doubt-connection
With your powerful vital
Will end in an unhappy disaster.
Try to develop
A beautiful friendship
With your prayerful and
  fruitful heart.

8

O my mind,
When did God tell you
That you are always destined
To do something stupid?

9

O my mind,
Ask your heart
Immediately for help.
You badly need help
From your heart
To see supremely good qualities
In all human beings.

10

O my mind,
Before God takes away
Your pleasure-life,
Can you not beg Him to
  grant you
His Compassion-
  Forgiveness-Treasure?

11

O my mind,
Your unhappy experiences
From human beings
Can never be an adequate excuse
For you to remain shockingly
  imperfect.

12

O my mind,
God is supremely proud of you
Only when He sees in you
A most sincere willingness
  to see good
In your fellow citizens of
  this world.

13

O my mind,
Since all your life
You have been giving
 undue importance
To what you know,
Can you not now
At least give due importance
To what you do not know at all?

14

O my mind,
Intolerance is an easy thing.
This is not something unknown
 to you.
Can you not try
To achieve something really
 difficult?
Love the world more,
Ever more.

15

O my mind,
My great task
Is to make you likable,
Nay, lovable by others — by all.
Of course, God is included!

16

O my mind,
What you need is cooperation
With the other members of
 your family.
Once you have that,
Then anger and frustration
Will run away from you
Faster than the fastest.

17

O my mind,
Invoke God the Forgiveness first,
And then invoke God the
 Compassion.
Then God the Justice
Will send you this message:
"My child,
I am glad to inform you
That you can surely escape my
 visit."

18

O my mind,
Negativity does not become you.
Be positive in everything
And in every way.
In you, with you and through you
God's Vision of the Beyond
Will be manifested.

19

O my mind,
Anything that is humanly right
May not always be divinely good.
But anything that is divinely good
Is undoubtedly always humanly
   right.

20

O my mind,
Do not feel sad
That you are rejected by mankind.
Just be humble and pure.
You will before long be protected
By the Absolute Lord Himself.

21

O my mind,
Do unfurl
Your hard-earned purity-banner
And champion the cause
Of self-offering.

22

O my mind,
If you do not care to acknowledge
Your own weaknesses,
How will you ever control
And perfect them?

23

O my mind,
In your newly discovered
Aspiration-life,
Do not permit procrastination.
What you call your
   procrastination,
God calls His starvation —
Starvation for reciprocal love,
Oneness and satisfaction-delight.

24

O my mind,
You have been my teacher
For a very, very long time.
From today on
I shall be your teacher.

O my mind,
You forced me to be your student,
But I shall swiftly awaken you
And unconditionally illumine
   you.

O MY MIND

25

O my mind,
Stop thinking that you are
The absolute authority on
    everything.

26

O my mind,
Because you are utterly stupid,
You think that you can overthrow
My heart's joy-government.

27

O my mind,
You must know
That nobody thinks highly of you
When you indulge in self-pity.

28

O my mind,
Before expecting
    world-perfection,
You must prove to the world
That you are perfectly faultless
And that you are a genuine
    student of peace.

29

O my mind,
Your stupidity
Makes you completely unaware
Of my heart's teeming admirable
    qualities.

30

O my mind,
You are nothing
But your own insecurity-success
And your own
    frustration-progress.

31

O my mind,
When are you going to become
Once more familiar
With your own long-forgotten
Tranquility-territory?

32

O my mind,
If you want to weaken
Your strongest pride,
Then start counting
Your missed opportunities.

33

O my mind,
Do you really want others
To be happy,
Or while others are suffering
   most deplorably
In utter helplessness,
Are you secretly enjoying
Selfish gratification?

34

O my mind,
If you allow yourself
Always to be a victim
To worries and anxieties,
Then it is you who have made
   yourself
A completely drunk driver
On the highway of your own
   aspiration-life.

35

O my mind,
When did God tell you
That you are every day destined
To do something great,
   very great?
Never!
But God did tell you
That every day
You have to be humility incarnate
And purity incarnate.

36

O my mind,
I shall no longer allow
Your callous rigidity
To overshadow
My heart's beautiful spontaneity.

37

O my mind,
I shall definitely enjoy
The separation between your
   dark doubts
And my heart's bright faith.
Needless to say,
I am all for my heart's faith.

O MY MIND

38

O my mind,
You are terrified of the unknown.
Look!
My heart not only admires
  the unknown
But is also fond of
  the Unknowable.

39

O my mind,
From this moment on,
My heart and I shall demand
Your deep respect.
No more will you be allowed
To belittle us!

40

O my mind,
One day you will wonder
Why you have not seen
My heart's unparalleled
  beauty before.

41

O my mind,
Do not pretend!
You cannot be nearly as innocent,
Sincere and pure
As you always try to appear.

42

O my mind,
Every day you are the inventor
Of confusion-monkey
And the discoverer
Of frustration-tiger.

43

O my mind,
In case you do not know,
I am telling you
That your happiness is fragile
But my heart's delight is
  everlasting.

44

O my mind,
Quite often you take vacations
From the aspiration-school.
I am ashamed of you.
Indeed,
That is an understatement.

45

O my mind,
Your wild restlessness,
My heart's calmness forgives.
But I cannot and I do not.
I do not even want to.

46

O my mind,
At long last
I have summoned the courage
    to tell you
That you are a shameless rogue.
My aspiration-heart and I
Will have nothing more
    to do with you.

47

O my mind,
Will you ever care for your
    perfection?
Take your own time;
I am not expecting
An immediate answer.

48

O my mind,
You exaggerate your strength
Far beyond your imagination.
Look!
My heart does not even want
    to advertise
Its God-given strength.

49

O my mind,
You buy a round-trip ticket
When you go to visit
The cottage of truth.
You quickly come back
To your falsehood-apartment.
My heart buys only a one-way
    ticket
To go to Truth-Palace.
Once it reaches Truth-Palace,
It does not return.

50

O my mind,
I am embarrassed
To see your over-confidence.
Your over-confidence ignores
Not only God the creation
But also God the Creator.

51

O my mind,
You depend on doubt.
Do you know that
The real name of doubt is
　frustration?
My heart depends on faith.
The real name of faith
Is satisfaction-jubilee.

52

O my mind,
So often you are befriended
By cynicism.
My heart and I are befriended
By the embrace of the
　universal man.

53

O my mind,
Because you do not have patience,
You badly fail.
Because my heart has patience,
God and my heart
Ultimately have each other
And enjoy each other.

54

O my mind,
Sincerity is powerfully knocking
At your door.
How long will you and your
　false pride
Ignore your unconditional
　well-wisher?

55

O my mind,
You must realise
That there is a vast difference
Between your great intentions
And my heart's good
　accomplishments.

56

O my mind,
Your life is nothing other
Than volcano-suspicion.
But my heart's aspiration-cry
And my Lord's
　Compassion-Light
Will never allow you to explode.

57

O my mind,
God does not want you
To make something great out
　of your suffering.
God does not want you
To idealise or idolise your
　suffering.
God wants you to take suffering,
When it comes,
As a valuable lesson.

58

O my mind,
No matter how often
Or how hard you try
To make others believe
Your falsehood-propaganda,
It will never pass for Truth.

59

O my mind,
If you deliberately remain
A stranger to purity and humility,
Then in God's
　Compassion-Heart-Home
You will always remain
Unexpected and uninvited.

60

O my mind,
Once more if you say
That you are depressed
And you need my sympathy,
I shall not remain silent.
I shall tell you the real reason.
The real reason for your
　depression
Is that you secretly and openly
Enjoy the pleasures of lethargy.

61

O my mind,
You are a constant trouble-maker,
But I shall not surrender to you.
I know that before long
My Lord Supreme will come
　to me
As my trouble-shooter.

62

O my mind,
Why are you so stupid?
As soon as you are inspired,
Why do you not go one step
    ahead,
And aspire to expedite
Your stupendous success-glory?

63

O my mind,
You can never be as serious
As you seem.
You can never be as pure
As you seem.
But you can be,
And you actually are,
As much of a doubt-monster
As you seem.

64

O my mind,
When I enter into my
    heart-room,
I clearly hear
The sweet melody of a
    golden flute.
But when you enter into my heart,
You command confusion-din
To accompany you.

65

O my mind,
When I think of your stupidity,
I feel sad.
When I think of your insincerity,
I am mad.
When I think of your imminent
And permanent surrender
To my truth-serving and
God-loving heart,
I become glad, supremely glad.

66

O my mind,
I do not trust you.
I am sure you know that.
I shall trust you
Only when you come to me alone,
And not with your dangerous
    doubt-friend
And useless uncertainty-friend.

67

O my mind,
You and I have been together
For a very long time.
But now I want to leave you
And go beyond you.
Do you want to know why,
After all these years,
I want to discontinue our
 association?
Only one reason:
You do not have soulful
 confidence.
What you have is either
Ridiculous over-confidence
Or confidence-famine.
I simply don't want either of
 the two.

68

O my mind,
You have made me ruthless.
You and I have become
Perfect strangers to sensitivity.
When are we going to realise
That kindness is the only key
To our real satisfaction?

69

O my mind,
My heart and I
Did not know ahead of time
That we would love each other
 so much.
And I never knew ahead of time
That you with your trickeries
And my vital with its aggressions
Would be so unthinkably hostile
To me and my heart.

70

O my mind,
It is simply useless to tell you
That unlike you,
Not only my heart
But also others' hearts
Are extremely beautiful and pure.
You have taken an oath
Not to listen to truth.

71

O my mind,
You secretly and shamelessly
Want to thrive
On the misfortunes of others.
Is that possible?
No, you fool, never!

72

O my mind,
Time and again
You have broken my heart
With false promises.
You are so cruel!
You are such a liar!
Even though my heart is broken,
It is healing the wounds
You have inflicted on
   my dedication-life.

73

O my mind,
Day by day
Your insincerity-breath
Is increasing its capacity.
Before you and your breath
   become immortal,
I must either illumine you or
   destroy you.

74

O my mind,
Are you blind?
Are you deaf?
Can you not see,
Can you not hear,
That the whole world is
   telling me
That my heart is the mother
Of Eternity's love
And Immortality's affection?

75

O my mind,
By defying my soul's authority
And by turning a deaf ear
To my heart's soulful requests,
You have become an object of
   contempt
And not of admiration.

76

O my mind,
Unlike you,
I appreciate, admire and adore
The human beings who take risks
To accomplish their
   dedication-services
To God the creation.

77

O my mind,
Instead of being a busy
 fault-finder
Can you not become
A busy, always busy,
God-lover?

PART XXIV

MY LORD SUPREME,
DO YOU HAVE A MOMENT?

MY LORD SUPREME, DO YOU HAVE A MOMENT?

1

My Lord Supreme,
Do tell me if You are in a mood
To answer a few spiritual questions.

"My child, I am always in a mood
To answer all your questions,
Spiritual and unspiritual."

2

My Lord Supreme,
Do You remember the first
   promise
I made to You?
Unfortunately,
I have totally forgotten it.

"My child, You have forgotten
   your first promise,
But I clearly and perfectly
   remember it.
Your first and foremost promise
Was to manifest Me in
   My own Way
At every moment here on earth."

3

My Lord Supreme,
Why do I limp along the path of
   impurity
Every day?

"My child,
You limp along the path of
   impurity
Every day
Because you and your mind
Do not want to study
At the prayer-school,
You and your heart
Do not want to study
At the meditation-college,
You and your life
Do not want to study
At the surrender-university."

4

My Lord Supreme,
Will You be happy if I become
The heart of greatness?
"Definitely, My child,
But I shall be infinitely happier
If you become the breath of
   goodness."

5

My Lord Supreme,
Is there any way that I can be
Constantly happy?

"Yes, My child,
Just make your day and night
My Command-Fulfilment-
   Satisfactions."

6

My Lord Supreme,
Please advise me
What You would like me to do.
Shall I put my arms around
   the world
Or place my head at the foot of
   the world?

"My child,
I want you to do both.
Your humility-mind
   will soulfully
Press the world inward —
Deep, deeper, deepest.
Your sincerity-heart
   will powerfully
Lift the world upward —
High, higher, highest."

7

My Lord Supreme,
Why is my inner progress-road
Always so bumpy?

"My child,
Your inner progress-road
Is always so bumpy
Because instead of ignoring
You are adoring your busy
   body-mind."

8

My Lord Supreme,
How can I arrest
The doubt-intruder?

"Easy, My child,
Just make friends
With the faith-protector."

9

My Lord Supreme,
Please be extremely honest
　with me.
Do You ever care
For my desire-deformation?

"My child,
To be extremely honest with you,
I do not have the time to care
For your desire-deformation."

Then, my Lord Supreme,
Do You have time to care for
　anything?

"Yes, I do, I do, My child.
I have always time to care
Only for your
　aspiration-perfection."

10

My Lord Supreme,
I know You are extremely busy.
Do You think You will be able
To ask my soul to be
My life's decision-maker?

"My child,
I can ask your soul
Only on one condition:
If you are ready to become
Your heart's sincerity-cry."

11

My Lord Supreme,
When I deliberately
Put destruction-thorns
In your beautiful Vision-Eye,
Do You not get hurt?

"No, My child, not at all.
But I do get hurt
When you do not dare to claim
Me
As your own, very own."

12

My Lord Supreme,
How can I make You
Extremely and eternally happy?

"My child,
You can make Me
Extremely and eternally happy
If you sleeplessly soar
With your soul's
　selflessness-wings
And make a solemn promise
　to Me
That you will at once become
A lifelong citizen of Heaven
　on earth
And a lifelong citizen of earth
　in Heaven,
For I sleeplessly need you
In My streaming human cries
And in My illumining divine
　Smiles."

13

My Lord Supreme,
Am I the only spoiled child
In Your Family?

"No, no, no, My child,
There are five more:
Your ingratitude-heart-sister,
Your impurity-mind-brother,
Your insincerity-vital-cousin,
Your stupidity-body-nephew
And your lethargy-life-niece."

14

A sincere
God-Forgiveness-heart-cry
Does not need
Stretching exercises.

15

Man surprises God by saying
That he needs nothing from Him.
God surprises man by proving
That He has already done
Everything for him.

16

I began my life
By sincerely believing
   the impossible.
I shall end my life
By unmistakably doing
   the impossible.

17

I soulfully love
My morning's folded hands.
I unreservedly love
My evening's silenced mind.

18

O my mind,
Instead of colliding
With a Godless past,
Why are you not embracing
A Godful future?

19

Yesterday what you had
Was a doubt-drenched mind.
Today what you are
Is a despair-air-filled balloon.

20

I entered into my mind's
   desire-room
At my own risk.
I am now entering
Into my heart's aspiration-room
At my Lord's unconditional
   expense.

21

Every tear
From every heart-eye
Is power unparalleled.

22

My sound-life
Is a man-feeding breakfast.
My silence-heart
Is a God-feeding dinner.

23

A gratitude-heart
Every day pioneers a new road
To arrive at
   compassion-height-palace.

24

Just as God has forgiven my past,
The Compassion-Lord is
   immortalising
My aspiration-heart and
   dedication-life.

25

A part-time seeker
I was.
A full-time sufferer
I am.

26

When God comes to me,
He tiptoes.
When I go to God,
I thunder.

27

No dream is a stranger
To my earth-illumining soul.
No reality is a stranger
To my God-manifesting life.

28

A completely surrendered life
Yesterday I tried.
Today I find it absolutely real.

29

My Lord Supreme,
Do You want to join
Our humanity's oneness-race
Which will soon start?

"My child,
I am simply dying to participate."

30

My Lord Supreme,
Do You have a moment?

"Yes, My child, I do."

Please tell me, my Lord,
Will I ever be
An unconditionally surrendered
    instrument
Of Yours?

"Certainly, My child, you will."

When, my Lord Supreme?

"The day, My child, you can
    sing for Me
Most soulfully
Your heart's surrender-life-song."

PART XXV

GOD IS KIDNAPPED

1. Preface

This book reveals a soulful conversation between a seeker and his heart.

— Sri Chinmoy

2

My heart, I love you.
Why?
Because you do not complain.

3

My heart, I love you.
Why?
Because you do not blame others
For your failures.

4

My heart, I love you.
Why?
Because you have enthroned
My Eternity's soul-child.

5

My heart, I love you.
Why?
Because in you God preserves
And treasures
His Immortality's Dream.

6

My heart, I love you.
Why?
Because of your soulful prayers
My Lord Supreme has shattered
My mind's doubt-vessels.

7

My heart, I love you.
Why?
Because of you,
Only because of you,
I know that God loves me.

8

My heart, I love you.
Why?
Because you pray
To my Lord Supreme
Not only for those who love you
But also for those who do not.

9

My heart, I love you.
Why?
Because of you I have
A God-protected life.

10

My heart, I love you.
Why?
Because of you I have become
A favourite child of God,
And because of you I shall remain
Forever so.

11

My heart, I love you.
Why?
Because of you, at any moment
I can have a glimpse of God's
Infinite Peace, infinite Light.

12

My heart, I love you.
Why?
Because of you
My songless mind,
My soulless mind
And even my godless mind
Will someday
Be totally transformed.

13

My heart, I love you.
Why?
Because of you,
Only because of you,
I am not so unimportant
And not so insignificant
Here on earth.

14

My heart, I love you.
Why?
Because of you,
Only, only, only because of you,
My Lord Supreme is
   transforming
My earth-bound desire
Into His Heaven-free Will —
Only, only, only because of you.

15

My heart, I love you.
Why?
Because you have
So compassionately
And so self-givingly taught me
How to love and fulfil
God's every Wish.

16

My heart, I love you.
Why?
Because at every moment
You are blessing me
With the whispered message:
"Self-reliance — no, no, no!
God-reliance — yes, yes, yes!"

17

My heart, I love you.
Why?
Because of your
Very strict vigilance
I do not dare to avoid or evade
Any of my earth-responsibilities.

18

My heart, I love you.
Why?
Because in you I see
Not my yesterday's failures,
But only my tomorrow's victories.

19

My heart, I love you.
Why?
Because you are the only one
Who is not interested
In seeing or feeling
My love for you,
But is only interested
In seeing and feeling
My sleepless and breathless
Love for God.

20

My heart, I love you.
Why?
Because no matter
How many times
I have fooled you
Since my adolescence,
You still love me.

21

My heart, I love you.
Why?
Because your purity-eye
Has silenced,
Once and for all,
My mind's clamouring thoughts.

22

My heart, I love you.
Why?
Because people
From all walks of life
And from all over the world
Tell me
That you are never, never, never
Inhospitable;
Because hospitality
Is the fragrance
Of your life-breath.

23

My heart, I love you.
Why?
Because day and night you tell me
To ask myself only one question:
"What is God's Will?"

24

My heart, I love you.
Why?
Because of your streaming tears,
I am sure that no mistake
In my life
Is unforgivable by God.

25

My heart, I love you.
Why?
Because no matter
How many times
I deliberately turn my back
On you,
I cannot escape
Your unconditional concern
For me.

26

My heart, I love you.
Why?
Because you inspire me
And illumine me
So powerfully
By telling me
That what I really need
Is not world-information
But my earth-life-transformation.

27

My heart, I love you.
Why?
Because of your constant concern
And compassion for me,
I can no longer remain
In the mire of complexity.

28

My heart, I love you.
Why?
Because it is you
Who have disarmed
My doubt-giant
With your ever-blossoming faith.

29

My heart, I love you.
Why?
Because you are the only one
Who does not turn away from
God
When your desires
Are not fulfilled.

30

My heart, I love you.
Why?
Because you are graciously
Telling me
That there are no
Serious stumbling blocks
In my path of self-perfection.

31

My heart, I love you.
Why?
Because long ago,
Most successfully,
You crossed the barriers
Of doubt, mistrust and suspicion.

32

My heart, I love you.
Why?
Because every day you take me
To either God's Compassion-Sky
Or God's Forgiveness-Ocean.

33

My heart, I love you.
Why?
Because of you
My God-realisation-destination
Is coming incredibly closer.

34

My heart, I love you.
Why?
Because you never forget
To tell me
Whose actually I am.

35

My heart, I love you.
Why?
Because you never give up
Your self-giving project.

36

My heart, I love you.
Why?
Because in you I see
My God-surrender-home-nest.

37

My heart, I love you.
Why?
Because your sincerity-tears
Purify my entire being.

38

My heart, I love you.
Why?
Because you are apt
To forgive and forget
Humanity's hypocrisies.

39

My heart, I love you.
Why?
Because you have free access
To God's most beautiful
And most powerful
Dream-Kingdom.

40

My heart, I love you.
Why?
Because you do not have to be
On the waiting list
To see the Smiles
Of God the Transcendental
And God the Universal.

41

My heart, I love you.
Why?
Because you always help me
In steering my life-boat
Towards God's Golden Shore.

42

My heart, I love you.
Why?
Because your very presence
Is a cure for doubt-disease.

43

My heart, I love you.
Why?
Because your untiring love
Helps me bring to the fore
New dreams out of old failures.

44

My heart, I love you.
Why?
Because you are always
A perfect stranger
To superficial sincerity.

45

My heart, I love you.
Why?
Because you inspire me
Most powerfully
By telling me it is never too late
To change.

46

My heart, I love you.
Why?
Because you feel
Most sincerely sad
When any human being
Walks away
From God's outstretched Arms.

47

My heart, I love you.
Why?
Because you are the only one
Who tells me
That if I do what I can,
Then God will do what I cannot.

48

My heart, I love you.
Why?
Because you are
My universal oneness within
And my universal fulness without.

49

My heart, I love you.
Why?
Because I see
Behind your sweetness-smile
A power-plant.

50

My heart, I love you.
Why?
Because you do not allow me
To make friends with my mind's
Splintered and scattered faith.

51

My heart, I love you.
Why?
Because you sleeplessly embody
God's Satisfaction-Fragrance.

52

My heart, I love you.
Why?
Because when my mind is
The question of questions,
In you I find
The answer of answers.

53

My heart, I love you.
Why?
Because you are
The pioneer-owner
Of surrender-garden
And gratitude-fragrance.

54

My heart, I love you.
Why?
Because every morning
You set off my aspiration-alarm
For me.

55

My heart, I love you.
Why?
Because your eagerness creates
Every day
So many golden opportunities
For me.

56

My heart, I love you.
Why?
Because in your kingdom
You have outlawed selfishness.

57

My heart, I love you.
Why?
Because everything good
That I do for mankind
Is due to your fast start
And strong finish.

58

My heart, I love you.
Why?
Because your sole goal
Is to leave the world
Far better than you found it.

59

My heart, I love you.
Why?
Because on willingness-road
You run the fastest.

60

My heart, I love you.
Why?
Because God proudly applauds
Your long surrender-steps.

61

My heart, I love you.
Why?
Because, unlike us,
You live to love.

62

My heart, I love you.
Why?
Because of you
I am genuinely loving
And surprisingly lovable.

63

My heart, I love you.
Why?
Because you tell me
That it is infinitely better
To be possessed by God
Than to try to possess God.

64

My heart, I love you.
Why?
Because, unlike us,
You never allow yourself
To be estranged from God.

65

My heart, I love you.
Why?
Because your
God-Satisfaction-dreams
Never fade,
But only grow and glow.

66

My heart, I love you.
Why?
Because you teach me so lovingly
How to become
A soaring progress-kite.

67

My heart, I love you.
Why?
Because your aspiration-flames
Have the capacity
To control and silence
My mind's thought-riots.

68

My heart, I love you.
Why?
Because your tremendous
And stupendous
Faith-productions
Amaze me.

69

My heart, I love you.
Why?
Because God is happily
And proudly
Publishing your silence-speeches.

70

My heart, I love you.
Why?
Because your sincerity-cry
Has an immediate access
To God's Compassion-Heart-Eye.

71

My heart, I love you.
Why?
Because in you
Humanity's hope is safe
And through you
Divinity's Promise is safe.

72

My heart, I love you.
Why?
Because you have taught me
The supreme truth:
Self-giving is the beginning
Of God-becoming.

73

My heart, I love you.
Why?
Because you are most graciously
Turning me into a psychic giant.

74

My heart, I love you.
Why?
Because in you is my Lord's
Brightest Confidence-Light.

75

My heart, I love you.
Why?
Because your inner cries
Have helped me achieve
Outer competence.

76

My heart, I love you.
Why?
Because you alone
Have the capacity
To unveil God's Face for me.

77

My heart, I love you.
Why?
Because humanity's
Frustration-stories
Cannot take away
Your love of God.

78

My heart, I love you.
Why?
Because every morning
You lovingly introduce me to
   God.

79

My heart, I love you.
Why?
Because of you
I have countless
Faith-friendship-flames.

80

My heart, I love you.
Why?
Because you surprise me
With your ever-increasing love
For God.

81

My heart, I love you.
Why?
Because you have inspired me
To feel
That God and God's Heaven
Can be won
With my life's patience-light.

82

My heart, I love you.
Why?
Because you so lovingly help me
Cling to my prayer-God.

83

My heart, I love you.
Why?
Because you have given me
The great capacity to arrest
The God-doubt-intruder.

84

My heart, I love you.
Why?
Because of you
The breath of goodness
Has entered my life.

85

My heart, I love you.
Why?
Because of you the whole world
Puts its long arms around me.

86

My heart, I love you.
Why?
Because you are
More than willing
To take care of my mind,
The completely spoiled child
In God's Family.

87

My heart, I love you.
Why?
Because you warn me
Not to walk
Along the resentment-path.

88

My heart, I love you.
Why?
Because you have given me
A large space
To bury my pride-giant
In your humility-garden.

89

My heart, I love you.
Why?
Because every day you inspire me
To soar on selflessness-wings.

90

My heart, I love you.
Why?
Because of your sleepless prayers
God has chosen me
To be on His Team
In the tug-of-war
Against ignorance-night.

91

My heart, I love you.
Why?
Because you never weaken,
But only strengthen,
All my divine resolves.

92

My heart, I love you.
Why?
Because God is proud of me
Only when I am in you,
With you and for you.

93

My heart, I love you.
Why?
Because you are my daily
God-Peace and God-Bliss
Supplier.

94

My heart, I love you.
Why?
Because your constant
Gratitude-fragrance-offering
Is my only hope of realising God.

95

My heart, I love you.
Why?
Because, unlike us,
You do not talk
About yourself;
You talk only about God.

96

My heart, I love you.
Why?
Because your philosophy is
The self-giving acceptance of life.

97

My heart, I love you.
Why?
Because your religion is
The universal oneness-song.

98

My heart, I love you.
Why?
Because your spirituality is
Perfection in self-transcendence.

99

My heart, I love you.
Why?
Because your yoga is
God for God's sake,
God's Satisfaction
In God's own Way.

100

My heart, I love you.
Why?
Because you want me, like you,
To embrace and lighten
The sufferings of humanity.

101

My heart, I love you.
Why?
Because you alone
Have the capacity
To kidnap God.

PART XXVI

EUROPEAN POEM-BLOSSOMS

1

My cheerful God-willingness
Is an immediate short cut
To my perfection-life.

2

I am so glad
That I am afraid
Of my desire-tiger-life.

3

An unreal life
I was.
A real heart
I now am.

4

What is humanity's mind doing?
It is drowning
In sleepless and endless
Attachment-oceans.

5

Doubt does not dare
To imprison
My purity's aspiration-heart
And
My duty's dedication-life.

6

No more
Ruthless punishment for me
From the past,
No more.

7

Self-discovery
Is
Infinity's Nectar-Delight.

8

Only stupidity incarnate
Does not mind
Preserving the tormenting past.

9

The absolutely correct definition
Of ego
Is slavery
And not bravery.

10

Fear,
You may love me,
But I cannot
And will not
Love you.

11

Desire is
A greedy mouth.
Aspiration is
A happy heart.

12

Don't take too long
To touch the Feet
Of God the Creator.

Don't take too long
To feel the Heart
Of God the creation.

13

My only real joy
Is my heart's
Gratitude-blossom.

14

O my mind,
Faith keeps calling you.
Why do you not respond?
Are you deaf?
If so, since when?

15

Because of your sincerity-heart
There will be
No last chance
For you.

16

To my utter astonishment,
I have come to realise
That even Heaven
Has very serious problems.

17

My Lord,
Before You decide
To admonish me,
Can You not decide
To abolish me,
My ignorance-world,
Once and for all?

18

Look, O world, look!
I am no longer
A desire-prison-inmate.

19

Alas, your impurity-mind
Has the capacity to imprison
Not only your present life,
But also your future life.

20

Where do I live?
I live in between
My Lord's Compassion-Tears
And His Forgiveness-Smiles.

21

Alas,
Unless my mind stops,
How can my heart start?

22

Can you imagine
What he has said
To God?
He has said to God
That he can create
A far better world.

23

What I need is
A sleepless and giant hunger
For my life's perfection-smile.

24

The voice of my silence
Is the fulness
Of my soul-fire.

25

My soul is there
Where my heart's
Dream-flowers blossom.

26

Who am I?
I am the possessor
Of desire-forests
And desire-deserts.

27

God's Justice-Light
Has forced him
To practise what he preaches.

28

Each human life
Is made of
Fragile hopes.

29

I must never lose
My heart's
Aspiration-pounds.

30

Each and every desire-dream
Is
Painfully false.

31

What am I doing?
I am amplifying
God's Silence-Voice.

32

Alas,
Each human life
Is an imperfection-cry.

33

I have chosen
The life
That knows how to bow.

34

Mine
Is the hope-elevator
That only goes up.

35

My soul and I
Are homesick
For God.

36

Steal, steal, steal
Your mind's
Darkest night.

37

Pray, pray, pray
For peace,
And never pay
For war.

38

To tame the vital-tiger
Is the supreme task
Of each human being.

39

A God-lover knows
What to give:
His heart.

A God-lover knows
How to give:
Unconditionally.

40

God's very first gift
To mankind
Was aspiration-flames.

God's very last gift
To mankind
Will be satisfaction-sun.

41

What I have
Is an inspiration-tree.
What I need
Is an aspiration-flower.

42

Two things of mine
I truly treasure:
My prayer-heights
And
My meditation-depths.

43

Each God-lover
Is commissioned to serve God
In a special way.

44

To me,
Patience-light means
Reality's fastest progress.

45

What does peace signify?
Peace signifies the love
Of togetherness.

46

Do not miscalculate
Your outer friends:
They are not as many
As you think.

Do not miscalculate
Your inner friends:
They are not as few
As you think.

47

You are at war
With your doubting mind.
That means you really love
Your aspiring heart.

48

Each self-giving thought
Is
A universal heart-embrace.

49

I just want to know
In which way
The human mind
Is better
Than a confusion-menagerie.

50

If you are desiring
An aspiration-short-cut,
Then you will have to be satisfied
With a lesser realisation.

51

Aspiration-discipline
I need.
Surrender-relaxation,
Too.

52

What does my mind do?
It cleverly plays the role
Of an irresponsibility-guide.

53

An impure thought
Is not even an inch away
From stark madness-danger.

54

Alas,
My dedication-bridge
Is always under construction.

55

God keeps my heart's cries
Inside the Satisfaction-Smile
Of His own Heart.

56

O pilgrim-soul,
Do come back
To your heart-home
Immediately.

57

I love, I love
And I always love
The Sweetness-Silence-Voice
Of my Lord Supreme.

58

My Lord Supreme
Blessingfully loves
The aspiration-perfection-plant
In my heart-garden.

59

Devotion
Self-givingly purified,
Man
Absolutely transformed.

60

A heart of delight
Sees not
The mind anywhere.

61

I am praying to God
For two things:
My body-vital-mind-collision
And my soul-heart-union.

62

Nobody knows,
Nobody even wants to know
How sleeplessly and badly
God suffers.

63

Man's attachment-fondness
Is his stupidity's
Greatest friend.

64

Where do I live?
I live in between
My heart's aspiration-pull
And my life's dedication-push.

65

A perfect attitude
Knows
No imperfect day.

66

What do I do every morning?
Every morning
I lovingly and carefully
Sow hope-seeds
Inside my heart-garden.

67

If you are trying
To escape God's Justice-Light,
Then your mind will fumble,
Your heart will stumble,
Your life will tumble.

68

O my clever mind.
You will not be able to fool
My God-blessed
Aspiration-cry-heart.

69

Insecurity
And its daily outbreak
Are so devastating.

70

I really do not want
To enjoy any more
My tortoise-aspiration-speed.

71

No climbing hope
Should be forgotten.
No fulfilling promise
Should be broken.

72

I am so sad
That my mind
Is so ruthlessly bound
By the past.

73

May my life become
An aspiration-mountain
And a dedication-fountain.

74

God's supreme Beauty
Is our love
Of togetherness-peace.

75

Shake not hands
Even in your dreams
With the doubt-giants.

76

His doubting mind
And his strangling vital
Are from the same forest.

77

If you choose
Not to see,
God will definitely allow you
To remain blind.

78

Where am I?
I am inside the heart-temple
Of Eternity's Cry
And Infinity's Smile.

79

Truth-seekers
Are good heart-cry-singers.
God-lovers
Are good soul-smile-dancers.

80

The human mind
Ruthlessly suspects.
The divine heart
Gladly accepts.

81

Doubt
Is a tricky question.
Faith
Is an easy answer.

82

To see your detractors
You do not have to
Keep your eyes open.
But to see your supporters
You have to.

83

Temptation-frustration
Was yesterday's bulletin-night.
Aspiration-satisfaction
Is today's message-light.

84

O world,
I am so fortunate and happy
That God has a totally different
Opinion of me.

85

The mind is nothing other
Than a cloud
In the heart-sky.

86

I trust myself
When I make something.
I love myself
When I give it
To my Lord Supreme.

87

I do not know
How to tell God
The right thing
To make Him happy.

God does not know
When to tell me
The right thing
So that I do not
Become unhappy.

88

Grievance is
A thorny forest.
Forgiveness is
A fragrant garden.

89

Lose what you
In your outer life have:
Impatience.
Lose not what you
In your inner life are:
Poise.

Notes to European Poem-Blossoms

1-37. These poems were written on a Pan Am flight from New York City, United States, to Zurich, Switzerland, on 2 June 1991.

38-57. These poems were written en route from Vaduz, Liechtenstein, to Lausanne, Switzerland, on 3 June 1991.

58-70. These poems were written on a Scandinavian Airlines flight from Zurich, Switzerland, to Oslo, Norway, on 4 June 1991.

71-89. These poems were written on a Sabena Airlines flight from Brussels, Belgium, to Vienna, Austria, on 6 June 1991.

PART XXVII

EVERY DAY A NEW CHANCE

EVERY DAY A NEW CHANCE

1

To my extreme joy,
There is no such thing
As a last chance
To please God!

2

My mind-prayer cries
For God the Power.
My heart-meditation dreams
Of God the Love.
My soul-surrender dines
With God the Satisfaction.

3

I could not realise God
In the heights of my reach.
But I did realise God
In the depths of my love.

4

I may not know what it means
To be perfect,
But I do know what it means
To be happy.

5

Today's hope
And tomorrow's promise
Are universal experiences.

6

The unknown
Can not only be known,
But can also be
And must be
Fully manifested.

7

God, I do not love You,
Yet You love me.
Why do You do that,
My Lord?
"My child, I cannot help it.
I just cannot do otherwise!"

8

I love God,
And next to God
I love the God-seeker
Who loves God infinitely more
Than I love God.

9

I have perfectly realised
Three important things:
My Lord's Compassion
Is never unwilling,
My Lord's Compassion
Is never slow,
My Lord's Compassion
Is never insufficient.

10

Faith is God's Power,
Loving, illumining and fulfilling,
In the hearts of
   His human children.

11

Freedom is God-discovery.
Freedom is self-mastery.
Freedom is satisfaction-recovery.

12

My freedom to choose:
A God-surrender-life,
A God-gratitude-heart!

13

Forgive
If you want to regain
The full freedom-joy
Of your mind and heart.

14

Yesterday I performed
Three real miracles,
And these three miracles
Lasted for the entire day:
I conquered my negativity-mind,
I proclaimed the victory
Of my willingness-heart,
And I became my life's
Unconditional surrender
To God's Will.

15

My aspiration-heart
And my dedication-life
Fondly and proudly
Depend on each other.

16

"God"
Is not the Name of God
But man's experience-description
Of God.

17

My aspiration-heart asks me
To look upward and see
    God's Feet,
Which are so merciful.
My dedication-life asks me
To look forward and see
    God's Eyes,
Which are so beautiful.

18

God forgives us
So that
His Compassion-
    Affection-Heart-Home
Does not remain empty.

19

Forgiveness is
The unparalleled capacity
To swim in the ecstasy-sea.

20

If you forgive the world,
God will use your fragrance-heart
As His cherished Throne.

21

I am in between
My Lord's blessingful Invitation
And my mind's awful rejection.

22

What my heart needs every day
Is lightning-speed
To serve humanity.

23

Hope-beauty starts
The inner journey.
Faith-purity completes
The inner journey.

24

My ego-balloon
Will soon burst,
For God's all-illumining
 Wisdom-Light
Has entered into my mind.

25

From God's point of view,
Honesty and integrity
Cannot be separated.

26

Willingness-capacity
Is at once
Most beautiful and
 most powerful.

27

May my life-dictionary
Have only four words:
Aspiration,
Dedication,
Gratitude,
Surrender.

28

Alas, my heart stands
In between
My delayed aspiration
And my decayed perfection.

29

The mind's happiness
Indicates
The heart's purity-prosperity.

30

Unlike my mind,
My heart does everything
Sooner rather than later
To please my Lord Supreme.

31

Not a fear-prompted prayer
But a love-inspired meditation
Can and does
Gladden God's Heart.

32

A fault-finding seeker
Is a colossal failure
In the aspiration-world.

33

God has categorically told me
That He will never listen
To my prayers,
No matter how sincere and pure
They are,
If I do not love my heart
Dearly
And show respect to my heart
Soulfully.

34

God is proud of me
When I have measureless
Enthusiasm.
God is disgusted with me
When I have bottomless
Depression.

35

An unconditional lover of God
Is the only human being
Who will always be a God-winner
At every hour of the day
And every hour of the night.

36

An ego-mind is by far
The best listener
To its own
    louder-than-the-loudest
Voice.

37

A sincere seeker
Deserves a truly God-realised
    Master.
A God-realised Master
Deserves at least one
Unconditionally surrendered
    disciple.

38

O my mind,
Be not a stupid stranger
To forgiveness!

39

A doubting mind
Is always at war
With itself.

40

Not one, but two new realities
I have discovered:
A breathless aspiration-heart
And a sleepless dedication-life.

41

I shall delay
No more
My unconditional
 surrender-joy-day.

42

Doubt, are you deaf?
Are you blind?
Can you not hear and see
That I am defying you
And saying good-bye to you?

43

If you are prepared
To trust God.
Only then should you test Him.

44

With his mind's capacities,
He is surprising the world.
With his heart's capacity,
He is obeying and pleasing
His Lord Supreme.

45

Strength indomitable
Comes not from outer exercise
But from inner awakening.

46

My earth-bound cries
Will eventually rest
In my Heaven-free smiles.

47

May each day for me
Usher in
A God-Satisfaction-hope.

48

The mind's jealousy
And the heart's insecurity
Like to coexist.

49

A sleepless
Surrender-heart-river
Runs fast, very fast,
Towards God's
Fulness-Satisfaction-Shore.

50

Alas,
Not even God's
Indulgent Compassion
Sees any progress
In my aspiration-heart.

51

Alas,
When God's Compassion-Eye
Called me,
Immediately my mind forced me
To run the other way.

52

Yesterday God the Compassion
Took away from me
My ego-bloated mind.

Today God the Satisfaction
Is receiving from me
My aspiration-flooded heart.

53

Instead of inventing excuses,
Why do you not prevent yourself
From making mistakes?

54

You can directly enter
Into aspiration-garden
Without tiptoeing
Through desire-forest.

55

When I am in my mind's
Possession-world,
My life is a problem.

When I am in my heart's
Renunciation-world,
My life is a privilege.

56

A doubting mind
Violently reacts.
An aspiring heart
Soulfully acts.

57

Never too late for the mind
To lose excessive doubt-weight
Or for the heart
To gain impressive faith-strength.

58

Finally I have dethroned
Ignorance-king
From my life-kingdom!

59

Illumination my mind needs.
Realisation my heart needs.
Transformation my life needs.
And what do I need?
I need God's Compassion-
    Forgiveness.

60

You do not need God
To tell you
If you have a pure heart.
God has already given you
The capacity
To examine your heart faultlessly.

PART XXVIII

GOD MINUS

GOD MINUS

1

A God-minus thought
Misleads
The searching mind.

2

A God-minus thought
Tortures
The aspiring heart.

3

A God-minus thought
Is
Happiness-starvation.

4

A God-minus thought of mine
Is a devastating blow
To my God-adoration-heart.

5

Each God-minus thought of mine
Eventually bursts
Into an utter failure-sigh.

6

Each God-minus thought
Compels the seeker
To enter into an abysmal abyss.

7

A God-minus life
Is
A spiritual failure.

8

A God-minus life
Must needs remain
A satisfaction-stranger.

9

A God-minus heart
Can never enjoy
God's Fondness-Oneness-
   Embrace.

10

A God-minus mind
Cannot escape
From the trauma of hopelessness.

11

A God-minus life
Is
Ignorance-confusion-immersion.

12

A God-minus man
Is
His own bondage-slave.

13

A God-minus day
Marks the seekers
Aspiration-shortage
And
Frustration-plethora.

14

A God-minus thought
Entangles the mind,
Enslaves the heart,
Endangers the life.

15

A God-minus day
Cannot free itself
From the knotted tentacles
Of suspicion.

16

A God-minus moment
Is when
Truth and I part ways.

17

A God-minus moment
Feeds doubt
And fondles suspicion.

18

A God-minus man
Loves
His ego-greed.

19

A God-minus man
Is totally empty
Of prayer-joy
And
Meditation-peace.

20

A God-minus man
Is obsessed
Only with others' mistakes,
Small or big.

21

A God-minus man
Plies his lifeboat
Between the mind's
　impatience-shore
And the heart's uncertainty-shore.

22

A God-minus man
Desires
World-supremacy-power
And not
World-ecstasy-hour.

23

A God-minus man
Can easily become
A negativity-monarch.

24

A God-minus man
Thinks
That he can never be wrong.

25

A God-minus morning
Marks
A soul-starvation-day.

26

A God-minus human being
Is found to be
Deplorably powerless
Over his own thoughts.

27

A God-minus breath
Is, indeed,
A spiritual death.

PART XXIX

GOD PLUS

GOD PLUS

1

A God-plus soul
Is
God-fulfilment-promise
On earth.

2

A God-plus heart
Knows
God's hiding place.

3

A God-plus mind
Is
A rare achievement.

4

A God-plus vital
Is
A God-manifestation-assurance.

5

A God-plus body
Is
An aspiration-dedication-fort.

6

A God-plus seeker
Is absolutely certain
That a desire-life is mortal
And
An aspiration-heart is immortal.

7

A God-plus seeker
Unmistakably feels
That God's Compassion-Eye
And
His Forgiveness-Heart
Are birthless and deathless.

8

A God-plus seeker
Is advised
By God Himself
To tell the world
To speak about God,
Only about God.

9

A God-plus seeker
Soulfully takes shelter
In God's
Sweetness-Fondness-Heart-Nest.

10

A God-plus seeker
Enjoys
The unseen company
Of angels, saints and seers.

11

A God-plus seeker
Spans
Earth-cries and Heaven-smiles
With his heart's
Unconditional surrender-light.

12

A God-plus seeker
Has
God the Satisfaction
To broadcast
His gratitude-heart
And surrender-life.

13

A God-plus seeker
Chooses
The freedom-life
From his ignorance-
    attachment-jungle.

14

A God-plus moment
Purifies my mind,
Intensifies my heart
And simplifies my life.

15

A God-plus dawn
Is
The harbinger of
A rainbow-delight-day.

16

A God-plus thought
Cannot be stolen
By temptation-thief.

17

A God-plus thought
Cannot be stabbed
By destruction-knife.

18

A God-plus thought
Cannot be devoured
By inconscience-night.

19

A God-plus journey's
Goal transcendental
Is destined.

20

A God-plus lover
Awakens
The sleeping humanity.

21

A God-plus aspirant
Is taught
By God Himself
How to sing
His nature's
Transformation-victory-song.

22

A God-plus aspiration-heart
Receives
The blessingful message
From God Himself
That his liberation-speed
Will be tremendous.

23

A God-plus server
Is a conscious
Ignorance-game-mastery-player.

24

A God-plus hunger
Is fed
By Immortality's nectar-delight.

25

A God-plus dedication
Of my life
Is accelerating
My God-satisfaction.

26

A God-plus aspiration
Of my heart
Is transforming
My confusion-mind
Into
My illumination-mind.

27

A God-plus gratitude-tear
Of my heart's inner hunger
Is always fondly blessed
By God the Creator
And
God the creation.

PART XXX

TWENTY-SEVEN
HEART-FRAGRANCE-DREAMS

TWENTY-SEVEN HEART-FRAGRANCE-DREAMS

1. One

My Beloved Supreme,
What will I do
If You ever cancel
Your Forgiveness-Compassion-
   Credit Cards?

2. Two

My love of God
Has many rivals
But no critic.

3. Three

Yesterday God came to me
As Hope-Seed.
Today God has come to me
As a Promise-Tree.
Tomorrow God will come to me
As a Fulfilment-Fruit.

4. Four

Only my soul,
The baby-God in me.
Has the capacity
To properly love my Supreme,
The Father-God in me
And around me.

5. Five

Oneness-heart-children
Have their homes
Everywhere.

6. Six

May my heart never study
Life's indifference-book.

7. Seven

My mind's sound-prayer
Is my first resort.
My heart's silence-meditation
Is my last resort.

8. Eight

God's Justice-Hand
Makes strict rules.
God's Compassion-Heart
Makes innumerable exceptions.

9. Nine

God's Compassion-Eye
Never uses
Justice-Glasses.

10. Ten

What my heart needs
Is cosmic beauty,
And not cosmetic beauty.

11. Eleven

Two things the mind
Does not want:
It does not want
To step back;
It does not want
God to lead.

12. Twelve

Each good thought
Adds a new God-dimension
To my dedication-life.

13. Thirteen

No
Oneness-heart-crop
No
Peace-life-harvest.

14. Fourteen

Even
At its infancy
Doubt
Is most dangerous.

15. Fifteen

My Lord's Heart
Is too compassionate
To contradict
My arrogance-mind.

16. Sixteen

My Lord Supreme cannot believe
That I spend daily
At least five hours
In my mind's
   complaint-department.

17. Seventeen

A gratitude-heart
Aspires.
An ingratitude-mind
Expires.

18. Eighteen

A limited mind
Houses unlimited thoughts.

19. Nineteen

A tiny heart
Embodies the Infinite.

20. Twenty

My mind-thought
Is a two-way street.
My heart-will
Is a one-way street.

21. Twenty-One

"I cannot love
And I do not love
God"
Is an old story
Of my mind.

22. Twenty-Two

"I can love
And I do love
God"
Is an ever-new song
Of my heart.

23. Twenty-Three

God teaches
Only the heart-singers
His peace-songs.

24. Twenty-Four

Who was I?
An anxiety-invaded mind.
Who am I?
A peace-expanded heart.

25. Twenty-Five

God always wants me to live
In my heart-industry.
But I always love to live
In my mind-factory.

26. Twenty-Six

God has forgiven me
So that I can once more
Love myself.

27. Twenty-Seven

God is extremely proud of
    Himself
Only when He can run to and fro
Between my
    heart's gratitude-tears
And my life's surrender-smiles.

PART XXXI

EACH HOUR IS A GOD-HOUR

EACH HOUR IS A GOD-HOUR

1

A sleepless server feels
That each hour is a God-Hour
To love God,
To serve God
And to satisfy God
In God's own Way.

2

When I pray to God,
I accumulate.
When I meditate on God,
I assimilate.

3

I wish to be the collector
Of soulful smiles
From God-lovers
Every day and every hour
Of my life.

4

Each good thought
Of my mind
Is welcomed
With my heart's
Congratulation-applause.

5

Eagerness-eye sees
God-fulfilment-opportunities
Here, there and everywhere.

6

When the aspiration-heart
Takes a long vacation,
It is bound to dream of God's
Compassion-disappearance.

7

Each good thought
Is a divine guard
That bravely protects
The mind-door.

8

The mind that soars
With inspiration
Is powerfully blessed
By God's Satisfaction-Heart.

9

Inner beauty
And outer enthusiasm
Are extremely fond of each other.

10

Uncertainty-stop signs
Are easily removed
By the heart's
Aspiration-intensity.

11

God always predicts
His Manifestation-Victory
In and through human aspiration.

12

It is simply impossible
For the soul to rely on
The leadership
Of the uncertain mind.

13

If you work out
In God's Gymnasium,
Then your manifestation-muscles
Are bound to be
Extremely powerful.

14

Each heart's
Affection-devotion-cries
Will definitely reach
God's Compassion-Eye.

15

Alas, I do not know
When and how
I shall be able to free myself
From this upside-down life!

16

In God's Eye
The power of surrender
Is infinitely superior
To any other power.

17

Real inner progress
Can be measured
Only in inches
And no other way.

18

O my stupid mind,
When will you give up
Your friendship
With your destruction-friend:
Dissatisfaction?

19

Insecurity-insects must be
   ignored
At every moment
If one wants to make
Solid progress
In the inner life.

20

To a heart of happiness
Each day is the best day
For meditation.

21

An unaspiring mind
Is always afraid of being tried
In the spirituality-court.

22

The real education,
Which is inner education,
Has to be always
Without compulsion.

23

Only a purity-heart
Can climb up
The towering and
Flowering heights.

24

To rely on one's mind
Is nothing short of
Relying on one's most inadequate
And imperfect resource.

25

A self-giving thought
Is always the sweetest
Of all earthly charities.

26

I do not want to live
Inside my mind's
All-encompassing stupidity.
I want to live
In my heart's
All-giving purity.

27

There will always come a time
When the pleasure-seeking mind
Will end in tearing suffering.

28

God blessingfully allows
His seer-poets
To consult His own Dictionary
Of the Beyond.

29

To manifest God's Light
Here on earth,
A oneness-heart
Is everything.

30

When the soul powerfully knocks
At the mind's door,
Eventually even the mind
Responds.

31

A mind of sincerity
And a heart of purity
Must become lifelong
    companions
To reveal divinity's height
Here on earth.

32

I am sure
That the undivine courage
Of the mind and the vital
Is bound to collapse
Sooner or later.

33

How can you make progress
In your spiritual life
If you suffer from
Confidence-shortage
In your aspiration-heart?

34

What you need is
A self-giving heart,
And not the spotlight of fame,
To conquer the heart of mankind.

35

Unfortunately, the mind-room
And impurity-dust
Are always fond of each other.

36

If you want to make
Quick and solid progress
In your spiritual life,
Then immediately move out
Of your mind's insecurity-room.

37

Each forgotten dream
Is a reminder
Of our failure-life on earth.

38

O my mind's inspiration-dawn,
Where are you?
O my heart's aspiration-day,
Where are you?
O my life's realisation-sun,
Where are you?

39

The battle of the ages:
The complete acceptance
Of truth
Or the utter rejection
Of truth.

40

God has infinitely more
Important things to do
Than to listen to your recitation
Of endless complaints.

41

My aspiring heart's faith-flower
I shall never allow
To be thrown away.

42

A heart
Of complete surrender
And a life
Of complete satisfaction
Inseparably live together.

43

The tears of my oval heart
Every day feed
God-blossoming meditations.

44

I shall pray and meditate
Soulfully, devotedly
And sleeplessly
So that the river of sorrow
Cannot wash away
My days and nights.

45

My inner strength is founded
On two things:
God's Forgiveness-Heart
And my gratitude-heart.

46

My Lord Supreme,
May my life from today on
Become a sweet, beautiful
And soulful
Progress-fountain.

47

Each soulful seeker
Is indeed a blessing-beacon
Of the fast-approaching
New century.

48

What I need is
A fast-growing prayer-plant
Inside my meditation's soul-soil.

49

Temptation-paradise
Is not meant for those
Who want to see God seated
On His Satisfaction-Throne.

50

Unless and until you have decided
To lose the breath of
Your ego-life,
You cannot expect God
To be mightily proud of you.

51

A self-giving moment
Is a sure way to know
The beauty and fragrance
Of your inner progress.

52

An aspiration-heart reminds us
Of the supreme fact
That life does not have to be
Long on deplorable shortcomings.
On the contrary, life can be
Long on striking capacities.

53

The insanity of the mind
And the vanity of the vital
Are either consciously
Or unconsciously
Extremely fond of each other.

54

Once you have touched
God's Forgiveness-Feet
And His Compassion-Heart,
Your life can never
Remain the same.

55

God tells us
That if we want to participate
In our self-transcendence-run,
Then we must plan to complete
The journey.

56

If you love God,
When you serve God
There is no such thing
As overtime.
It is all undertime!

57

O my past,
You are powerless.
O my present,
You are helpless.
O my future,
You will be useless
If I do not wake up
To love and serve
My Lord Supreme.

58

My Lord Supreme,
I pray to You
To make me and my heart
Two eternal gratitude-students.

59

Hard is it
Always to clear
Fear and doubt-hurdles
In the life of aspiration
And dedication.

60

We start our upward journey
On beautiful imagination-wings,
And we continue
On soulful aspiration-wings.

PART XXXII

MY LIFE-BOAT'S
DREAM-REALITY-SHORE

MY LIFE-BOAT'S DREAM-REALITY-SHORE

1

Every day I challenge myself.
I forgive the unforgivable —
My mind.

2

Every morning my Lord Supreme
Helps me renew
My heart-committee-membership.

3

Peace is more than
A friendship-story.
Peace is a oneness-song.

4

My Lord,
Each time I look at
Your Sweetness-Eye,
You give me a portion
Of Your Fulness-Heart.

5

My Lord,
My mind desires
Many things from You.
But my heart desires
Only a small space
At Your Compassion-Feet.

6

I owe nothing to my face.
But I owe everything to my heart.

7

Every day
At least for an hour,
I enjoy a heart-to-heart talk
With my soul.

8

My Lord Supreme
Compassionately tells me
That there is no "cut-off time"
for my nature's transformation.

9

Where do I see my mind?
I see my mind inside
 withering hopes.
Where do I feel my heart?
I feel my heart inside
 blossoming promises.

10

With his mind's capacities
He is surprising the world.
With his heart's capacities
He is obeying and pleasing
Only His Lord Supreme.

11

Strength indomitable
Comes not from outer exercise
But from inner awakening.

12

May each day for me
Usher in
A God-satisfaction-hope.

13

Yesterday God the Compassion
Took away from me
My ego-bloated mind.

Today God the Satisfaction
Is receiving from me
My aspiration-flooded heart.

14

Illumination my mind needs.
Realisation my heart needs.
Transformation my life needs.
And what do I need?
I need God's
 Compassion-Forgiveness.

15

You can enter directly
Into the aspiration-garden
Without tip-toeing
Through the desire-forest.

16

Hope-beauty starts
The inner journey.
Faith-purity completes
The inner journey.

17

Never too late for the mind
To lose doubt-weight
And for the heart
To gain faith-strength.

18

Yesterday I performed
Three real miracles,
And these three miracles
Lasted for the entire day:
I conquered my negativity-mind.
I proclaimed the victory
Of my willingness-heart,
And I became my life's
Unconditional surrender to
    God's Will.

19

My aspiration-heart
And my dedication-life
Fondly and proudly
Depend on each other.

20

Freedom is God-discovery.
Freedom is self-mastery.
Freedom is satisfaction-recovery.

21

I could not realise God
In the heights of my grasp.
But I did realise God
In the depths of my love.

22

My aspiration-heart asks me
To look upward to see God's Feet,
Which are so merciful.
My dedication-life asks me
To look forward to see
    God's Eyes,
Which are so beautiful.

23

If you forgive the world,
God will use your fragrance-heart
As His cherished Throne.

24

Willingness-capacity is at once
Most beautiful and most
   powerful.

25

Alas, my heart stands
In between
My delayed aspiration
And my decayed perfection.

26

Not a fear-prompted prayer
But a love-inspired meditation
Can and does gladden
   God's Heart.

27

When I am in my mind's
Possession-world,
My life is a problem.

When I am in my heart's
Renunciation-world,
My life is a privilege.

PART XXXIII

WAR: MAN'S ABYSMAL ABYSS-PLUNGE,
PART 1 AND 2

WAR: MAN'S ABYSMAL ABYSS-PLUNGE

1

War is
The most nourishing food
For the senile.

2

War is
Man's self-exposed
Stupidity.

3

War is
Man's self-imposed
Futility.

4

War-story:
Stupidity fights.
Futility wins.

5

War
Is life's fastest
Backward march.

6

War
Is ignorance-slavery.

7

War
Is treasured
By ignorance-princes.

8

War
Is ego's self-made
Crown and throne.

9

War
Is complete and unconditional
Surrender to ignorance-forces.

10

War
Is the glad acceptance
Of destruction-invitation.

11

War
Is the destruction-discovery
Of the stupidity-mind.

12

Now
Is the only time
To end any war.

13

War
Is the mind's
Stark impurity-dance.

14

War broadcasts
The stupendous victory
Of Satan.

15

War compels
The heart's wisdom-light
To surrender to
The mind's stupidity-night.

16

War
Is the mind-temptation
Within
And life-destruction
Without.

17

War
Is the undivine
   confidence-presence
Of the hostile forces in man.

18

War
Is man's instigation-story
And not God's Inspiration-Song.

19

War
Is a self-styled stranger
To God's Compassion-Eye.

20

War
Is the greatest victory
Of inconscience-night.

21

War
Is world-possession-greed-
  satisfaction.

22

War wants to prove
That the human mind
Has no greatness
And that the human heart
Has no goodness.

23

War invites
War-lovers
To come and participate
In a destruction-dance.

24

War
Is the joint
Elephant-madness
Of supremacy-hungry nations.

25

War
Is the irresistible sadness
Of the universal heart.

26

War
Is the utter disgrace-failure
Of the hostile minds.

27

War says:
"O man-made Compassion-God,
Where are You?"
God-made God-Peace answers:
"Shut up, you villain!
I am sleeplessly sick of you
And I am breathlessly
Disgusted with you."

28

In the inner world
War-mongers are
Pitiful fear-hostages.

29

Man's familiar war-excuse:
I was not responsible.
He, only he.

30

A man of war
Does not actually need anything
But wants everything immediately.

31

Alas, the heart
Cannot understand
Why and how
The mind's war-insanity
Is escalating.

32

We do not need
Heaven-born saints
But just earth-born seekers
Who believe in peace
And want to live in peace.

33

War-mongers are first-class
Insecurity-coward-singers.

34

He who loves war
Is undoubtedly
The abysmal terrorist.

35

God-lovers long for
Ever-advancing peace.
War-lovers desire
Ever-multiplying destruction.

36

A war-lover,
No matter how long
He chases after satisfaction-deer,
Will never succeed.

37

It is the height of absurdity
When the war-mongers interpret
In their own way
God's all-fulfilling Peace-Delight.

38

No human stupidity
Can take the place
Of the animal brutality:
War.

39

War enjoys
Helplessness-cries.
Peace enjoys
Fulness-smiles.

40

A man of war thinks
It is beneath his dignity
To visit a mental asylum
Although he is absolutely
The perfect patient.

41

War is the victory-drum
Of the animal consciousness.

42

War is the stupid winner
Of futility
And the unavoidable loser
Of dignity.

43

A man of war is, indeed,
The worst possible
Self-doubt-sufferer.

44

A man of war
Does not care for his heart
As long as he knows that
He has a world-devouring mind.

45

War is at once
Mind the thief
And heart the grief.

46

War shows me
The utter helplessness of earth
And the shocking indifference
Of Heaven.

47

War-enjoyers cannot answer
The simplest question,
Which any child can:
"What is life?"

48

A man of war
Has the face of shameless pride
And the heart of deathless
   insecurity.

49

War is man's
Mind-prison-slavery.

50

A war-monger is destined
To be a sorrow-millionaire.
A peace-lover eventually becomes
A joy-billionaire.

51

In the inner world
War-lovers are
Insecurity-dancers.

52

War-mongers do not respond
Even to God's
Urgent emergency Calls.

53

War-lovers are never permitted
To enter into the heart-kingdom.

54

War is man's
God-Satisfaction-promise-
   devourer.

PART XXXIV

I KNOW WHY I AM HELPLESS

I KNOW WHY I AM HELPLESS

1

I know why I am helpless.
I am helpless
Because
I want to take a prominent part
In the desire-drama.

2

I know why I am helpless.
I am helpless
Because
I do not believe
In my illumination-whispering
   heart.

3

I know why I am helpless.
I am helpless
Because
I feel that opportunity
Is another name for forced
   responsibility.

4

I know why I am helpless.
I am helpless
Because
I am afraid of climbing up
The reality-tree.

5

I know why I am helpless.
I am helpless
Because
I do not want to accept
That my desire-life
Is indeed a frustration-heart.

6

I know why I am helpless.
I am helpless
Because
I like constant sound-success
And not sleepless
   silence-progress.

7

I know why I am helpless.
I am helpless
Because
I do not allow patience
To feed me.

8

I know why I am helpless.
I am helpless
Because
I have turned my mind
Into a self-importance-volcano.

9

I know why I am helpless.
I am helpless
Because
I want to succeed
In substituting my
    mind-cleverness
For my heart-soulfulness.

10

I know why I am helpless.
I am helpless
Because
I always carry a doubt-dagger
Wherever I go.

11

I know why I am helpless.
I am helpless
Because
I am afraid of training my mind
To hope.

12

I know why I am helpless.
I am helpless
Because
I do not want to accept the fact
That because of my
    unbending mind
My life has become an
    unending darkness.

13

I know why I am helpless.
I am helpless
Because
I want to live
Inside a binding and blinding
Desire-room
And not inside
An illumining and liberating
Aspiration-palace.

14

I know why I am helpless.
I am helpless
Because
I am always quick to anger
And slower than the slowest
   to smile.

15

I know why I am helpless.
I am helpless
Because
I never want to become
An expert in self-giving.

16

I know why I am helpless.
I am helpless
Because
I never pray to God
For a oneness-heart.

17

I know why I am helpless.
I am helpless
Because
I have never learned the
   silence-language
That is needed to talk to God.

18

I know why I am helpless.
I am helpless
Because
I have never dared to anchor
   my heart
In implicit faith-harbour.

19

I know why I am helpless.
I am helpless
Because
I never believe
That God has kept
　His Heart-Door
Wide open for me.

20

I know why I am helpless.
I am helpless
Because
I am afraid of
Life-transforming dreams.

21

I know why I am helpless.
I am helpless
Because
Every day I bury myself
In thought-mud.

22

I know why I am helpless.
I am helpless
Because
I do not enjoy
Doing my will-drills.

23

I know why I am helpless.
I am helpless
Because
I have a questioning mind
And not a listening heart.

24

I know why I am helpless.
I am helpless
Because
I enjoy my mind's
Constant unwillingness-grumbles.

25

I know why I am helpless.
I am helpless
Because
I do not place every day
Fresh hope-flowers
On my heart-shrine.

26

I know why I am helpless.
I am helpless
Because
I have allowed outer calamities
And inner frustrations
To befriend me.

27

I know why I am helpless.
I am helpless
Because
Every day I feel the end
Of my life's fleeting span.

28

I know why I am helpless.
I am helpless
Because
I carry thickening
    disappointments
Of decades.

29

I know why I am helpless.
I am helpless
Because
I care only for what is gone
And not for what remains.

30

I know why I am helpless.
I am helpless
Because
My name is ego-indulgence.

31

I know why I am helpless.
I am helpless
Because
My name is oneness-starvation.

32

I know why I am helpless.
I am helpless
Because
I dearly enjoy
Sleepless ignorance-appetite.

33

I know why I am helpless.
I am helpless
Because
I have never developed
A distaste for ignorance-food.

34

I know why I am helpless.
I am helpless
Because
My inner faith
Has deserted me for good.

35

I know why I am helpless.
I am helpless
Because
I have not yet discovered the antidote
To my expectation-poison.

36

I know why I am helpless.
I am helpless
Because
I am afraid of taking
Aspiration-fitness-course.

37

I know why I am helpless.
I am helpless
Because
I do not ignore
Constant anxiety-punches.

38

I know why I am helpless.
I am helpless
Because
I do not dare to think
That God the Creator is within me
To awaken me
And God the creation is for me
To please me.

39

I know why I am helpless.
I am helpless
Because
I think that my life
Is a curse of the devil
And not a Love-Gift from God.

II — MINE IS A GOD-DREAM

40

Mine is a God-dream
That can never be shattered.

Mine is a God-dream
That can never be shaken.

41

Mine is a God-dream
That never forgets
Its God-appointment Hour.

42

Mine is a God-dream
That tells me
That my heart's aspiration
Is nothing other than
My life's re-creation.

43

Mine is a God-dream
That embodies only
The mountain-silence-peace.

44

Mine is a God-dream
That knows only
My heart's rising aspiration-sun
And never the setting
Of the aspiration-sun.

45

Mine is a God-dream
That is always empty
Of doubt-poison.

46

Mine is a God-dream
That is always triumphant
Over my earthly human fate.

47

Mine is a God-dream
That tells me
It is not sadness but selflessness
That makes us very special to
　God.

48

Mine is a God-dream
That is indeed my passport
To God's celestial
　Country-Home.

49

Mine is a God-dream
That does not allow
My God-manifestation-heart-song
To remain unsung.

50

Mine is a God-dream
That bravely swims
Across the ocean of impossibility.

51

Mine is a God-dream
That always finds
My Lord Beloved Supreme
　available
Inside my heart-home.

PART XXXV

THE BEGINNING AND THE ARRIVING

THE BEGINNING AND THE ARRIVING

1

The beginning
Gives me
Always more joy
Than the arriving.

2

God's Compassion
Silences
Man's justice.

3

My endless imperfections
Keep God
Sleeplessly busy.

4

God's Greatness
Puzzles
My mind.

5

God's Goodness
Awakens
My heart.

6

Faith earns.
Doubt steals.

7

Faith
Pitifully cries.
Doubt
Shamelessly laughs.

8

Nature is at once
The mother
And the child
Of a miracle.

9

Nature does not know
How to divide.
Nature only knows
How to unite
And multiply.

10

The shallow mind
Questions.
The deep heart
Answers.

11

Fear and self-torture
Regularly play
Hide and seek.

12

The mind
Is afraid
Of silence.

13

The heart
Is afraid
Of Infinity.

14

Silence
Is beyond
Both the knower
And the known.

15

Desire
Is
An insecurity-prisoner.

16

Competition-game
God does not know
How to play.
What is strange,
He does not even want
To learn it.

17

Yesterday
I was a sweetness-desire.
Today
I have become
Bitterness-frustration.

18

Unwillingness-thorn
Was
My yesterday's choice.

19

My today's choice
Is
Willingness-flower-fragrance.

20

Go forward!
Go forward!
Be not afraid
Of even
A marathon-obstacle!

21

I need
Only one thing:
A divinely inspired
Warrior-eye.

22

My unconditional heart
Receives from God
The sunshine
Of His Peace-Sky.

23

Humanity's
Self-giving smiles
Are Divinity's
New God-manifesting
Creations.

24

A life without prayers
And meditations
Is nothing other than
An agonising emptiness.

25

My life swims
Every day
In the sweet sea of hope.

26

Yesterday
I was
My competition-eye.

27

Today
I am
My competence-heart.

28

My prayers
Are my heart's
Experience-flowers.

29

My meditations
Are my life's
Realisation-fruits.

30

My heart
Teaches me
God-obedience.
My life
Teaches me
God-obeisance.

31

My unconditional surrender
Is the topmost branch
Of my life-beauty's tree.

32

God's dancing ankle-bells
Are only for
The aspiration-heart
To hear.

33

Each desire
Is a bottomless
Nothingness-abyss.

34

To an unconditionally
Surrendered soul,
God does not come alone.
He comes with His Breath,
Blissfully embracing.

35

Alas,
My life is nothing other than
An ingratitude-dagger.

36

An indifference-mind
Is indeed
A destructive knife.

37

My Lord,
Every day
Do make my heart
A new gratitude-prayer.

38

I may allow myself
To lose all my other resolves
But never, never
My God-satisfaction-resolve.

39

With my aspiration-heart
I began my journey.
With my dedication-life
I shall forever continue.

40

My heart
Is always eager
To give my mind
God-lessons
Free of charge.

41

A singing heart
Is
A flying life.

42

Fear
Binds the body.
Doubt
Blinds the eyes.
Suspicion
Blights the heart.

43

Good-bye, ego,
Good-bye.
Hello, surrender,
Hello.

44

My Lord,
May I make every day
A new gratitude-prayer.

45

Nothing
Can be more powerful
Than eagerness.

46

Nothing
Can be more fruitful
Than surrender.

47

Nothing
Can be more beautiful
Than forgiveness.

48

A soulful smile
Can create a blissful
Transformation-life.

49

Today
I am determined
To honour
All my promises
To God.

50

Nature means
Life-enlightenment
And not
Mind-confinement.

PART XXXVI

BEAUTY-DISCOVERY

BEAUTY-DISCOVERY

1

The inner
Beauty-discovery
Is the outer
Life-mastery.

2

The beauty of the sound-life
Fades.
The beauty of the silence-life
Forever lasts.

3

A God-seeker thinks
That God is powerful.
A God-lover knows
That God is beautiful.

4

The beauty
Of a simplicity-life
And the beauty
Of a self-giving heart
Have no equal.

5

May beauty be my mind's
Immediate choice.
May beauty be my heart's
Perfect voice.

6

Beauty is
My surrender-flower-life.
Beauty is
My gratitude-fragrance-heart.

7

My mind's readiness-beauty
And my heart's willingness-
    beauty
Are two things I enjoy deeply.

8

Ugliness
Is self-reliance.
Beauty
Is God-reliance.

9

Beauty
Is my heart's
Mind-transcendence-hope.

10

I dearly love
My mind's invincible
Determination-volcano-beauty.

11

Beauty
Is my heart's
Expectation-hope-collection-
 dreams.

12

My heart's aspiration-beauty-
 flames
Are destined to climb
The transcendental Heights
Of the Beyond.

13

My heart
Is
Affection-nest-beauty.

14

My yesterday's willingness
Looked beautiful.
My tomorrow's devotedness
Will look beautiful.

15

Beauty is in
My child-heart-cries.
Beauty is in
My child-eye-smiles.

16

When I look at a child,
He gives me
His soul-beauty-dreams.

17

Beauty is in my today's
Life-acceptance.
Beauty is in my tomorrow's
Self-transcendence.

18

The very purpose
Of inner aspiration-beauty
Is to be shared
With the rest of the world.

19

My Lord Supreme,
Do make me a sleepless dreamer
Of soulfully beautiful dreams.

20

Immortality's Beauty
Is the feast
Of silence-light.

21

Alas,
My heart's beauty
Is as fleeting
As my mind's silence-peace.

22

Not the rise, but the fall
Of my mind's ego-empire
Is extremely beautiful.

23

God Himself has made our
  heart's
Oneness-aspiration-beauty
And our life's
Oneness-dedication-beauty
Unfathomable.

24

Self-offering-beauty
Is at every moment
On the increase
Ad infinitum.

25

Beautiful is a purity-seed.
Soulful is a purity plant.
Powerful is a purity-tree.

26

Eternity's Beauty
Is in my mind's
Self-control.

Infinity's Beauty
Is in my life's
Transformation-goal.

27

The mind's silence-beauty
Does not contradict.
The heart's peace-beauty
Does not question.

28

The mind prefers
To remain uninformed
About the fully formed,
Exclusive beauty
Of the heart.

29

Attachment-beauty
Has a very short life.
Detachment-beauty
Is Eternity's Breath.

30

I look divinely beautiful
When I say my last farewell
To my ego-life.

I look supremely beautiful
When I welcome
The universal oneness-home.

PART XXXVII

BEAUTIFUL IS MY WHISPERING SOUL

BEAUTIFUL IS MY WHISPERING SOUL

1

Beautiful is my whispering soul.
Beautiful is my climbing heart.
Beautiful is my willing mind.
Beautiful is my uncomplaining vital.
Beautiful is my serving body.

2

I look beautiful
When I accept
Impossibility-challenges.

3

I look beautiful
When I play with
My silence-mind.

4

I look beautiful
When I am not tortured
By jealousy, insecurity
And doubt.

5

I look beautiful
When my mind divinely enjoys
The endless process
Of transformation.

6

I look beautiful
When each thought of mine
Grows into angelic perfection.

7

I am supremely beautiful
Only when I become
The nothingness of my own life.

8

I am supremely beautiful
Only when I become
The fulness of my soul.

9

I am challenging
The haughtiness
Of untruth.

10

I am challenging
The tyranny
Of impurity.

11

I am challenging
My mind's
Confusion-jungle-thoughts.

12

I am challenging
My ingratitude-mind.

13

I am challenging
My long-standing
    helplessness-life,
Hopelessness-life
And fruitlessness-life.

14

I am challenging
My failure-pangs
And pathos-sighs.

15

I am challenging
My worst enemy:
Self-indulgence.

16

I am challenging,
On God's behalf,
His oldest enemy:
My ignorance-night.

17

I am challenging
The death
Of my God-manifestation-dream.

18

I am challenging
My heart's
Anxiety-chains.

19

I am challenging
The fruitless desert
Of my mind.

20

I am challenging
The bite
Of my loneliness-vital.

21

I am challenging
My desire-snakes.

22

I am challenging
My mind's
Unwillingness-supremacy.

23

I am challenging
My satisfaction-punctured heart.

24

I am challenging
The failure of my soul's mission
On earth.

25

I am challenging
My expectation-frustration-
    graveyard.

26

I am challenging
The inevitable doom
Of human life.

27

I am challenging
The wasteful regret
Of my failure-life.

28

I am challenging
My mind's sincerity:
Does it really love God?
Does it really need God?
Can it really live without God?
Can it really dare to doubt God?

29

No more
Shall I suffer
From binding and blinding
  anxieties.

30

No more
Shall I enjoy
Aspiration-vacation.

31

No more
Shall I indulge
In dedication-retirement.

32

No more
Shall I suffer
From an incomplete heart.

33

No more
Shall I tolerate
My mind's surrender-bankruptcy.

34

No more
Shall I be afraid
Of my heavy responsibilities.

35

No more
Shall I be with those
Who tell me that I am not
God's choice instrument.

36

No more
Shall I ignore
My heart's peace-hunger.

37

No more
Shall I allow my mind
To take the expectation-
    frustration-course.

38

No more
Shall I allow my mind
To think of any human being
As a dangerous stranger.

39

No more
Shall I allow my vital
To love suspicion-wrestling.

40

No more
Shall I allow my mind
To feed on doubt-boxing.

41

No more
Shall I cherish
My mind's ego-feast
And my heart's
    oneness-starvation.

42

I am more.
I am more
Than my mind's sincerity.

43

I am more.
I am more
Than my heart's purity.

44

I am more.
I am more
Than my life's spontaneity.

45

I am more.
I am more
Than my outer appearances.

46

I am more.
I am more
Than my inner experiences.

47

I am more.
I am more
Than my readiness.

48

I am more.
I am more
Than my willingness.

49

I am more.
I am more
Than my fulness.

50

Who am I actually, then?
I am my Eternity's Dream-Boat
Heading towards
My Immortality's Reality-Shore.

PART XXXVIII

FRIENDSHIP-BIRDS FLY

FRIENDSHIP-BIRDS FLY

1

O my friend,
Let us claim each other first.
Then let us walk together
Towards our destined goal.

2

Friendship is
No fragile human bond.
Friendship is
A strong oneness-bridge.

3

I am so proud of my friends,
For all of them are
Genuine peace-prophets.

4

Each and every friend of mine
Rightly deserves
My heart's gratitude-tears.

5

A real friend may be
Far, very far in miles,
But near, very near
In heart-smiles.

6

Sincerity-bud-beauty
Is my mind's safeguard-friend.
Purity-blossom-fragrance
Is my heart's safeguard-friend.

7

A new friend is a new hope-sea
Inside my heart.
A new friend is a new hope-sky
Inside my mind.

8

Friendship openly persuades our minds
To do the right thing
And secretly convinces our hearts
To become the right person.

9

Friendship-birds
Can fly
Only on the wings of sincerity.

10

Friendship is the mind's readiness,
The heart's willingness
and the life's oneness.

PART II: I AM SO HAPPY

11

I am so happy
That I have done
The right thing:
I have destroyed
My monarch-ego.

12

I am so happy
That I have done
The right thing:
I have not allowed
My receptivity-heart
To fall asleep.

13

I am so happy
That I am immersed
In my self-giving service.

14

I am so happy
That I have not allowed science
To inflate my spiritual mind.

15

I am so happy
That I do not have the smile
Of a world-conqueror.

16

I am so happy
That I have the smile
Of a world-lover.

17

I am so happy
That I do not immortalise
My mind's frustrations
And my mind's miseries.

18

I am so happy
That I gladly accept
All the proposals of my heart
And execute them immediately.

19

I am so happy
That I never allow my mind
To oppose my heart's
God-inspired and
   God-initiated proposals.

20

I am so happy
That my heart and I
Every day sing together
Our unconditional life-songs
To God.

21

I am so happy
That the ideal in me
And the real in me
Have most cheerfully
Become inseparable.

22

I am so happy
That I have fortified
My aspiration-breath
With ever-increasing faith.

23

I am so happy
That my aspiration-heart
And my dedication-life
Sleeplessly long for the
   inner grace
And not for the outer space.

24

I am so happy
That at long last I have become
The big man who sympathises,
And that I am no longer
The little man who criticises.

25

I am so happy
That my desire-life
Has been completely
And permanently illumined
By my aspiration-heart.

26

I am so happy
That my heart hears
Enchanting, illumining
And fulfilling God-melodies
Wherever I go.

27

I am so happy
That my mind is no longer a member
Of the doubt-society.

28

I am so happy
That my heart no longer lives
Inside an insecurity-cave.

29

I am so happy
That I have a new name:
Gratitude-fragrance-heart-smile.

30

I am so happy
That at long last
I have the capacity
To claim only my Lord
    Beloved Supreme
As my own, very own.

PART III: MY MIND AND MY HEART

31

My mind tells me
That it is too soon
For me to realise God.

My heart tells me
That it is already late
For me to realise God.

32

My mind tells me
That what I need is a finish line.

My heart tells me
That what I need is a
   progress-run.

33

My mind wants me
To enjoy pleasure-harvest.

My heart wants me
To enjoy faith-feast.

34

My mind wants me
To go out
And be part of
The outer world.

My heart wants me
To come home
And remain a member of
The inner family.

35

Opportunity is the only thing
That my mind craves.

Preparation is the only thing
That my heart longs for.

36

My mind-teacher tells me
That time is a circle.

My heart-teacher tells me
That time has no birth
And no death.

37

My mind is afraid
Of the aspiration-life.

My heart is afraid
Of the desire-life.

38

My mind loves
Daring intensity.

My heart loves
Illumining immensity.

39

My mind wants me
To be a world-shaking warrior.

My heart wants me
To be a world-elevating inspirer.

40

My mind's supremacy
Wants to change the world.

My heart's ecstasy
Wants to arrange the world.

41

Hesitation
Precedes my mind.

Satisfaction
Precedes my heart.

42

My mind loves to take
Confusion-extension exercises.

My heart loves to take
Confusion-extinction plus
Illumination-expansion exercises.

43

My mind asks God,
"God, do You live for me?"

My heart asks God,
"My Lord, will I always
Live only for You?"

PART XXXIX

GOD THE EYE AND GOD THE HEART

GOD THE EYE AND GOD THE HEART

1

God the Eye
Tells me to be perfect.

2

God the Heart
Shows me how.

3

God the Eye
Commands me:
"Go home!"

4

God the Heart
Whispers to me:
"Here is your Home,
My child."

5

God the Eye
Tells me:
"Give Me!
I shall give you
Much more
In return."

6

God the Heart
Tells me:
"Give Me
What you have.
I shall give you
What I am —
My Infinity's Wealth —
In return."

7

God the Eye
Tells me:
"Be careful!
Danger
May be ahead!"

8

God the Heart
Tells me:
"Be wakeful,
Prayerful and soulful.
Danger ahead
You can escape."

9

When I ask
God the Eye
How old God is,
The immediate
Answer is:
"Birthless and
Deathless."

10

When I ask
God the Heart
The same question,
The sweet answer is:
"I am exactly as
Young
As your heart is."

11

God the Eye
Shows me my present
Imperfections
Impartially.

12

God the Heart
Promises me my
Future perfection
Compassionately.

13

God the Eye
Is not always
Satisfied with me.

14

God the Heart
Has repeatedly
Promised to me
That He will never
Give up on me.

15

God the Eye
Tells me:
"Look!
Your mind is cloudy."

16

God the Heart
Tells me:
"Your mind can be
Sunny.
Just try for it!"

17

God the Eye
Tells me that I am
Indeed
A possibility-fulfiller.

18

God the Heart
Tells me that I am
Undoubtedly
An impossibility-challenger.

19

God the Eye
Wants me to achieve
Quickly.

20

God the Heart
Wants me to receive
Smilingly.

21

God the Eye
Arouses
My God-hunger.

22

God the Heart
Feeds
My God-hunger.

23

God the Eye
Chases
My restless mind.

24

God the Heart
Embraces
My peaceful heart.

25

God the Eye
Definitely
Loves me.

26

God the Heart
Sleeplessly
Caresses me.

27

God the Eye
Asks me:
"Where
Have you been?"

28

God the Heart
Asks me:
"How are you?"

29

God the Eye
Shows me the Way.

30

God the Heart
Hastens my Goal.

31

God the Red Eye
Threatens
And frightens me.

32

God the Blue Heart
Immediately
Comes to my rescue
And
Starts perfecting me.

33

When necessity
Demands,
God the Eye
Tells me to shut up.

34

At that very
Moment,
God the Heart
Pleads with me
To wake up:
"My child, wake up!"

35

God the Eye
Tells me:
"You must not have
A negative thought!"

36

God the Heart
Tells me:
"You must be
A positive will!"

37

God the Eye
Tells me that
The Road is very long.

38

God the Heart
Tells me that
The Goal is eagerly
And sleeplessly
Waiting for me.

39

The very presence of
God the Eye
At times
Chills my mind.

40

The very presence of
God the Heart
Always
Thrills my heart.

41

God the Eye
Tells me:
"What I need from you
Is genuine aspiration."

42

God the Heart
Tells me:
"My child,
What we mutually
Need
From each other
Is satisfaction."

43

God the Eye
Tells me that
My success depends
On my mind's
Strength-expression.

44

God the Heart
Tells me that
My progress depends
On my heart's
Length-expansion.

45

God the Eye
Tells me that
My success comes
From the beauty
Of my determination.

46

God the Heart
Tells me that
My progress comes
From the purity
Of my aspiration.

47

God the Eye
Wants my mind to see
What is happening.

48

God the Heart
Wants my heart to feel
What is becoming.

49

God the Eye
Declares my victory.

50

God the Heart
Parades my victory.

PART XL

MY GOD-MASTER

MY GOD-MASTER

1

My God-Master
Is
My Absolute Lord Supreme.

2

My God-Master is
The one Master,
The real Master,
My only Master.

3

My God-Master has given me
His own Map to study
So that my life's journey
Most successfully reaches
Its destination.

4

My God-Master does not want
  me to be
A talking miracle,
But a living gratitude.

5

My God-Master is telling me
Not to act like a fool.
My greed for greatness
Will end in helpless uselessness.

6

My God-Master is telling me
That His Closeness to me
Is all that I need
In my entire life.

7

My God-Master is advising me
To discard my pride-flooded,
All-knowing mind
Once and for all.

8

My God-Master is telling me
In supreme secrecy
That if I have a purity-flooded
Surrender-heart,
Then I can easily have Him
For the asking.

9

My God-Master is telling me
Not to blame anybody,
Not even myself,
But to open my heart's eye every day
To a new horizon.

10

My God-Master wants me
To surrender to Him alone
If I want to heave a sigh of relief
From the world's untold tension.

11

My God-Master wants me
To make friends with adventure
So that every day I can grow
Into something more beautiful
And someone more perfect.

12

My God-Master wants me
To stop criticising
His Body — mankind —
If I want to please Him
In His own Way.

13

My God-Master wants me
To become a good listener.
But I must also try to become
An iota of wisdom-light.

14

My God-Master wants me to
   know
That the desire-life
Anybody can have,
But the aspiration-life
Is always meant for the few.

15

Unless I accept my God-Master
As my own, very own,
Useless nothingness will never
   leave me.

16

Behold, my God-Master is
   blessing me
With His own Plane
So that I can fly far above
My stupidity-mind's
   confusion-turbulence.

MY GOD-MASTER

17

My God-Master is telling the
   whole world
That a oneness-purity-heart
Can easily prove His Existence
   on earth.

18

I want happiness
From my God-Master.
My God-Master wants from me
A heart of blossoming faith.

19

My God-Master does not see
Any difference between
A needless life and a
   faithless mind.

20

Because I have given my
   God-Master
My undivided attention,
He is blessing me with
His unreserved Compassion.

21

My God-Master is telling me that
My mind is His own experiment,
My heart is His own experience
And my life is His own progress.

22

My God-Master is telling me
That I give not only too much
   importance
But also exorbitantly useless
   importance
To my failure-heart.

23

My God-Master is asking me
Not to allow my heart
To be stabbed by fear.

24

My God-Master is telling me
That if I live inside His Heart,
I will never be lost
On the way to the Golden Shore.

25

My God-Master is not so cruel
As to tell me
That I have to find
My own way.

26

Today my heart is
My God-Master's Dream-Seed.
Tomorrow my heart will be
My God-Master's Reality-Tree.

27

Each time I think of my
   God-Master,
I try to feel that it is
A new awakening-flash
   of inspiration-light.

28

I am my God-Master's
Heart-Prosperity-Fragrance.

29

I cannot measure
My God-Master's limitless
   Heart-World
With my tinier-than-the-tiniest
Doubt-tape.

30

My God-Master asks me
To share my doubt-demon
Only with Him
And with nobody else.

31

I am listening to my God-Master.
He is telling me that
I do not have and can never have
An ugly heart.

32

My God-Master is so happy
   with me
And so proud of me
Because my willingness-heart
Is never empty.

33

I am my God-Master's
Satisfaction-Dream-Fulfilment.

34

My God-Master is so sad
Because my heart has eloped
With despair-ignorance-beggar.

35

I can be my God-Master's
Supremely chosen instrument
Only when my heart
Hungers only for Him.

36

I am asking my mind to cry
For my God-Master's Light
Like my heart.
My God-Master will definitely
Forgive and illumine
My mind's countless crimes.

37

My unconditional surrender-life
Is my God-Master's fondest
Pride.

38

My God-Master does not want
   me to be
A desperate cry
Inside my mind's desire-jungle.

39

At least for one solitary day
I shall show my God-Master
My divinity's enthusiasm-heart.

40

My God-Master tells me
That neither I
Nor anybody else
Is a loser in the spiritual world.

41

In secrecy supreme
My God-Master comes to me
To enjoy my heart-rose-
　fragrance-petals.

42

My God-Master wants me
To take every day
Soulfulness-heart-lessons
　from Him.

43

I am listening to what
My God-Master is telling me.
He says that my mind's
　volcano-eye
Is not worth even a penny!

44

If I become a heart-sprinter,
My God-Master Himself
Will amazingly increase
My enthusiasm-stride.

45

My God-Master is the only one
Who wants me to stop carrying
My heavy imperfection-load.

46

According to my God-Master,
My mind's insincerity-boat
Will definitely capsize
Long before the destination.

47

My God-Master does not
　want me
To play with
My restlessness-thought-
　monkeys.

48

Inside my God-Master's
Compassion-Eye
I must feel
My devotion-bliss.

49

Why do I not feel
That I break my
   God-Master's Heart
When I deliberately enjoy
My mind's cyclone-confusion-
   fury?

50

It is my bounden duty
To ask my mind's sincerity
And my heart's purity
To breathe inside
My God-Master's Heart.

51

My God-Master wants me
Only to live
Inside my own aspiration-heart
And not die
From expectation-greed.

52

My God-Master
Proudly treasures
My gratitude-heart-blossoms.

53

Can I not hear what
My God-Master is telling me?
He wants me to stop playing
Self-indulgence-game.

54

My God-Master wants me to be
Only one thing:
My heart's happiness-fountain.

55

My God-Master's Love-Sky
I can easily span
With my gratitude-rainbow-heart.

PART XLI

MY GOD-PRAYERS AND MY GOD-MEDITATIONS

MY GOD-PRAYERS AND MY GOD-MEDITATIONS

1

Prayer
Cries for God.
Meditation
Dreams of God.

2

Prayer
Longs to know.
Meditation
Longs to be.

3

Prayer
Is fear-extinction.
Meditation
Is confidence-manifestation.

4

Prayer
Is a Heaven-climbing bird.
Meditation
Is all-spreading wings.

5

Prayer
Is God's fond child.
Meditation
Is God's responsible son.

6

Prayer
Is simplicity's beauty.
Meditation
Is responsibility's capacity.

7

Prayer
Thinks God dwells
Far above the human head.
Meditation
Feels God's Presence
Deep inside
The aspiring heart.

8

Prayer
Goes to
The Eternal Saviour.
Meditation
Goes to
The universal Dreamer.

9

Prayer
Is affection-lesson.
Meditation
Is wisdom-lesson.

10

Prayer
Is upward self-offering.
Meditation
Is inward self-digging.

11

Prayer
Is a hope-pilgrim.
Meditation
Is a promise-traveller.

12

Prayer
Is fond of
God the Power.
Meditation
Is fond of
God the Silence.

13

Prayer
Glorifies God.
Meditation
Beautifies God.

14

Prayer
Is mind-purification.
Meditation
Is heart-expansion.

15

I pray to God
To receive
His Compassion.
I meditate on God
To receive
His illumination.

16

Prayer loves
God the Drummer
And God the Drum.
Meditation loves
God the Flutist
And God the Flute.

17

I pray to God
To bless me
With His Protection.
I meditate on God
To bless me
With His Peace.

18

I pray to God
To make me
A choice instrument of His.
I meditate on God
To make me
An unconditional seeker
And server of His.

19

I pray to God
To give me
A truth-seeking mind.
I meditate on God
To receive
A self-giving heart.

20

When I pray,
God blesses my head.
When I meditate,
God feels my heart.

21

I pray to God
To become
His Heart-Flower.
I meditate on God
To become
His Soul-Fragrance.

22

When I pray,
God charmingly whistles.
When I meditate,
God sweetly whispers.

23

Prayer
Is at once
A giver and receiver.
Meditation
Is at once
A diver and explorer.

24

Prayer
Is
My God-journey-preparation.
Meditation
Is
My God-journey-excavation.

25

When we pray,
We usually pray
For success.
When we meditate,
We invariably meditate
For progress.

26

The highest height
Of prayer
Is unconditional surrender.
The deepest depth
Of meditation
Is sleepless gratitude.

27

A beautiful thought
Is the result
Of a sincere prayer.
A fruitful experience
Is the result
Of a deep meditation.

28

I pray to God
To push aside
My destructive
Doubt-mind.
I meditate on God
To increase the beauty
And fragrance
Of my blossoming
Faith-heart.

29

The Christ
Prayed and prayed
And then declared:
"I and my Father
Are one."
Sri Krishna
Meditated and meditated
And then declared:
"I am
The Lord
Absolute Supreme."

30

I pray and pray
To become
The direct representative
Of God
The transcendental Dreamer.
I meditate and meditate
To become
The direct representative
Of God
The universal Liberator.

31

I pray and pray
Because
I wish to see
The beauty
Of the higher worlds.
I meditate and meditate
Because
I wish to smell
The fragrance
Of the inner worlds.

PART XLII

I AM SURE

I AM SURE

1

I am sure,
You cannot tell me lies
When you allow God
To speak through you.

2

I am sure,
Your soul at least knows
Where God is.

I am sure,
Your heart at least knows
Who God is.

3

I am sure,
Although you do not have
Much faith in God,
You are eager
To see God
At least once a day.

4

I am sure,
God asks you every day
Not to speak ill of
His beloved creation.

5

I am sure,
God has repeatedly told you
That I am not as bad
As you think.

6

I am sure,
God will not stop asking you
To be my friend,
Real friend,
Once again.

7

I am sure,
God has already told you
That you cannot live
Even one single day
Without enjoying
Your ego-feast.

8

I am sure,
Like me,
You too do not work hard
To please God.

9

I am sure,
Like me,
You too forget to offer
A gratitude-prayer to God
Every day.

10

I am sure,
My ingratitude-sword
Is not as destructive
As yours.

11

I am sure,
Like me,
Every morning you forget
To say hello to your soul.

12

I am sure,
Although you do
Not want to,
Something within you
Forces you to accept me,
Or at least tolerate me.

13

I am sure,
What you need
At every moment
Is to breathe the purity
Of your
Heart-blossom-fragrance.

14

I am sure,
God never, never has heard
A single word
Of appreciation
From you about me.

15

I am sure,
You admire
Your so-called huge mind
Infinitely more
Than it rightly deserves.

16

I am sure,
Your fully blown ego
Is not interested in singing
World-oneness-songs.

17

I am sure,
You cannot possibly
Please God
More than I do.

18

I am sure,
You are not working hard
To break the chain
Of your desire-life.
But I can't blame you.
There are many who are
Sailing in your boat.
Perhaps I am no exception.

19

I am sure,
Even your own heart
Laughs and laughs
At your mind's bombastic
God-manifestation-promises.

20

I am sure,
God has asked you
Many times
To sing every day
A new aspiration-song.
And you just do not,
Not that you cannot.

21

I am sure,
God does not hate you
So much
As to give up on you.

22

I am sure,
Your excessive fondness
For your clever mind
Pains your poor heart
Deeply.

23

I am sure,
Many people have already
Told you
That your computer-mind
Is soulless.

24

I am sure,
There is not a single day
That you do not blame God
For your
Mind-frustration-life.

25

I am sure,
God never
Takes you seriously
When you make your life's
Perfection-promises to Him.

26

I am sure,
You have never
Looked for God
With your heart's
Soulful obedience-cries.

27

I am sure,
When you wake up
In the morning
You do not think of
God the Supreme Lover,
But you think only of
God the Supreme Power.

I AM SURE

28

I am sure,
By now your soul
Has given up its
    God-manifestation-dreams
In and through you on earth.
Why?
Because it is an extremely
Difficult task.

29

I am sure,
You never want to learn
That it is infinitely better
To love the world
Than to expect anything
From the world.

30

I am sure,
What everybody needs
From you
Is affection and nothing else.

31

I am sure,
You want the whole world
To understand,
But do you ever care
To understand
The poor world?

32

I am sure,
Your loveless heart
Has made your life
Utterly helpless.

33

I am sure,
When it comes to offering
Your service to the world
Unconditionally,
Even for a day,
You enjoy
Your precious absence.

34

I am sure,
You are suffering
From the universal disease:
Indifference.

35

I am sure,
No matter what
The world thinks of you,
God has unmistakably
Chosen you
To be a choice instrument
Of His.

36

I am sure,
Every morning
You wake up and wonder
Why nobody loves you
And nobody needs you.

37

I am sure,
There shall come a time
When even you
Will be totally transformed
By God's Forgiveness-Heart
And Compassion-Eye.

The question is:
When?
The answer is:
Now,
Right at this very moment.

PART XLIII

MY MIND-CONFUSION OUT,
MY MIND-ILLUMINATION IN

MY MIND-CONFUSION OUT, MY MIND-ILLUMINATION IN

1

My mind
Was a slow
God-Wisdom-learner.
Now the story
Is completely changed.
My mind has become
A fast God-Wisdom-lover.

2

My mind
Was a quick
Man-critic.
Now my mind
Has given up totally
Man-criticism-profession.

3

My mind
Was a perfect stranger
To gratitude.
Now my mind
Is a devoted member
Of the gratitude-family.

4

My mind
Was not a believer
In God-service.
Now my mind
Has become
A spontaneous God-server.

5

My mind
Was a quantity-lover.
Now my mind
Is a quality-chooser.

6

My mind
Thought that God
Was a strict
Oneness-Examiner.
Now my mind
Not only thinks
But also knows
That God is a compassionate
Oneness-Heart-Tutor.

7

My mind
Vehemently disliked
My silence-heart.
Now my mind
Is enamoured of
My silence-heart.

8

My mind
Used to follow
Success-glory-path.
Now my mind
Follows
Progress-fragrance-path.

9

My mind
Was proud of
Its complexity.
My mind
Now is fond of
Its simplicity.

10

Either my mind
Did not know
Or did not care to know
That pleasure
Is perishable and fleeting.
Now my mind
Is fully aware
Of pleasure's perishability
And the real name
Of pleasure:
Futility.

11

My mind
Believed
Only
In rich results.
My mind
Now believes
Only
In self-offering-efforts.

12

My mind
Used to ridicule
My heart's silver dreams
And golden promises.
Now my mind
Has become
An ardent adorer
Of my heart's
Dreams and promises.

13

My mind
Used to question
The sincerity
Of the God-seeking hearts.
Now my mind
Not only admires
But loves
The God-seeking hearts.

14

My mind
Was a long-dead hope.
Now my mind
Is a newborn hope
Flooded with
God-fulfilment-promises.

15

Right or wrong,
My mind
Used to accuse others.
Now,
Even when others
Are wrong,
My mind does not hesitate
To excuse them.

16

I was
A hesitant
Mind-walker.
Now
I am a confident
Mind-runner.

17

My mind
Did not care for
God's Compassion.
Now my mind
Is a superb
God-Compassion-distributor.

18

Mine was the mind
That was
Doubt-ridicule.
Mine is the mind
That is now
Faith-thrill.

19

My mind
Enjoyed
Self-appreciation-stories.
My mind
Now enjoys only
God-satisfaction-songs.

20

My mind
Used to explode
When it noticed
Imperfections
In any human being.
My mind
Now explores
All possibilities
For the perfection
Of the human race.

21

My mind
Cherished
The tantrum of impatience.
My mind
Now cherishes
The sky-vast patience.

22

Ruthless
And
Endless worries
Used to engulf
My mind.
Shadowless
And
Priceless dreams
Now adorn
My mind.

23

My mind
Never welcomed
Aspiration-guests.
My mind
Now has become
A sleepless open door
To all aspiration-guests.

24

My mind
Used to ply
Its life-boat
Between
The confusion-shore
And
The suspicion-shore.
My mind
Now plies
Its life-boat
Between
The compassion-shore
And
The illumination-shore.

25

My mind
Was God's
Tolerance-limit.
My mind
Is now
God-redolence-delight.

PART XLIV

MY GOD-COMMITMENTS

1

Every day
My soul reminds me
Of my God-commitments.

2

God proudly treasures
The beauty
Of my God-aspiration,
The purity
Of my God-dedication
And the divinity
Of my God-manifestation.

3

To be a better aspirant,
I helplessly cry within
And
Powerfully smile without.

4

If you do not want
To listen to God
Even once a day,
Why should God allow you
To remain inside
His Heart-Garden?

5

O my Lord Supreme,
Do ask my heart
Not only to forgive my mind,
But also to lead
And guide my mind
To reach the golden
Destination-Shore.

6

From now on
I am determined
To love and serve God
Sleeplessly, blindly
And unconditionally.
Who cares if my ex-friend,
Ignorance,
Suffers?

7

Each serious mistake
Leads to either
An outer punishment
Or an inner enlightenment,
Or both.

MY GOD-COMMITMENTS

8

My soul-friend
Wants me to make progress
Only through
My inner and outer
Happiness.

9

The inner experience-height
Is the beginning of
The outer freedom-delight.

10

Very happily and proudly
God watches
My humility and His Divinity
Playing together.

11

Can there be anything
More fruitful than
My sweetness-fragrance
Progress-heart-home?

12

Why do I love and look at
The beauty and purity
Of the world?
Because
They take away instantly
My own ugliness
And impurity
For my much-needed
Transformation.

13

Ignorance-torture
Unconsciously
Has awakened me
To pray for God-rapture.

14

The world
Is really beautiful
Because
So my heart
Has imagined it.

15

God will never allow
A true God-seeker
To waste time,
For each moment
In God-aspiration,
In God-realisation
And
In God-manifestation
Is so important.

16

Even from an iota
Of my patience,
I have come to learn
How wise, illumining
And fulfilling
God eternally is.

17

If you are a true seeker
And
Want God-manifestation,
How can you then enjoy
Your chronic
Self-absorption?

18

No matter
What the world
Thinks of me,
I am, indeed,
A God-lover
In my own right.

19

Gratitude
And surrender-flights
Know no turbulence
In the sunlit sky.

20

My heart and I
Are so happy
That insecurity
Has finally drawn
Its last breath.

21

Surrender, surrender,
Surrender unconditionally!
Yours will be an inner
Ecstasy-flooded life.

22

Alas,
How I wish
Somebody would tell me
What my heart's
Daily true needs are!

23

Every day
I meet God
In His Heart's
Silence-Illumination-Sea.

24

Alas,
It is my own jealous mind
That destroys
My heart's
Sweet hope-dreams.

25

O my unaspiring mind,
You are neither needed
Nor wanted.
You are just tolerated.

26

What I always need
Is not a publicity-mind
But a purity-heart.

27

O my silence-rainbow,
May I fly
With your
Heaven-climbing wings?

28

If you are
A chosen God-dreamer,
Then before long
Your life's
Ignorance-nightmare
Will come to an end.

29

Only
A tranquillity-flooded heart
Can be the possessor
Of beautiful, soulful
And fruitful tears.

30

As love of God
Without prayer
Is impossible,
Even so,
Peace of mind
Without meditation
Is impossible.

31

Harmony shall echo
And re-echo
Throughout the length
And breadth of the world
When each human being
Values the beauty
And divinity
Of self-offering.

32

In my universal
Oneness-heart-nest,
No earth-bound desire-bird
Will ever be allowed
To take rest.

33

Nothing is impossible.
There shall come a time
When I shall definitely
Be able
To move my searching mind
From ignorance-pathways.

34

The unwillingness
Of the mind
Has to surrender eventually
To the streaming tears
Of the heart.

35

O my mind,
I do not think anybody
Is willing to pay attention
To your
Ruthless and shameless
Indifference-life.

36

God neither imposes
Nor exposes.
He just proposes
Out of His infinite
Compassion-Light.

37

O my mind,
Do you not remember
That there was a time
When you loved God
Most dearly?
If you do not
Remember the time,
Let me tell you.
It was before the time
When you made friends
With fear, doubt,
Anxiety and despair.

38

O my life, O my life,
My heart must do
What it has to do.
You cannot and must not
Stand in my heart's way.

39

My Lord,
Please tell me why
You have created thoughts:
To punish me
Or to illumine me?
"My child,
The thoughts
That your mind creates
For you
Are for your punishment.
The thoughts
That I create for you
Are for your
Enlightenment."

40

When God comes to you,
He brings with Him
His transcendental Dream.
When you go to God,
You should take with you
Your earth-liberated reality.

41

As a glimpse of God
Can give you
A taste of trance,
Even so,
A glimpse of God
Can make you
His direct representative
On earth.

42

I have two teachers:
The soul and the mind
The soul teaches me
God-acceptance-songs.
The mind teaches me
Life-possession-dance.

43

God and God's Peace-Hours
Are fast approaching me
Because
I am now grown into
My heart's
Unconditional breath.

44

Every day
My Lord Supreme
Wants me to multiply
My heart's
Sincerity-purity-smiles.

45

Alas,
I do not know why and how
I have lost
My heart's
Aspiration-hunger
And my life's
Dedication-thirst.

46

The indomitable
Power of faith
Will eventually conquer
All mountain-barriers
Of our desiring and
Unaspiring mind.

47

God does not want
To expose
Your mind's stupidity
And your heart's impurity.
He just wants to plant
His own Divinity
Inside your Heaven-longing
Necessity.

48

O my mind,
You are helping
The wrong parties
If you are siding with
The haughtiness
Of your vital
And
The laziness
Of your body.

49

May invisible inspiration
Be found inside my mind.
May invisible aspiration
Be found inside my heart.
May invisible enthusiasm
Be found inside my vital.
May invisible awareness
Be found inside my body.
May invisible perfection
Be found inside
All that I do
And all that I become.

50

The God-hunger-song
Of the ancient sages
Must be learned
By the modern world
To please
The Absolute Lord Supreme
Once more in His own Way.

51

What I need
Is a quenchless thirst
For the perfection of
My mind
And the satisfaction of
My Lord Beloved Supreme.

52

There can be
No iota of confusion
In the shrine of my heart.
But confusion
Can be endless
Inside my mind-temple.

53

My Lord,
Were You looking for me?
Alas, I was in
My darkness-mind-room.
My Lord,
Will You once more
Look for me?
This time
You will definitely find me
Inside
My aspiration-heart-room.

PART XLV

MORNING INVITES MY HEART. EVENING INVITES MY LIFE

MORNING INVITES MY HEART. EVENING INVITES MY LIFE

1

Morning invites
My aspiration-heart to ascend.
Evening invites
My dedication-life to transcend.

2

What do I need?
I need sleepless courage.
What for?
To enjoy breathless happiness.

3

Since the beginning of creation
Self-giving and happiness
Have been oneness-friends.

4

Without patience-peace
Nobody can and nobody will
Win the progress-race.

5

To God I give what I have:
My heart-patience-seed.
To me God gives what He is:
His Heart-Satisfaction-Tree.

6

The very nature of the heart's
 purity
Is to remain beautiful,
Soulful and fruitful.

7

God does not want
My heart to remain
An invisible seeker.

8

God wants me to study
Carefully
My heart's aspiration-history.

9

O my mind,
Your intimacy with
   ignorance-prince
Is extremely dangerous.

10

Is there any human being
Who is not addicted
To his own desire-fulfilment?

11

Outer wealth is properly spent
Not to gratify our vital
But to fulfil and please
The Supreme in our lives.

12

You have told God
To let you know
When He is in need.
But can you not see
That poor God is always
Badly in need
Of your self-offering?

13

It is the doubting mind
That says:
"If he doesn't perform miracles
At every second,
He is not the Saviour."

14

Because you have sincerely
   accepted
The spiritual life,
Your soul now expects to take you
Happily and proudly to God.

15

The best and most effective way
To rectify your mistakes
Is not to repeat them.

16

You want to cure your
   humanity-friend?
You may not know about the
   outer medicine,
But you do know the
   inner medicine:
Prayer.

17

When you do not value
God's creation-flowers,
God feels like a gardener
Whose work is not appreciated.

18

If you cannot listen
To your Master-Lord's soulful
   requests,
Why should he be responsible
Throughout Eternity
For your spiritual life?

19

He was such a careless
And useless seeker
That God finally decided
Not to continue His
   Compassion-Stupidity
In this lifetime.

20

O unfortunate seeker,
You have forced God
To have a new name:
Disappointment.

21

God is offering His
   Gratitude-Heart
To all His seeker-children
For the good things
They have done for Him
And for the bad things
They have not done.

22

You expect from God
And God is more than willing
To give you
His Blessings, Love and Concern.
But where is your receptivity,
Alas?

23

God's blessingful Eye has asked
Each and every seeker
To do many things inwardly
   and outwardly.
To His great sorrow,
There is not a single seeker
Who has passed his examination
To God's true Satisfaction.

24

Now is the time for you
To run, run, in your inner life,
And pay no attention to
 wrong forces
Trying to devour you.

25

If you want to sail
In the boat of ignorance
Which is certain to capsize,
Who can prevent you?
No, not even your Pilot Supreme.

26

Do not wait indefinitely for
 others.
Go forward and reach your
 highest.
The Supreme will give you
Infinitely more strength
To care for humanity.

27

Do not expect anything
From anybody.
Just do everything cheerfully
To transcend your own capacities.

28

What a rank fool!
He refused to be part and parcel
Of God's Vision and Mission,
Yet he wanted God's Attention
At every moment.

29

Do not look around at others.
Just go forward!
For you, and you alone,
Will be accountable for your
 inner progress.

30

God's urgent Question:
"Are you ready?"
Your immediate answer-prayer:
"Take me, take me!"

31

It is up to you
To choose the most difficult
 obstacle
In your spiritual life
And fight against that very
 obstacle.

32

True,
You have failed God
Again and again.
But now is the time
To challenge that failure
And succeed at last.

33

There is no such thing as
   impossible
In the spiritual life.
When you achieve the so-called
   impossible,
Then all your problems,
Inner and outer,
Will be solved.

34

Do not allow your doubting mind
And frustrated vital
To attack poor God.
God will survive,
But your aspiration will be weaker
And your spiritual death will be
   sooner.

35

Offer all your problems to God
As you would offer Him flowers.
He will be more than happy
To accept them,
And to make your problems
His problems.

36

Alas,
When his desires were not
   fulfilled,
He kept them to use as
   destructive weapons
Against God
Instead of dedicating them
To God.

37

Undivine thoughts offered to God
Become beautiful flowers
At His Feet.
Undivine thoughts cherished
Become powerful weapons
To attack God.

38

Be careful what you do
With your thoughts,
For each thought has and is
An atomic power.

39

Spirituality means fighting —
Fighting against ignorance —
Nothing else.
A true seeker must always be
 ready
To fight to the very end.

40

The Supreme is always ready
To transport us to our
 own natural
Divine consciousness,
But alas, we have clothed
 our minds
In the heaviness of thought.

41

When your mind's
 thought-arrows
Assail you,
Hear only one word
Exploding like a bomb
In your meditation:
Your heart's constant "No!"

42

Who is going to win ultimately
In the tug-of-war?
You, the seeker,
And not your unaspiring
 thoughts.

43

Have faith in God,
Have faith in your own
 spirituality.
You will definitely be the victor
If you just continue walking
Along the inner path.

44

God will not fail us,
And if we are wise,
We also will not fail Him
In any way.

45

Let us not lose touch with our
Inner Pilot
By neglecting and ignoring Him
And giving undue importance
To our outer life.

46

If you have not already
   discovered,
Then now is the time for you
   to discover
Your inseparable
   Eternity's oneness
With your Lord Supreme,
Who is all for you.

47

The faster we can run toward
   our goal
The better for us,
For once we reach our destination
We come to realise that it is not
The ultimate destination,
But a new beginning.

48

If you don't see anything in God,
Then in God's entire creation
There can be no greater fool
   than you!

49

Alas, for a few days
Humanity remembers
God's supreme Message,
And then it goes back
To its life of oblivion.

50

Do not transfer to
 ignorance-school,
For when you come back
To wisdom-school
You will have to start again
From the very beginning.

51

Be sincerely brave
To accept God's criticism.
Be braver still
To abide by His Requests,
Inner and outer.

52

Your absolutely most
 important task
Is not to make friends with doubt
Either in your own life,
In the life of your Master
Or in the Life of your
 Beloved Supreme.

53

You feel that action alone
Is progress.
But I am saying that non-action
Is also necessary.

54

The rogue-vital says:
"How I wish God would not
 call me.
I am so exhausted!"
The clever mind supports
 the vital.
But the willingness-heart says:
"I will always keep the receiver on
So that God can call me at
 any time
On my inner telephone!"

55

Everything God is doing for you
Is for your good.
Everything He is not doing
 for you
Is also for your good.
God will not do anything
To lower your consciousness
Or to take you away from
 His Heart.

56

How to make progress?
Expand your heart,
Expand your consciousness,
And become happy
By establishing your oneness
With the world.

57

If you are divinely happy,
You are absolutely perfect.
Your happiness is your progress
And God's Satisfaction.

58

God is in my hand
And God is also in my eye.
My Hand-God is acting
And my Eye-God is watching.

59

When the God inside you
Serves others with purity and
   divinity,
The God inside others
Appreciates your highest
   consciousness.

60

The very best ending
Of any year
Is only gratitude
For the things that have
   happened
In your life.

PART XLVI

THE ONENESS-HEART-UNIVERSITY

THE ONENESS-HEART-UNIVERSITY

1

The beauty of the start
Gives me much more joy
Than the bounty of the end.

2

Nobody can reach
The perfection-pinnacle
Without studying at the
Oneness-heart-university.

3

The mind-professors
Are not qualified
To teach
The heart-students.

4

God's proud heart
Broadcasts my humble
Aspiration-dedication-progress.

5

A man of peace
Is destined to play
A most significant role
In the
World-transformation-drama.

6

A seeker must realise
That each
Earth-bound desire of his
Is a giant destructive animal.

7

There is no real choice
Between a self-giving heart
And a God-becoming life.

8

No more depressing news.
There is plenty of hope
For each and every
Human being on earth.

9

False alarm!
God and God's
Justice-Anger-Eye
Are not coming.

10

The outer man
Cries to increase
His earthly power.

The inner man
Cries to increase
The world's happiness.

11

Yesterday
My mind greedily desired
Only power.

Today
My mind is wisely desiring
Only love.

Tomorrow
My mind will be
Self-givingly desiring
Only God-satisfaction.

12

Everybody needs a friend.
Therefore, I have decided
To have
My Lord's Compassion-Eye
As my friend,
Only friend.

13

My illumination-soul
Is teaching
My aspiration-heart
How to live
In the Eternal Now.

14

Jealousy is destined
To die eventually
Under the heavy weight
Of insecurity.

15

Self-challenge:
The first glorious attempt
At perfection-excellence-
Achievement.

16

O my mind,
Aspire, aspire!
Otherwise,
You will never be able
To come out of
The darkness-forest-thought.

17

From each and every
Wrong deed
We are forced to wake up
One day
And complete our
One-way trip
To the God-realisation-land.

18

Alas!
Will the negativity-mind
Of the world
Ever be transformed into
A God-receptivity-heart?

19

How do you expect God
To bless and appreciate
Our lip-deep prayers
For world peace?

20

At long last
I was able to say good-bye
To my
Confusion-professor-mind.

21

Alas!
I kept my mind's desire-door
Wide open.
And what do I see?
My heart's aspiration-bird
Has flown away.

22

A God-unwillingness-mind
Is not only ruthless
But also useless.

23

Each day I love
More and more dearly
And
More and more powerfully
The God-created
God-Hunger in me.

24

May
The morning of everything
Be beautiful,
Divinely beautiful
And supremely beautiful.

May
The evening of everything
Be peaceful,
Divinely peaceful
And supremely peaceful.

25

What I need
Is a progressive heart
And not a possessive mind.

26

Anger blasts.
Poise outlasts.

27

Acceptance can freely
Go everywhere;
Rejection, nowhere.

28

Two creators:
God and I.
God created
A togetherness-heart,
And I am creating
A separateness-mind.

29

The mind knows how
To ask,
The heart knows how
To urge,
And the soul knows how
To whisper.

30

The ordinary man
Is a self-binder.
The extraordinary man
Is a self-revealer.

31

Darkness
Is a self-admirer.
Light
Is a God-adorer.

32

God arrives
Because of
My purity-heart.

God departs
Because of
My haughty mind.

33

God needs
My heart's eagerness
And not
My mind's cleverness.

34

The mind's hostility
Ultimately surrenders
To the heart's humility.

35

My mind is a
Thunder-drummer-boy.
My heart is an
Aspiration-perfection-flutist.

36

A dry mind finds
No house anywhere.
A soft heart finds
Home everywhere.

37

"Am I constantly
Self-giving?"
Is the question
That torments my heart.

38

My heart's silence-smiles
Are every day blessed
By God's Ecstasies.

39

A soulful meditation
Is
A powerful heart-castle.

40

A doubting mind
Is doomed to have
A wasted life.

41

The birth of
Aspiration-hunger
Liberates
The desire-possession.

42

The Compassion-God
Never allows anybody
To work overtime for Him.

43

God tells me that
He never wants me
To vegetate.
He wants me only
To navigate.

44

God and I are sailing
In the same boat.
We have too many critics.

45

My Lord Supreme,
Were You looking for me?
"My child,
Were you thinking of Me?"

46

Each willingness-thought
Is a branch of
God-Fulfilment-Tree.

PART XLVII

PEACE: GOD'S FRAGRANCE-HEART

1

I feel immense peace
The moment my heart
Opens its forgiveness-door.

2

The sunlit smile
Of your eyes
Comes directly from
The peace of your heart.

3

I lose my peace of mind
Even when I unconsciously
Turn away from
God's blessingfully extended
   Hands.

4

If you really desire peace
In your life,
Then dissolve your stupid mind's
Resentment-stone.

5

My soul most compassionately
Teaches my heart
How to play peace-melody
On my life-flute.

6

Every morning my
   Lord Supreme
Happily comes and hears
My heart's silence-peace-songs.

7

If your mind's name
Is synonymous with
Unaspiring thoughts,
How can you ever have
An iota of peace?

8

My Lord,
I do not want Your Love,
I do not want Your Joy,
I do not want even Your Peace.
But I do want from You
The capacity to obey You
Sleeplessly.

9

The peace-bird flew
Into my heart-nest
The moment I showed
My life's gratitude-passport
To my Lord Supreme.

10

Peace is not
A man-written story.
Peace is
A God-composed Song.

11

Today I am so happy
And proud of my mind
Because it has fully accepted
My Lord's blessingful Peace-Advice.

12

In my heart-garden
Each peace-flower-plant
Has a unique inspiration-fragrance.

13

Of all God's
Blessing-Gifts,
Peace
Is my most favourite.

14

If your mind is surrounded
By a cloud of insecurity,
And your heart
By a cloud of impurity,
Then how can you have peace?

15

To swim in the peace-river,
I prayed to God
To make me a choice instrument.
But God made me
His loving partner instead.

16

When I soulfully
Think of peace
And prayerfully
Talk about peace,
I clearly see that
The Prince of Peace
Is coming closer to my life.

17

O Compassion-Lord Shiva,
Do bless me today
From Your Himalayan
Peace-Peak-Trance.

18

I acquire peace
Not from solitude
But from my world-servitude.

19

Peace in abundant measure
I feel
Inside my heart's cry,
And not in my life's sigh.

20

Sweetness-sorrows
Give me
A very special kind
Of peace.

21

My inner peace
Does not select anybody,
Does not reject anybody.
My inner peace
Always self-givingly projects
　itself.

22

Peace is
Divinity's strength
That covers
Infinity's length.

23

My mind's success-dance
Does not give me peace.
My heart's progress-song
Gives me peace.

24

Inside my mind-ailments
Peace is my medicine.
Inside my heart-garden
Peace is my fragrance.

25

Peace is not
In my death.
Peace is in
My self-giving breath.

26

The love of your mind
May not be for all,
But the peace of your heart
Is definitely for all.

27

Peace is
My soul's property
And my life's prosperity.

28

We may not see God,
But we do feel
The Breath of God,
Which is peace.

29

O world of unrest!
We peace-lovers
Are trembling for you
Inside our
    aspiration-heart-garden.

30

My heart of peace
Is my life's
Self-giving immortality.

31

I love
The human beings
Who embody peace.
I even love
The human beings
Who sincerely and soulfully
Long for peace.

32

A life of peace
Is the beginning
Of Heaven's
Cheerful and powerful descent.

33

Peace is the beauty
Of my heart.
Like the beauty of nature,
I cannot hide it.

34

Unlike other friends of mine,
Peace is the only friend
That begs me not to enter
Into the desire-land.

35

My Lord asks me to develop
A special kind of fondness
For the sweetness
Of my purity-heart-peace.

36

You must stop postponing
Your heart's surrender to
    God's Will
If you want to have
Divinity's Love and
    Immortality's Peace.

37

Bid your fear, doubt and anxiety
A hasty farewell.
You will be able to enjoy
Immediate peace.

38

Peace always chooses
Our hearts
To be its perfect home.

39

How can you have peace
If you cannot come out of
Your mind's
Insecurity-imprisonment-cave?

40

When God saw in me
Sincere and perfect helplessness,
He gave me His Heart of Love
And His Breath of Peace.

41

A man of peace is
The fragrance of
God's beautiful Garden-Heart.

42

Do you want to know
Where the residence of peace is?
It is inside
Your expectation-free existence.

43

If you are a man of peace,
Then you are divinely great.
But if you share your peace
With the world unreservedly,
Then you are unquestionably
Supremely and unsurpassably
   good.

44

Peace is my soul's
Brightest readiness-smile
In all kinds of life-weather.

45

Your heart's peace
Is bound to be suffocated
Inside your mind's sealed
   and unlit
Expectation-caves.

46

Your volleyball-heart
With its restlessness-game
Will not be able to see, feel
Or receive even an iota of peace.

47

My peace
Is my soulful glimpse
Of my Lord's
Infinite Liberation-Light.

48

How can you have
A mind of joy and a heart of peace
If you have chronic
Superiority-inferiority complex relapses?

49

The mind's imperfection-philosophy
Is empty of peace
And the heart's perfection-song
Is full of peace.

50

Peace is not to be found
In my prayer-success-mind.
Peace is to be found only
In my meditation-progress-heart.

51

While walking
Along Eternity's Peace-Road,
I need only one thing
From my Beloved Supreme:
A powerful Smile.

52

His mind has boundless peace.
Do you know why?
Because his mind is sheltered
Twenty-four hours a day
By a purity-sky.

53

At long last
Today I am able to say hello
To my long-lost, long-forgotten
Very old, dear friend,
Peace.

54

My heart's gratitude-tears
And my life's surrender-smiles
Are the products of my life's
Immortalising peace.

55

Sing, my heart,
Sing Eternity's oneness-song.
You will before long feel
Infinity's fulness-peace.

56

My aspiration is my bridge
Between
My Lord's Compassion-
 Satisfaction-Eye
And my heart's silence-peace-
 thrill.

57

God's Peace-Fragrance-Heart
Is not meant for those
Who live in self-indulgence-
 world.

58

You are telling me
That you have no peace of mind.
Such being the case, I am asking
 you
To turn your self-doubt
Into earth-trust.
Try, you certainly can!

59

You do not have to climb up
To the highest height
Of the aspiration-mountain.
Just start climbing up the
 mountain
Soulfully and unconditionally.
God will bless you
With his blessingful Love,
Blessingful Joy and blessingful
 Peace.

60

When we give God
What we have,
He gives us
His Readiness-Smile-Eye.
When we give God
What we are,
He gives us
His Fulness-Peace-Heart.

61

In Heaven
I do not know what
I shall precisely need.
But on earth
I do know what
I desperately need:
Peace, an iota of peace.

62

Your heart's oneness-peace
Is not real
If it cannot fly
Across the vastness-ocean.

63

I call it
My heart's peace.
My Lord calls it
My perfection-life.

64

My peace is
My heart's unconditional
Self-offering.

65

The divine in me tells me
That peace is infinitely
More powerful
Than anything else.

The human in me
Asks the divine in me:
"But, brother,
Tell me where it is."

66

Peace in stone statues
Has inspired and helped the
   world
Infinitely more
Than the present-day
Self-acclaimed peace-possessors.

67

My peace is my heart's
Highest education-diploma
From my Lord Beloved Supreme.

68

My satisfaction-peace
Is not the success
Of my outer smile
But the progress
Of my inner cry.

69

How can you have
A wisdom-mind
If you do not have
A peace-heart?

PEACE: GOD'S FRAGRANCE-HEART

70

Great human beings may not be
Always wise,
But a heart of peace
Is unmistakably
And perpetually wise.

71

My Lord does not visit
My heart-garden.
Do you know why?
Alas, it is because
My heart-garden does not have
A single peace-plant.

72

I call it
My peace-heart.
But my Beloved Supreme calls it
His Treasure-Kingdom.

73

A real man of peace
Is he who works sleeplessly
With God the creation
And eats hungrily
With God the Creator.

74

First believe
That there is something called
   peace,
And then try to feel it.
Indeed, this is the proper way,
The only way.

75

Mine is the heart
That cannot conceal peace.
Mine is the mind
That cannot reveal peace.

76

A heart of peace
Has the supreme authority
To predict the immortal birth of
   peace
In the outer life.

77

Peace is not
Property-prosperity-achievement.
Peace is
Self-enlightenment-attainment.

78

A life of peace
Is the perfect perfection
Of the heart.

79

God has not forgotten
To give us peace.
He is just waiting for us
To ask for it.

80

Peace is
My heart's sacred book.
Oneness is
My life's devoted reader.

81

Peace has no imperfection.
It never prompts us
To do anything wrong.
On the contrary, it only helps us
To do everything
Soulfully, unconditionally
And perfectly.

82

God has always been extremely
 proud
Of the human beings
Who have peace,
And He always will be.

83

Poor is he
Who does not have peace.
Poorer is he
Who does not need peace.
Poorest is he
Who does not want to hear
People talking about peace.

84

Nothing is as high as peace.
Nothing is as deep as peace.
Nothing is as God-pleasing as
 peace.

85

Peace is the only silence-power
That I need
To live happily with mankind
Without any fear.

86

Peace is
The only divine wisdom-light
That successfully operates
In human affairs.

87

I love you
Not because you have
    tremendous power,
But because
You are all peace.

88

Because you have peace,
You are divinely great.
Because you want to share your
    peace
Lovingly and cheerfully with me,
You are supremely great,
    plus perfect.

89

Power is the most difficult thing
To work with.
Peace is the easiest thing
To work with
And also the most rewarding.

90

The wings of peace
Carry my heart
High, very high.
The shoulders of peace
Carry my mind
Far, very far.

91

When we pray for peace,
God tells us
That we rightly deserve to be
    heard.

92

Patience and sacrifice
Are my life's newly discovered
Peace-allies.

93

Defy the existence of fear.
You will have peace.
Deny the existence of doubt.
You will have more peace.
Embrace the existence of oneness.
You will have Infinity's Peace.

94

O my ingratitude-mind-sovereign,
You and my peace-heart
Will remain perfect strangers
To each other.

95

A man of boundless inner peace
Is indeed
A self-discoverer.

96

When you kneel
To a higher authority,
You unmistakably receive
Needed peace.

97

At every moment
Celebrate the Hour of God
Inside your gratitude-heart.
Then you are bound to feel peace.

98

There are many different
  approaches
You can make to God
For peace in your mind.
If you fail in one,
Then keep making new
  approaches.
Sooner or later fulfilment-peace
Will inundate your entire being.

99

Do not allow the past
To impose itself on you.
Do not allow the future
To come to you unduly fast.
Just try to live
In your today's peace-world.

100

Responsibility-evading
   human beings
Will never be blessed with
God's Joy-Peace-Satisfaction.

101

Do not allow your mind-fort
To be invaded by
   doubt-suspicion-devils.
You will be blessed
With faith-blossomed peace.

102

An iota of peace-satisfaction-
   result
Is infinitely better
Than thousands of imaginary
   expectations.

103

Name-fame-hunger-fascination
Cannot have even a glimpse
Of satisfaction-peace-sea.

104

With a serenity-mind
And a purity-heart
If you can look in the
   God-mirror,
God will give you
What you need most:
   Peace.

105

Never entertain your insecurity,
   jealousy
And impurity-acquaintances.
They will definitely destroy
Your peace-cottage-mind.

106

The heart definitely wants
To make a peace-deal,
But the mind
Vehemently refuses.

107

My aspiration-heart's
Oneness-responsibility
Is my dedication-life's
Fulness-peace.

108

If I want peace,
Then there should be no space
Between
My unconditional surrender-heart
And God's Compassion-
　Satisfaction-Eye.

109

I feel tremendous peace
Inside my heart
Not when I answer the question
"Who am I?"
But when I answer the question
"Whose am I?"

110

I can have immediate peace
If I allow others
To be the rulers of their lives
The way I like to rule
My own life.

111

Do not try to experience others
In your own way.
Just try to experience yourself
In your own way
And, if possible, in God's Way.
Then you will have real peace,
God-created peace.

112

I gave God
My gratitude-heart.
God gave me
His Plenitude-Peace.

113

A continuously blossoming peace
Is the fragrance-heart
Of my silence-mind.

114

God blessingfully visits
My heart's meditation-peace-
　garden
Every day.

115

No peace in austerity-cave.
Peace is in temptation-grave.

116

If not today,
Then in the distant future,
The voice of peace will conquer
Insurmountable disharmony-
　obstacles.

117

Aspiration-exercises strengthen
Our peace-loving heart-muscles.

118

Doubt says to peace,
"Peace, I can easily erase you."

Peace says to doubt,
"No, you cannot erase me.
Can you not see that I am
　embracing you
To transform you totally?"

119

God does not allow
My peace-heart
To hear anything
About my doubt-mind.

120

My heart's
Enlightenment-peace-progress
Is my life's
Detachment-revelation-success.

PART XLVIII

YESTERDAY, TODAY, TOMORROW

YESTERDAY, TODAY, TOMORROW

1

Yesterday
God asked me
To come and visit Him
Inside
His Heart-Home.

2

Today
God is asking me
To study
At His Inner School.

3

Tomorrow
God will be asking me
To take
My first lesson
From Him.

4

Yesterday
God's Eye
Frightened me.

5

Today
God's Heart
Is feeding me.

6

Tomorrow
God's Feet will be
Sheltering me.

7

Yesterday
I adored
God's Beautiful Eye.

8

Today
I am loving
God's Peaceful Heart.

9

Tomorrow
I shall be worshipping
God's Powerful Feet.

10

Yesterday
I pleased
God the Power.

11

Today
I am pleasing
God the Love.

12

Tomorrow
I shall be pleasing
God the Compassion.

13

Yesterday
I gave God
My aspiration-heart.

14

Today
I am giving God
My dedication-life.

15

Tomorrow
I shall be giving God
My surrender-breath.

16

Yesterday
God cradled me
Between
Desire and aspiration.

17

Today
God is cradling me
Between aspiration
And Realisation.

18

Tomorrow
God will be
Cradling me
Between Realisation
And
Self-Transcendence.

19

Yesterday
God was happy to see
My aspiration-bird.

20

Today
God is happy to see
My dedication-wings.

21

Tomorrow
God will be happy
To see
My ever-transcending
Flight.

22

Yesterday
God showed me
And gave me
His Greatness.

23

Today
God is showing me
And giving me
His Goodness.

24

Tomorrow
God will show me
And give me
His Fulness.

25

Yesterday
God looked at
My head
And said to me:
"My child,
Your head is full
Of stupidity."

26

Today
God is looking at
My head
And saying:
"My child,
Your head is full
Of sincerity."

27

Tomorrow
God will look at
My head
And say:
"My child,
Your head is full
Of humility."

28

Yesterday
I ascertained my love
For God.
God said to me:
"Terrific,
My child."

29

Today
I am revealing my love
For God.
God is saying to me:
"Marvellous,
My child."

30

Tomorrow
I shall be manifesting
My love for God.
God will say to me:
"Perfect,
My child."

31

Yesterday
God called me
A desire-beggar.

32

Today
God is calling me
An aspiration-lover.

YESTERDAY, TODAY, TOMORROW

33

Tomorrow
God will be calling me
A Perfection-Dreamer.

34

Yesterday
My life-book read:
God does not care
For me.

35

Today
My life-book reads:
God does not love me.

36

Tomorrow
My life-book
Shall read:
God cares for me.
God loves me.
God even needs me.

37

Yesterday
I went to God
With my
Expectation-heart.

38

Today
I am going to God
With my
Aspiration-heart.

39

Tomorrow
I shall go to God
With my
Emancipation-heart.

40

Yesterday
God pleaded with me
To become
A perfect
Human being.

41

Today
God is
Commanding me
To become
A perfect
Human being.

42

Tomorrow
God will either
Touch my feet
Or break my head
Or do both.
Tomorrow
He will definitely
Make me
A perfect
Human being.

43

Yesterday
I made
No spiritual progress.
God scolded me
In private.

44

Today
I have made some
Spiritual progress,
But not
To God's Satisfaction.
God has scolded me
In public.

45

Tomorrow
I shall make
Stupendous progress.
God will turn me into
His own Heart's
Satisfaction-Smile.

46

Yesterday
God asked me
To be His
Victory-roaring lion.

47

Today
God is asking me
To be His
Lightning-speed-deer.

48

Tomorrow
God will be asking me
To be His Heart's
Fondness-lamb.

49

Yesterday
God asked me
To sing one song
For Him
Soulfully.

50

Today
God is asking me
To sing one song
For Him
Self-givingly.

51

Tomorrow
God will be asking me
To be
His own Heart-Song.

52

Yesterday
God gave me
One special name:
Obedience.

53

Today
God is giving me
Two special names:
Enthusiasm and
Eagerness.

54

Tomorrow
God will be giving me
Three special names:
Gratitude, surrender
And perfection.

55

Yesterday
God wanted me
To be His spokesman.

56

Today also,
He wants me
To play the same role.

57

Tomorrow
God will be reversing
The roles.
He will be my
Spokesman.

PART XLIX

IMMEDIATELY START!

IMMEDIATELY START!

1

Immediately
Start
Loving yourself.

2

Immediately
Start
Counting your God-Blessings.

3

Immediately
Start
Taking mind-transforming
  lessons.

4

Immediately
Start
Singing heart-crying songs.

5

Immediately
Start
Disowning your self-doubts.

6

Immediately
Start
Claiming your faith-fountain.

7

Immediately
Start
Clasping God the Creator's Eye.

8

Immediately
Start
Serving God the creation's body.

9

Immediately
Start
Daring temptation-invasions.

10

Immediately
Start
Invoking the silence-life of the
Beyond.

11

Immediately
Start
Being the fragrance of
　self-offering.

12

Immediately
Start
Clearing your dangerous
　mind-jungle.

13

Immediately
Start
Loving and enjoying
Your heart-garden-beauty-
　fragrance.

14

Immediately
Start
Loving the lovable
Simplicity-mind-child of yours.

15

Immediately
Start
Adoring the adorable
Sincerity-heart-child of yours.

16

Immediately
Start
Saying to yourself
That God's Compassion-Eye
　loves you
Infinitely more than you can
　love yourself.

17

Immediately
Start
Surrendering
Your unwillingness-
　disobedience-life
To your illumination-flooded
　soul.

IMMEDIATELY START!

18

Immediately
Start
Unlearning your old
　division-mind-stories.

19

Immediately
Start
Learning your new oneness
　heart-songs.

20

Immediately
Start
Plucking and distributing
Your soul-peace-blossoms.

21

Immediately
Start
Dreaming of a
　surrender-excellence-mind.

22

Immediately
Start
Dreaming of a
　gratitude-perfection-heart.

23

Immediately
Start
Dreaming of a
　God-satisfaction-life.

24

Immediately
Start
Feeling that God needs you
　desperately
To participate cheerfully
In His Cosmic Drama.

25

Immediately
Start
Being contemplative
And not competitive.

26

Immediately
Start
Realising that the compassionate
    Lord Supreme
Can and does smile
Even through the eyes of
    your enemies.

27

Immediately
Start
Realising that God wants
You and everybody to be
    desirable
And nobody to be preferable.

28

Immediately
Start
Pleasing the world
With your heart's benevolence
And not with your
    mind's eloquence.

29

Immediately
Start
Commanding your mind
To shut up
And wake up
And look up.

30

Immediately
Start
Demanding happiness
From your unwilling and
    unbending mind.

31

Immediately
Start
Being spiritually evolved
And not emotionally involved.

32

Immediately
Start
Having a generous heart
And not a stupendous mind.

IMMEDIATELY START!

33

Immediately
Start
Telling your mind
That you want your mind
To be a sleepless God-lover
And not a ruthless God-examiner.

34

Immediately
Start
Dreaming and daring
And not calculating and
   measuring.

35

Immediately
Start
Having a resourceful
   fountain-life
And not having
A remorseful mountain-mind.

36

Immediately
Start
Thinking and feeling
That nobody has anything
To tell God against you.

37

Immediately
Start
Knowing that God wants you
   to have
A doubt-free mind
And an insecurity-free heart.

38

Immediately
Start
Avoiding and ignoring and
   discarding
Your complexity-duplicity-mind.

39

Immediately
Start
Valuing the moment,
For each moment
Is not only significant but also unique.

40

Immediately
Start
Being a God-beloved religious heart
And not a man-applauded genius-mind.

41

Immediately
Start
Claiming
Your experience-rainbow-heart-roses
And discarding
Your experiment-cloud-mind-thorns.

42

Immediately
Start
Singing the hope-bird-reality-songs
In the soul-dream-delight-tree.

43

Immediately
Start
Jumping out of the tiny success-ferry
And entering into the progress-oceanliner
To arrive at your destined Golden Shore.

44

Immediately
Start
Drinking without hesitating and suspecting
God's unconditional Nectar-Delight.

45

Immediately
Start
Telling the world frankly
That your mind-analysis
Has given birth
To your heart-paralysis.

46

Immediately
Start
Telling the world
That you are learning
The supreme art
Of cheerful and unlimited
   self-offering.

47

Immediately
Start
Telling God
That not your mind but your
   heart
Is leading your life-breath.

48

Immediately
Start
Broadcasting that you are
   no longer
At the beck and call
Of ignorance-king.

49

Immediately
Start
Telling God that He has the
   last word
In everything in your life.

50

Immediately
Start
Telling God that from now on
You are determined to please
Him
Cheerfully, sleeplessly and
   unconditionally,
Come what may.

PART L

IMMEDIATELY START AGAIN!

IMMEDIATELY START AGAIN!

1

Immediately
Start again
Blooming and flowering
With the infinite Delight
Of your Inner Pilot
Lord Beloved Supreme.

2

Immediately
Start again
To pray to the Forgiveness-Heart
Of your Lord Absolute Supreme.

3

Immediately
Start again
To meditate on the
　Compassion-Eye
Of your Lord Absolute Supreme.

4

Immediately
Start again
To take shelter at the
　Protection-Feet
Of your Lord Absolute Supreme.

5

Immediately
Start again
Begging your Lord Supreme
To pilot your life-boat
With His boundless Compassion.

6

Immediately
Start again
Singing your soul-immortality's
God-satisfaction-songs.

7

Immediately
Start again
Planting the seeds
Of your God-revealing smiles.

8

Immediately
Start again
To bring down
The smiling Kingdom of Heaven
To suffering earth.

9

Immediately
Start again
Devoting your inner breath
And outer life
To God-manifestation.

10

Immediately
Start again
To remember the beauty and
    delight
Of God-satisfaction
Inside your crying heart
And smiling eyes.

11

Immediately
Start again
To transform your
    confusion-mind
Into your illumination-mind.

12

Immediately
Start again
To come out of
Your age-old
    doubt-flooded mind-room.

13

Immediately
Start again
To declare that yours is not
A self-broadcasting
But a God-promoting task.

14

Immediately
Start again
Feeling that you have to play
A most significant role
To establish silence-peace-
    oneness-world.

15

Immediately
Start again
To discard your confusing,
   binding
And strangling doubts.

16

Immediately
Start again
Praying to God to protect you
From the unreal
   earth-enamoured reality.

17

Immediately
Start again
To soulfully help God
Create a new universe
Of joy, perfection and
   satisfaction.

18

Immediately
Start again
To feel that your heart
Is God-Infinity's Dream
And your life
Is God-Immortality's Reality.

19

Immediately
Start again
Loving and acquiring
The Heaven-loved
   simplicity-mind,
Sincerity-heart and purity-life.

20

Immediately
Start again
To avail yourself sleeplessly
Of God-loving, God-serving
And God-manifesting
   opportunities.

21

Immediately
Start again
To stop the proud life-
　　extinction-exhibition
Of ignorance-night.

22

Immediately
Start again
To believe that God definitely
　　hears
Your life's morning
　　surrender-songs
And your heart's evening
　　gratitude-songs.

23

Immediately
Start again.
Yours is not the life
Of a loser's lamentation,
But yours is the heart
Of a winner's exhilaration.

24

Immediately
Start again.
This time you must realise
That the heart and not the mind
Is the safest and most effective
　　place
For prayer.

25

Immediately
Start again.
This time you must realise
That God comes to you
In the form you need Him
Not in the form you want Him.

26

Immediately
Start again
To climb to the
　　God-Pinnacle-Height
Is indeed arduous,
But never, never impossible.

27

Immediately
Start again.
You must put an end
To the worldwide shortage of
   peace.

28

Immediately
Start again.
Your prayers and meditations
Must no longer be pitiful,
But surprisingly fruitful.

29

Immediately
Start again
To bring to earth
The living presence of
   peace-smile.

30

Immediately
Start again
To see the whole world
Through your
Affection-compassion-heart-
   window.

31

Immediately
Start again.
Be no more a self-lover and
   self-server,
But be a selfless lover and
   selfless server.

32

Immediately
Start again.
From now on you must be
A non-stop server
Of God-hungry seekers.

33

Immediately
Start again.
Do not allow your mind to think
That it has been rejected by God.
On the contrary, convince your
   mind
That God has special and
   unconditional Compassion
For the mind's total
   transformation.

34

Immediately
Start again.
Never be intimidated by
    self-doubt,
But be inundated with
    God-confidence.

35

Immediately
Start again.
Be sleeplessly self-giving.
Then God Himself will sign
Your heart's love-oneness-
    perfection-letter
To the world.

36

Immediately
Start again.
This time do not allow your mind
To be afraid of silence.
Turn your mind into
An open God-Silence-channel.

37

Immediately
Start again
Using the secret combination
To open your heart-safe.
The numbers are:
One for love,
Two for devotion,
Three for surrender.

38

Immediately
Start again.
I assure you that your heart
Will no more suffer from
    starvation
In aspiration-famine.

39

Immediately
Start again
To disconnect your
    mind-telephone.
This time disconnect it
    permanently.

40

Immediately
Start again
To live in a world
Independent of expectation.

41

Immediately
Start again
With your willingness-mind
And selflessness-heart
To be an unconditionally
   choice instrument
Of your Inner Pilot.

42

Immediately
Start again
To obtain
Your ignorance-death certificate.

43

Immediately
Start again
To remember that God does
   not need you
To be on His Advisory
   Committee,
But He wants you to be a
   member
Of His World-Service-Boat.

44

Immediately
Start again
To be on excellent terms
With your heart's
   aspiration-fragrance.

45

Immediately
Start again
Spreading your sparkling
   heart-smile.

46

Immediately
Start again
To become the joy
Of your soaring heart-bird.

47

Immediately
Start again
To become the lion-soul
And roar powerfully and
 relentlessly
At your ignorance-flooded
 outer life.

48

Immediately
Start again.
This time do not be torn
Between your mind's desire-world
And your heart's aspiration-world.
Aspiration-world is all
That you sleeplessly need.

49

Immediately
Start again
To relinquish your authority
 over everything.
Be a seeker and lover of
 everything,
And not a doubter and
 examiner of everything.

50

Immediately
Start again.
This time, no more
 heart-aspiration-vacation
And no more
 life-dedication-vacation.

PART LI

IMMEDIATELY STOP!

IMMEDIATELY STOP!

1

Immediately
Stop
Hating yourself.

2

Immediately
Stop
Belittling
Others' lofty achievements.

3

Immediately
Stop
Wallowing in the pleasures
Of ignorance-life.

4

Immediately
Stop
Advising the world
What it should do
And what it should not do.

5

Immediately
Stop
Flying your mind's ego-kite
High, higher, highest.

6

Immediately
Stop
Ignoring each precious moment,
For each moment is the source
Of a unique fulfilment.

7

Immediately
Stop
Making friends
With chronic insecurity
And obsessive individuality.

8

Immediately
Stop
Hurting, criticising and
 disgracing
Those very few
Who love God only.

9

Immediately
Stop
Being the possessor
Of an ingratitude-heart.

10

Immediately
Stop
Staying inside
The doubt-insecurity-domain.

11

Immediately
Stop
Limiting
Your silence-oneness-peace-life.

12

Immediately
Stop
Trusting
Your surrender-fractured-heart.

13

Immediately
Stop
Doubting and criticising
God-lovers.

14

Immediately
Stop
Remembering the huge failures
Of the deplorable past.

15

Immediately
Stop
Rejecting God's choice,
   illumining
And fulfilling Voice
In every sound.

16

Immediately
Stop
Withdrawing from the
   outer world
Of God-ordained responsibility.

IMMEDIATELY STOP!

17

Immediately
Stop
Avoiding the Inner Pilot,
Who so compassionately steers
Your life-boat.

18

Immediately
Stop
Masking your inner fears
With your outer smiles.

19

Immediately
Stop
Underestimating the
　unparalleled values
Of a gratitude-heart and a
　surrender-life.

20

Immediately
Stop
Predicting the outer
　world-perfection-day
And the inner
　world-satisfaction-day.
World-perfection and
　world-satisfaction
Will definitely take place
At God's choice Hour.

21

Immediately
Stop
Disregarding
Your aspiring heart's
　ecstasy-flames.

22

Immediately
Stop
Cancelling foolishly or roguishly
Your God-appointments.

23

Immediately
Stop
Lingering
In yesterday's, today's and
    tomorrow's
Desire-storms.

24

Immediately
Stop
Discovering
Man-perfection and
    God-satisfaction
On television.

25

Immediately
Stop
Looking for the
    satisfaction-dance
In temptation-lance.

26

Immediately
Stop
Cherishing the despair-desert
Of your heart's streaming tears.

27

Immediately
Stop
Mimicking secretly
God-dependent seekers.

28

Immediately
Stop
Discouraging
The impossibility-
    challenger-hearts.

29

Immediately
Stop
Dancing
With your hallucination-mind.

IMMEDIATELY STOP!

30

Immediately
Stop
Neglecting
Your ancient wisdom-light.

31

Immediately
Stop
Visiting
The rumour-clamour-parlour.

32

Immediately
Stop
Multiplying
Your imaginary heart-fears.

33

Immediately
Stop
Ignoring
God's Silence-Peace-Dictates.

34

Immediately
Stop
Ignoring the climbing flames
Of your soul's beauty.

35

Immediately
Stop
Singing the tearful songs
Of your self-styled loneliness.

36

Immediately
Stop
Covering your mind-sky
With your
    insincerity-impurity-clouds.

37

Immediately
Stop
Forgetting your heart's
   aspiration-beauty
And your life's
   dedication-fragrance.

38

Immediately
Stop
Denying
Your universal oneness-heart.

39

Immediately
Stop
Dissecting
Your heart's hope-song-flowers.

40

Immediately
Stop
Paying attention to your past
Failure and discouragement-life.

41

Immediately
Stop
Turning your face towards
Your mind's ignorance-abyss.

42

Immediately
Stop
Being a rebellious mind,
A ferocious vital
And a duty-escaping life.

43

Immediately
Stop
Starving your heart's
God-pleasing feelings.

44

Immediately
Stop
Doubting God's compassionate
    descent
Into the aspiration-heart
Of every human being.

45

Immediately
Stop
Cherishing
Even a fleeting desire-smile.

46

Immediately
Stop
Living in your mind's
Ever-lengthening
   confusion-chains.

47

Immediately
Stop
Being ignorant of the futility
Of fear and doubt.

48

Immediately
Stop
Ridiculing
Your heart-ennobling ideals.

49

Immediately
Stop
Being instigated
By your sophisticated mind.

50

Immediately
Stop
Ignoring the goodwill
Of your flower-heart-fragrance.

51

Immediately
Stop
Hiding.
Come out and bravely fight.
God wants you to be a hero
   supreme
On the battlefield of life.

PART LII

MY BONDAGE-LIFE IS
MY SELF-INVENTION

1

Little do I know
Or care to know
That my bondage-life
Is my self-invention.

2

Prayer-tears
Are indeed pure.
Meditation-smiles
Are supremely sure.

3

We cannot solve life's riddles
On our own.
Each riddle of life
Needs a special
Compassion-Smile from God
For its liberation.

4

We celebrate
The supremacy
Of the division-mind,
Which is absurdity itself.
We must celebrate
The satisfaction-ecstasy
Of the oneness-heart.

5

Ego and fear
Chase each other.
Doubt and faith
Chase each other.
Confidence and insecurity
Chase each other.

6

Forgiveness
Is a matter
Of luminous choice.
Forgiveness
Can enter
And does enter
The heart
Of progress-delight.

7

We do not need a mind
Of constant contradiction.
What we need is a heart
Of constant
Heaven-climbing aspiration.

MY BONDAGE-LIFE IS MY SELF-INVENTION

8

Aspiration-shortage
Is a very old story.
Let us write
A new story:
Aspiration-plenitude.

9

May each seeker's love of God
And surrender to God's Will
Be a fragrance-flooded
One-way street
With no U-turn.

10

Our world-attachments
Will vanish
Only when our minds
Sincerely care for
The world-transforming
Illumination.

11

Alas,
Long lost are
My God-loving days
And
God-worshipping nights.

12

At last wisdom-light
Has dawned in my heart.
No more
Shall I be trapped
In the net
Of unhealthy,
Earth-bound thoughts.

13

The complexity-challenges
Of life
Are outwardly hurtful
But inwardly fruitful.

14

The triumphant
God-loving hearts
Are happily treasured
By God's Compassion-Eye
And Satisfaction-Heart.

15

Each seeker-heart realises
That his Master-Saviour
Is an extraordinary member
Of God's immediate Family.

16

Mortal
Is the life of hope.
Let us try to place
Immortality
Inside the heart-breath
Of hope.

17

Aspiration and dedication
Are by far
The best instruments
Of the God-manifesting souls.

18

Let us abandon
Our yesterday's minds.
Let us deal with
Our today's
God-manifesting hearts.

19

When I treat others
As God-manifesting
Divinity-souls,
I feel that I am
Safely on my way
To God-manifestation-lands.

20

Try to live
According to your heart's
Aspiration-wisdom-dictates.

21

The man-made life
Is too weak to climb up
To the highest.
The God-made life
Remains always
At the summit-heights.

22

Be not infatuated
With money-power
Or possession-power,
For their lives
Are extremely short.
Frustration
And
Destruction
Quickly follow them.

23

The failure
Of desire-life
Is the satisfaction
Of earth's
Aspiration-victory.

24

The capacities
Of the inner man
Far transcend
The impossibility-barriers
Of the outer life.

25

Continued effort
Is the open secret
Of success-life.
Continued surrender
Is the open secret
Of progress-heart.

26

My success-choice
Has made my life
Miserable.
My progress-choice
Will make my heart
Always laudable.

27

O man, hide not
Your earth-bound desires.
Bring them to the fore,
Illumine them
And help them reach
Their destined goal:
Satisfaction divine.

28

Since the mind-prison
Is never locked,
Insincerity and impurity
Frequently visit there.

29

Blameless people
Never dream of blaming
The blighted
Imperfection-world.

30

When I invite
God the Voice
To fulfil me,
I reach the heart
Of my own
Perfection-choice.

31

He who has
The abundant capacity
To forgive others
Sees that he has
Nobody to forgive.

32

To forgive
Is to identify oneself
With
God's God-Satisfaction.

33

Nobody else
Causes my suffering.
My own choices
Are the only cause
Of my suffering.

34

My mind
Wants to change
The minds of others.
My heart
Does not want to change
Any other heart.
It only wants to become
Part and parcel
Of all hearts.

35

Listen to the soundless voice
To give you the capacity
To make the perfect choice
In your outer life.

36

Mine is the choice
Either to blindly bind
Or to smilingly liberate
The world.

37

Spirituality is not like
A scientific experiment.
Spirituality is divinity's
God-fulfilment-experience.

38

He who has faith
In abundance
Can never lose
The reality,
For he has already
Become the reality.

39

The clever man does not know
That God is great.
The wise man knows
That God is not only
Divinely great
But also supremely good.

40

The congregation
Of aspiring hearts
Is the liberation
Of binding lives.

41

Each man must try
Not only to curtail
But actually to end
His self-indulgence
Pleasure-life.

42

To see
The perfection-divinity
In a human being
Is the most precious
Opportunity
Of a lifetime.

43

The mind is always eager
To export stupidity.
The heart is always eager
To import wisdom.

44

My life's
Heavenward journey
Is the liberation
Of my mind's
Ignorance-night.

PART LIII

MY EAGERNESS-HEART

MY EAGERNESS-HEART

1

My eagerness-heart
And my self-giving life
Always win
The inner race.

2

Alas,
When can I put an end
To my confrontation
With self-doubt?

3

Although my prayers
And meditations
Do not reach
Their usual height,
I am basking in the Lord's
Constant Forgiveness-Light.

4

Alas,
What can I do with the mind
That is always hostile
To change?

5

Something
Supremely important:
My oneness-willingness-heart
With the Will
Of my Lord Supreme.

6

If there is no positive effort
To change our life,
How can we ever fulfil
Our God-manifestation-dreams?

7

Small-minded people
Are always finding fault
With everything
And everyone.

8

You cannot always
Avoid suffering,
But you can always try
To transform suffering
Into happiness.

9

In my silence-dream
I become a citizen
Of the perfection-land.

10

What do I pray for?
I pray for an elevator ride
To God's
Compassion-flooded Floor.

11

The outer world demands.
The inner world commands.
I am totally lost in between.

12

In vain
My heart every day
Tries to establish
A close friendship
With my mind.

13

I want to love God.
That is all.
I do not want to know
Why and how.

14

If you have a self-giving heart
For the world,
Then the happiness
Of your Beloved Supreme
Will be yours.

15

An inner pilgrimage
Without love, devotion
And surrender
Will be utterly disastrous.

16

You think
That God's Wisdom
Cannot speak
Through all human beings.
But you are mistaken.
His Wisdom-Light can speak
Even through
The worst possible fool.

MY EAGERNESS-HEART

17

When my life
Is in my division-mind,
No matter what I choose,
Eventually
I am totally frustrated.

18

When my life
Is in my oneness-heart,
Not only do I have everything,
But also
I become everything.

19

My Lord Supreme,
Since the entire universe
Belongs to You,
You can give me shelter
Anywhere You want to.
But I would like to remain
Only in
Your Compassion-Heart
Or at
Your Forgiveness-Feet.

20

God tells us
That there is only one way
For us to be cured
Of our ignorance-disease,
And that is by
Consciously and sleeplessly
Loving Him more.

21

A surrender-heart
Is the most perfect place
To embark
On our highest soul-journey.

22

The frequent visits
Of self-doubt
Have made us
Not only helpless
But also useless.

23

When you become
Your willingness-mind
And eagerness-heart,
Perfection
Fast approaches you.

24

Our greatness
Is in climbing up
To the top of the tree.
Our goodness
Is in becoming
The tree itself.

25

O God-satisfaction-dreams,
Fly far beyond
Humanity's happiness-horizon!

26

The very nature of love
Is to forgive,
And forgiveness is
God's ever-transcending
Universal experience.

27

What I need
Is the purity
Of goodness,
And not the prosperity
Of greatness.

28

Only a surrender-heart
Will have the confidence
To march bravely
Into the land unknown.

29

When the newness-mind
Serves the fulness-heart,
Life grows into
Harmony, peace
And perfection.

30

You are displeasing God
By cherishing
Your doubting mind.
You are disappointing God
By not using
Your confidence-light.

31

My bossy ego
And my busy ego
Move together to arrive at
A hallucination-created
Destination.

32

Ignorance-lethargy-sleep,
I shall prove to you
From now on
That I can and I shall be
Your absolutely worst foe.

33

To a divinely peaceful
Oneness-heart,
No door can remain closed.

34

My God-hunger-hour
Is the right time,
And
My God-nourishment-heart
Is the right place.

35

Two things I truly love:
My life's
Prayer-mountain
And my heart's
Meditation-fountain.

36

O audacity-mind,
I am not afraid of you.
O tenacity-vital,
I am not afraid of you.
O God the Power,
I am not afraid of You.
O God the Compassion-Tears,
I am indeed afraid of You.

37

The heart-university teaches
Both the unity and diversity
Of life
To the humanity-students.

38

A life without fear of death
Comes only from
The beauty and fragrance
Of a God-surrendered breath.

39

God's Compassion-Eye
Teaches me.
God's Satisfaction-Heart
Rewards me.

40

O heart of optimism,
I love you immensely.
O mind of pessimism,
I detest you vehemently.

41

If you do not spend
Your heart's time
In prayer and meditation,
Then there will be
No Heaven-home for you.

42

In the depth
Of each human life
There is a fulfilling breath
Of the Lord Supreme.

PART LIV

MY GRATITUDE-HEART-GARDEN

MY GRATITUDE-HEART-GARDEN

1

My Lord,
May my life
Every day blossom
Inside
My gratitude-heart-garden.

2

O my mind,
What are you looking for?
As long as you think
That desire-fulfilment
Is happiness,
Then there can be
No happiness
For you.

3

The mind that
Does not believe in
God's Compassion
Has to believe in
Endless frustration-night.

4

Only your ceaseless
God-hunger
Can make you win
Membership in
God's Parliament.

5

Why do you look always
In your mind-mirror?
Can you not look
Once and for all
In your heart-mirror?
To your wide surprise
You will be so happy to see
Your own exquisite beauty.

6

I wish to be
My heart-passenger-boat
And ply between
My own aspiration-shore
And
God's Compassion-Shore.

7

It is the mental hallucination
Of a human being
To think that
He can deliberately ignore
God's Compassion
If he wants to.
God's Compassion
Is not only omniscient
And omnipotent,
But also omnipresent.

8

My Lord,
If You do not give me
The eyes that shed tears,
I shall not mind.
But if You do not give me
A heart with
Streaming tears,
Then I shall feel miserable.

9

An obedience-mind
Is an illumination-life.
An obedience-heart
Is a fulfilment-breath.

10

Your unconditional surrender
And your sleepless gratitude
Will definitely help you stand
At the top of God's
God-manifestation-list.

11

When the hour strikes,
If you do not offer
Your heart's gratitude-tears
To your Lord Supreme,
Then all your capacities
Will unmistakably
Be paralysed.

12

An insecurity-mind
Is exiled from the world
Of happiness-smiles.

13

The very presence
Of an enthusiasm-heart
Will compel
The frustration-mind
To breathe its last.

14

The suspicious mind-station
Is the place from where
The doubt-trains
Arrive and depart.

15

God will ask you
To be His spokesman
Only after you have become
The beauty of your heart's
Silence-smile.

16

Self-offering
Is the sunlit path
For the heart-pilgrim
To arrive at the destination.

17

An urgent message
From the soul to the heart:
"Be good
And not great.
Be a God-lover
And not a God-possessor."

18

Pleasure perishes.
Joy lasts.
Delight forever lasts.

19

At the moment,
God is asking you
To pray for
Genuine aspiration
And not for
Perfect perfection.

20

A true seeker
Definitely has the capacity
To implant faith
In the heart of
All and sundry.

21

The breath of hope
May not last.
The breath of promise
May not last.
But the breath of
Self-offering
Forever lasts.

22

We must learn to value
The world-saving divinity
Of invaluable peace.

23

Human pride
Is followed by
The unmistakable tears
Of the divine in man.

24

The new Dream of God
Will not allow me
To remain imperfect
Any more.

25

God wants me
Always to keep my heart
Visible and serviceable.

26

Anything that is unwilling
In our mind
Is actually worthless
And useless.
Anything that is willing
All the time in our heart
Will prove to fulfil God's Will
In His own Way.

27

No more depression,
No more frustration,
No more hallucination.
In me I see a new dawn —
A dawn that will reveal
Divinity's life-fulfilment
On earth.

28

Not an easy task
To reach the highest height
Of perfection-light,
But you must try.
You are bound to succeed,
For you are, indeed,
An exception.

29

When I offered
My heart's gratitude-tears
To my Lord Supreme,
He immediately told me
That from now on
His Heart-Home-Door
Will always remain open
For me.

30

Each time
I challenge myself,
God sings
His own Excellence-Songs
To herald
My supreme victory.

31

My Lord Supreme
Compassionately tells me,
"Wake up, My child,
From your ignorance-sleep!"
I tell my Lord Supreme,
"I shall definitely
Wake up soon.
But a little more rest I need,
Just a little more."

32

This morning I kept
My heart's aspiration-door
Wide open,
And whom did I see
At my door?
God,
With His Perfection-Eye
And His Satisfaction-Heart.

33

The more I love God
Soulfully and self-givingly,
The sooner God
Unburdens me
From my mind's
Ignorance-cherishing
Desire-loads.

34

My Lord Supreme,
This is Your creation.
I do not want to know
From You
When this creation of Yours
Will be perfect.
I just want to know
If this creation of Yours
Will ever be perfect
To please You
In Your own Way,
To make You really happy.

35

My Lord,
My aspiration-heart
And my dedication-life
Have once more left behind
The world of
Ignorance-lethargy
To please You,
This time only to please You
In Your own Way.

36

My Lord Supreme,
My life's only desire
Is to be on my knees
Before You,
For my life's transformation
And for my heart's
Inseparable oneness
With Your Heart.

37

If we have
A soulfulness-heart
And an eagerness-breath,
Then there can be nothing
That we cannot accomplish
For
Our Lord Beloved Supreme.

38

O my mind,
If you are unwilling
To separate yourself
From doubt-clouds,
Then how can
God bless you with
His Divinity's Fulness-Sun?

39

The illumination of the soul
Does not frighten
The confusion of the mind.
The illumination of the soul
Only brightens
And enlightens
The confusion of the mind.

40

God does have the power
To change your life
In the twinkling of an eye.
But alas, when God arrives
Out of His infinite Bounty,
You are not available.
You are
Nowhere to be found.

41

Your yesterday's glory
Has today become
A dry flower.
Therefore, do not try to live
On yesterday's success,
But try to live
On your
Ever-transcending progress.

42

An insecure heart
And an impure mind
Can never be members
Of God's
Perfection-Satisfaction-Family.

43

When you sing
Your heart's gratitude-song,
God proudly tells you
How to navigate your life
And the lives of
Aspiring humanity.

44

There is always
The Satisfaction-Sunrise-Might
Of my Lord Supreme
In the heart
Of my gratitude-sky.

45

My success-life
Cannot show me
How close God is to me.
My progress-heart
Not only shows me
How close God is,
But also tells me
To claim God
As my own, very own.

PART LV

MY GRATITUDE-TEARS AND GOD'S SATISFACTION-SMILES

MY GRATITUDE-TEARS AND GOD'S SATISFACTION-SMILES

1

God tells me that
My gratitude-tears
Are as beautiful as
His Satisfaction-Smiles.

2

There are
Countless human beings
On earth
Who every day cherish
A multitude
Of fruitless fantasies.

3

Science is soulless.
Therefore, to me,
For my spiritual perfection,
Science is useless.

4

The heart
Has to sleeplessly give
If the life
Is to achieve
Something beautiful,
Meaningful
And fruitful.

5

I have surprised my heart
With my mind's sincerity.
I have surprised my soul
With my heart's purity.

6

If you want freedom
From your unhappiness,
Then pray to your soul
To cultivate smiles
In your heart-field.

7

You want freedom
From your unhappiness.
I want you to have freedom
From
Your mind's unwillingness.

8

Yours will be a life
Of divine surprises
If you give up
Your endless
Desiring thoughts.

9

When everything
You hold dear
Is taken away,
And you remain
Happy and peaceful,
That is the time
God considers you to be
His choicest instrument.

10

If faith is absent
From your heart,
Then God does not want
To live inside your heart,
For fear of suffocation.

11

Your fear of God
Is unjust.
Your love of God
Is just.
Why do you not always
Do the right thing?

12

Each
Enthusiasm-eagerness-attempt
Helps us come out of
The mind's prison.

13

Alas, alas,
My heart's insecurity
And my mind's anxiety
Have paralysed
My inspiration-aspiration-
 dedication-life.

14

Each inner cry
Is indeed
A hope-strengthening
God-Smile.

15

God, how I wish
I could smile like You!
"My child,
If you can cry
Like Me,
Then certainly
I shall teach you
How to smile
Like Me."

16

Do you want to escape
From your mind-prison?
If so, remember
Your perfection-life-promise
To God.

17

My Lord,
Smash me asunder
When I become
The pride of ignorance-night.

18

A confused desire-mind
Can never experience
The heart's
Gratitude-ecstasy.

19

You can become
God's dearest
Manifestation-instrument
If you can turn your life into
A sleepless surrender-song.

20

The fear of the mind
And
The hope of the heart
Must not live together.
They must remain
Perfect strangers.

21

Every day
God helps me
Climb my heart's
Loftiest dream-mountain.

22

Take a deep purity-breath.
God will immediately
Make you
His constant
Satisfaction-Delight.

23

If necessity demands,
For a perfection-life
God changes everything
And everyone.

24

Unlearn your mind's
Doubt and fear-messages.
Learn only your heart's
Self-giving and life-smiling
Messages.

25

Life is true.
Life is meaningful.
Life is fruitful.
If your mind does not agree,
Then remain far beyond
The snares
Of your mental thoughts.

26

God wants me to live
In the city
Of heart's prosperity,
And not in the city
Of mind's aridity.

27

As I love
The divinity
Of God's Answer,
Even so, God loves
The purity
Of my question.

28

May my life
Forever remain
A student at
The God-obedience-school.

29

If the past's misdeeds
Chase you,
Then run
Faster than the fastest,
And remain always
Far ahead
With your present virtues.

30

My ancient God-memories
Are not only pleasant
But are also the pathfinders
Of my
God-realisation-destination.

31

Whenever I take
A big purity-breath,
I escape
My mind's darkest jungle.

32

My Lord,
Do awaken me,
Bless me,
Prepare me
And finally make me
All Yours.

33

Not your mind's pride
But your oneness-heart
Has the capacity
To carry the weight
Of the entire world.

34

To make my life
Supremely fruitful,
I live between
My heart's hope
And
My mind's patience.

35

If you know only
How to love yourself
And how to care
For yourself,
Then God will never
Invite you
To be a member
Of His Perfection-
Manifestation-Team
On earth.

36

I do not need
Any other treasure
As long as I can
Safely keep my heart
As my only treasure.

37

Alas,
My poor aspiration-heart
Is being strangled
Between my leisure-mind
And my pleasure-vital.

38

O my mind,
I no longer need
Your false
Freedom-fantasies.
I now only need
My heart's true
Freedom-ecstasies.

39

God wants me to be
Divinely loyal
To my dear friends
And
Supremely magnanimous
To my so-called enemies.

40

If fear guides us,
Then death nears us
Sooner than the soonest.

41

Sometimes I feel
That God does not know,
Even does not care to know,
What is happening
In my life.
But God tells me that
He does not have to know
What is happening in my life
If my life is only for myself.

42

O seeker,
You can be divinely happy
And supremely perfect
If your heart's aspiration
Tops the list
Of your life's values.

PART LVI

GOD THE MOTHER AND GOD THE FATHER

1

God the Mother tells me:
"My child, wake up!"

God the Father tells me:
"My son, stand up!"

2

God the Mother tells me:
"My child,
Give Me all your problems."

God the Father tells me:
"My son,
Be not afraid.
Challenge and conquer
All your problems."

3

God the Mother tells me:
"My child,
I am always inside
Your streaming tears."

God the Father tells me:
"My son,
I am always inside
Your brightening smiles."

4

God the Mother tells me:
"My child,
Walk along
My protection-blessed
Road."

God the Father tells me:
"My son,
March along
My confidence-flooded
Street."

5

Inside my unfulfilled desires
I see God the Mother's
Compassion-Heart.

Inside my unfulfilled desires
I see God the Father's
Wisdom-Mind.

6

The very presence
Of God the Mother
Always comforts me.

The very presence
Of God the Father
Quite often frightens me.

7

A partial transformation
Of my nature
God the Mother expects.

A complete transformation
Of my nature
God the Father demands.

8

When God the Mother
Blessingfully comes to visit me,
She always carries with Her
Her Eternity's Patience-Depth.

When God the Father
Hurriedly comes to call on me,
He always carries with Him
His immediacy's Power-Height.

9

God the Mother tells me:
"My child,
If you do not drink
Nectar-Delight,
I shall also not drink it."

God the Father tells me:
"My son,
Like Me, you can and you must
Drink Nectar-Delight."

10

Whenever God the Mother
Sees me, She asks me:
"How are you today,
My child?"

Whenever God the Father
Sees me, He asks me:
"What is your schedule for today,
My son?"

11

God the Mother
Has a very special love
For the soulful singer
In my heart.

God the Father
Has a very special love
For the powerful warrior
In my life.

12

God the Mother
Gives me the chance
To obliterate my mistakes.

God the Father
Gives me the chance
To rectify my mistakes.

13

This morning God the Mother
Blessed me
With a very special gift:
An aspiration-flute.

This morning God the Father
Blessed me
With a very special gift:
A determination-drum.

14

God the Mother wants me
To utilise my time properly.

God the Father wants me
To economise my time
   judiciously.

15

God the Mother appreciates
Even my remote willingness.

God the Father appreciates
My willingness
Only when it is followed
By immediate readiness.

16

God's Omnipresence
Is predominant
In God the Mother.

God's Omnipotence
Is predominant
In God the Father.

17

God the Mother comes to me
To feed my happiness-hunger.

God the Father comes to me
To feed my majesty-hunger.

18

God the Mother asks me
To come into my heart-room
And rest.
God the Father asks me
To come out of my heart-room
And blossom everywhere.

19

God the Mother tells me
To stay where I am
If I want to see Her.

God the Father tells me
To climb up
High, higher, highest
If I want to see Him.

20

God the Mother
Is my heart's sympathy-expander.

God the Father
Is my life's capacity-expander.

21

My patience-progress
Makes God the Mother
Extremely happy.

My determination-success
Makes God the Father
Extremely happy.

22

God the Mother
Is my readiness
And enthusiasm-Teacher.

God the Father
Is my obedience
And perseverance-Teacher.

23

My uncaring heart
Deeply hurts
God the Mother.

My doubting mind
Ruthlessly tortures
God the Father.

24

I can give surprise-joy
To God the Mother
The moment I achieve
Something great.
But it is almost
An impossible task
To give surprise-joy
To God the Father.

25

My incapacity-heart
Pains God the Mother.

My incapacity-mind
Astonishes God the Father.

26

God the Mother tells me:
"My child,
Start walking.
I shall follow you."

God the Father tells me:
"My son,
Follow Me.
I am marching."

27

God the Mother
Loves the beauty
Of the world-cradle.

God the Father
Loves the peace
Of the world-grave.

28

God the Mother
Hurriedly comes to me
To stop my heart's
　　streaming tears.

God the Father
With great strides comes to me
To increase my soul's smiles.

29

God the Mother asks me
To sleeplessly keep
My heart-door wide open.

God the Father asks me
Never to stop
My ignorance-devouring roaring.

30

I become an ecstasy-sea
When I see God the Mother
In my dreams.

I become a freedom-sky
When I see God the Father
In my dreams.

31

God the Mother
Lovingly plays with me
And my prayer-tears.

God the Father
Seriously plays with me
And my meditation-smiles.

32

God the Mother tells me:
"My child, I am going to listen
To all your complaints.
You should try
To obey Me afterwards."

God the Father tells me:
"My son, obey Me first
And then I shall listen
To all your complaints
And see what I can do
With you and with them."

33

Nothing gives God the Mother
More Joy
Than my heart's
Satisfaction-smiles.

Nothing gives God the Father
More Joy
Than my life's
Self-transcendence-promises.

34

My heart's love-gift
God the Mother
So proudly shows
To the cosmic goddesses.

My life's surrender-gift
God the Father
So proudly shows
To the cosmic gods.

35

I pray to God the Mother
To save me
From the hostile forces.

I pray to God the Father
To forgive me
All my sins.

36

God the Mother
Is never tired
Of my unwillingness-mind.

God the Father
Is never tired
Of my unfulfilled promises.

37

Whenever God the Mother
Approaches me,
The very first thing I do
Is look at Her sea-blue Eyes.

Whenever God the Father
Approaches me,
The very first thing I do
Is look at His Thunderbolt-Feet.

38

After committing
Even a Himalayan blunder,
I am not ashamed
Of going to
God the Mother.

After committing
Just a trifling mistake,
I am sincerely afraid
Of approaching
God the Father.

39

God the Mother
Is my sweetness-home.
God the Father
Is my vastness-kingdom.

40

When God the Mother
Comes to visit me,
She always brings me food
And we eat together.

When God the Father
Comes to visit me,
He asks me:
"Son, do you have
Anything special
For Me to eat today?"

GOD THE MOTHER AND GOD THE FATHER

41

God the Mother helps me
Carry my heart-garden
And place it carefully
Inside my mind-jungle.

God the Father helps me
Carry my mind-jungle
And throw it abruptly
Into my heart-garden.

42

God the Mother
Just loves my stupendous
Success-stories.

God the Father
Just loves my precious
Progress-poems.

43

God the Mother
Thinks that I am only
Six months old.
Therefore She does not expect
Anything from me.

God the Father
Thinks that I am
Twenty-seven years old,
And He expects me
To fulfil my responsibilities
In accordance with my age.

44

When I fail in something,
God the Mother
Cries with me
And with my sincerity.

When I fail in something,
God the Father
Not only laughs at my stupidity
But also laughs at me
Mischievously.

45

God the Mother
Wants me to be
Her Breath-fragrance.

God the Father
Wants me to be
His Heart-garden.

46

When I desperately
And truly need something,
God the Mother
Unconditionally gives it.

When I desperately
And truly need something,
God the Father
Helps me unconditionally
To acquire the thing myself.

47

When the hour strikes
For me to get up and meditate,
God the Mother
Is more than willing
To grant me another
Fifty-nine minutes to rest
Before I start to meditate.

When the hour strikes
For me to get up and meditate,
God the Father tells me:
"It is already high time
For you to meditate.
Start immediately."

48

God the Mother
Teaches me privately.

God the Father
Examines me openly.

49

To make God the Mother happy,
I start.

To make God the Father happy,
I continue and complete.

GOD THE MOTHER AND GOD THE FATHER

50

I am made of
The soulfulness and newness
Of my God the Mother.

I am made of
The seriousness and fulness
Of my God the Father.

51

God the Mother
Wants me to close my eyes
While meditating,
So I will not be affected
By the imperfection-world.

God the Father
Wants me to keep my eyes open
While meditating,
So that I can see
The world's imperfections
And perfect them.

52

God the Mother
Assuages my heart-pangs.

God the Father
Dries my life-tears.

53

When I am in front of
God the Mother,
I somehow feel
That my life's sincerity
Is on trial.

When I am in front of
God the Father,
I somehow feel
That my heart's purity
Is on trial.

54

I need God the Mother
As my character-reference.

I need God the Father
As my credential-reference.

55

To God the Mother
I offer all my mind-anxieties.

To God the Father
I offer all my heart-insecurities.

56

I just tell
God the Mother
What I have in my heart.

I think twice before I tell
God the Father
What I have in my mind.

57

God the Mother
Is always ready
To sweeten my heart.

God the Father
Is always ready
To quicken my life.

58

To God the Mother
I give my heart
For consolation.

To God the Father
I give my mind
For illumination.

59

Lo, God the Mother
Is entering into my heart
With a fresh supply of ecstasy.

Lo, God the Father
Is opening a new embassy
Inside my mind.

60

My heart's ingratitude-weeds
Do not sadden
God the Mother.

My life's gratitude-flowers
Do gladden
God the Father.

61

My desire-dust
Has blinded
God the Mother's Eye.

My aspiration-thirst
Has thrilled
God the Father's Heart.

62

My devastating shortage
Of happiness
Has turned
My God the Mother
Insane.

My devastating shortage
Of faith in myself
Has turned
My God the Father
Insane.

PART LVII

A LOVE-BATHED HEART

1

A love-bathed heart
Will always have
A cheerfully blossoming faith.

2

The man of the mind
Quite often is forced
To live in self-exile.

3

True, right now
I do not know how,
But there must be a way
For me to satisfy
My Lord Supreme
In His own Way.

4

God's Compassion
Makes us feel
That we are really important.
But God's Compassion
Can easily remain
Independent of our service.

5

God's Compassion
And God's Affection:
These are my only
Trusted companions.

6

Every day I am aspiring
For a newborn hope
To break asunder
My mind's bondage-chains.

7

May the flames of peace-torch
Kindle and awaken
Each and every world-citizen.

8

God wants me to be
The commander of my mind
And not
The servitor of my mind.

9

If you live
Always in the mind,
Then you are bound to arrive
At the dry shores
Of nothingness.

10

I bow
To every God-seeking heart.
I salute
Every God-searching mind.

11

I shall definitely succeed,
For my eyes
Are full of dreams,
And my heart
Is full of promises.

12

Mine is the mind
That does not know
When to embark on
The God-journey.

Mine is the heart
That does not want to know
When to stop
The God-journey.

13

Whom are you trying to fool —
God the Wisdom
Or God the Compassion?
You fool!
You cannot deceive either one.

14

He who tells us
There is no use
In running further,
Will die
With his pessimistic cries.

15

Beautiful
Is the sunrise of the heart.
Peaceful
Is the sunset of the mind.

16

With peace
In your mind-pocket,
You can never be
A poor truth-seeker
And God-lover.

17

May my inner life be
A constant
Aspiration-practice-joy.

May my outer life be
A constant
Dedication-practice-joy.

18

A child of God-dreams
Lives not
In the mind of the future,
But in the heart
Of the eternal Now.

19

Actions dictated by insecurity
Will never be able
To see the face
Of life-satisfaction-victory.

20

No matter how hard I try,
I cannot escape from
A doubtful mind,
A fearful heart
And a sorrowful life.

21

When I pray,
I try to pray
With the beauty
Of a flower-mind.

When I meditate,
I try to meditate
With the fragrance
Of a flower-heart.

22

What I need
Is a gratitude-heart-compass
That always points
In God-Satisfaction-direction.

23

Is there any day
When God does not suffer
From His own
Unanswered Calls?

24

A thought-bound life
Is undoubtedly
Mankind's
Ignorance-inheritance.

25

God does not mind
If you do not give Him credit
For your outer success
And inner progress.
But God does mind
If you make friends
With pride and haughtiness
When success and progress
Bring you forward.

26

The mind's absurd statement is:
God's Compassion-Voice
Remains unheard.

27

There is nothing to choose
Between
An illusion-mind
And a confusion-life.

28

No, the human life
Is not meant to be
A long desire-walk,
But a fast aspiration-run.

29

When the heart cries
From devotion-depths,
God's Compassion-Light
Cannot remain hidden.

30

Both the cries of a child-heart
And the smiles of a child-heart
Are destined to fly
In God's unhorizoned Sky.

31

Until the soul's illumination
Takes place,
The confusion of the mind
Will blind us,
Threaten us
And frighten us.

32

No mind-discovered
Philosophy
Can ever nourish
A God-hungry heart,
Not to speak of
God-envisioning soul.

33

You are bound to succeed fast,
Very fast,
In the inner life,
If you cheerfully
And soulfully feed
Each and every
Aspiration-flame
Of your heart.

34

Every day
My soul compassionately
Whispers to my mind:
"My child, move out of
The desire-neighbourhood
Immediately.
Do not delay."

35

May my life be found
Only in my high
Aspiration-hopes,
And nowhere else.

36

My Lord is always happy
To be able to be proud
Of my continued
Progress-smile-eyes.

37

In vain the doubting mind
Tries to keep
The aspiring heart
From its daily
God-correspondence.

38

By singing only God-songs,
We can strengthen
Our upward longing
And inward diving.

39

The hope
Of my heart dies
When my mind
Does not cry.

40

God's Forgiveness
Does not mind
When we blame God
For our mistakes.
But God's Forgiveness
Does mind
When we blame
Other human beings
For our mistakes.

41

A life empty of devotion
Cannot be free from
A ceaseless desire-hunger.

42

Love the world
With your heart's dreams.
Serve the world
With your life's promises.

43

My Lord,
Will You ever smile at me?
I have completely exhausted
All my capacities
Inner and outer
To make You smile at me.

44

The sincere heart
Works for God
Untiringly.

The clever mind
Works for God
Only when God is looking.

45

God's Justice-Hand slaps us
Not to hurt us,
But to perfect us
And remind us
Of our divine destiny.

46

Desire-hunger does not know
What God-Satisfaction is.
Aspiration-hunger does not
Even want to know
Anything other than
God-Satisfaction.

47

The strength of the body,
The energy of the vital,
The clarity of the mind,
The purity of the heart,
And the divinity of the soul
God created
To please the capacity
Of His own Vision-Eye.

48

Even for a fleeting second
If you make friends
With doubt,
You may suffer from
A tragic aspiration-shortage.

PART LVIII

LOVE, COMPASSION, FORGIVENESS

LOVE, COMPASSION, FORGIVENESS

DEDICATION

Lovingly,
Affectionately
And
Gratefully
I am dedicating this book
To the President Gorbachev,
The Himalayan
Peace-Dreamer
On earth.

1

Long
Is the Love-list of God.
Longer
Is the Compassion-list of God.
Longest
Is the Forgiveness-list of God.

2

Doubt is a sin
Of the mind.
Faith is a virtue
Of the heart.

3

I breathe out
Oldness-despair.
I breathe in
Newness-hope.

4

The mind
Blames the world.
The heart
Claims the world.

5

Purity's beauty
Knows no bounds.
Purity's smile
Is a direct descendant
Of God.

6

God wants
Me to live
Either inside
My willingness-heart
Or inside
My cheerfulness-mind.

7

The mind likes
To chase God.
The heart loves
To embrace God.

8

The mind cries
For God's Sanction.
The heart cries
For God's Direction.

9

My mind is afraid
Of seeing God the Power.
My heart is afraid
Of falling God the Lover.

10

Patience
Is heart-born.
Persistence
Is mind-born.

11

Silence is
Eternity's Choice.
Sound is
Infinity's Voice.

12

My mind does not
Care to know
What God is doing
At this very moment.
My heart is dying
To know
What God is dreaming of
At this very moment.

13

Yesterday
I called it
Desire-sweetness.
Today
I call the same thing
Frustration-bitterness.

14

When I soulfully
Love God,
He asks me to claim
His myriad Dreams
As my own, very own.

15

The mind
Complains and assails.
The heart
Steers and sails.

16

Prayer
Expects.
Meditation
Selects.

17

My mind wants
To challenge the whole world.
My heart longs
To change the whole world.

18

O my gratitude-heart-garden,
Where are you?
O my ingratitude-mind-jungle,
Where are you not?

19

My mind is
A world-story-teller.
My heart is
A God-Song-Singer.

20

I shall not allow myself
To stay in between
My yesterday's failures
And
My tomorrow's anxieties.

21

My Lord,
Your Nearness is so sweet.
"My child,
Your gratitude-tears
Are sweeter.
Your surrender-smiles
Will be the sweetest."

22

Yesterday I prayed
I became
A God-possibility-bud.
Today I shall meditate.
I shall become
A God-reality-flower.

23

When God sees
My heart's streaming tears,
He tells me, "My child,
I have not come alone.
I have brought with Me
My Forgiveness-Heart."

24

Enthusiasm
Brings me
To the right path.
Willingness
Leads me.
Eagerness
Quickens my speed.

25

A God-obedience-mind
Is a most precious
Achievement.

26

I may not claim God
As my own, very own,
But God's Compassion-Eye
And
His Forgiveness-Heart
Have already claimed me.

27

I must not forget
That I have made
Appointments
With Eternity's Silence-Heart
And
With Infinity's Sound-Mind.

28

My heart's
Gratitude-smile
Is my life's
Love-devotion-surrender
In action.

LOVE, COMPASSION, FORGIVENESS

29

God's blessingful Compassion
Is determined to end
Even the last vestige
Of human pride.

30

At long last
I am brave enough
To successfully build
A funeral pyre
For my desire-mind.

31

How can God
Ever be pleased with you,
When you proudly cherish
Your ruthless indifference
To humanity?

32

I greet the morning
With my heart's
God-gratitude-cries.
I greet the evening
With my life's
God-surrender-smiles.

33

In the morning
I prayerfully, soulfully
And gratefully need
A Glimpse of God's Eye,
A Smile from God's Heart,
A Song from God's Breath
And
A Whisper from God Himself.

34

Of all the most beautiful
And most powerful Limbs
Of my Lord Beloved Supreme
I have chosen
His Compassion-flooded
Protection-Feet.

35

Greed
Is my mind-thirst.
Need
Is my heart-hunger.

36

My Lord,
For me, no old way,
No new way.
For me, there is
Only one way,
Your Heart's Way,
My Lord!

37

Every day I must renew
My closest friendship
With my sweetest heart
So that I can receive
God's highest Blessings
To fly far beyond
My happiness-horizon.

38

My Lord Supreme,
No more shall I try
To surprise You
With my stupendous
Aspiration-progress.

39

My Lord Supreme,
No more shall I try
To shock You
With my most deplorable
Dedication-failures.

40

My Lord Supreme,
From now on
Every morning I shall
Offer You
My sincere devotion-flooded
   eyes,
And every evening
I shall offer You
My pure gratitude-flooded heart.

41

My Lord Supreme,
Your Head was aching
Because
I was not pleasing You
In Your own Way.

42

My Lord Supreme,
Your Heart is bleeding
Because
I am not pleasing You
In Your own Way.

43

My Lord Supreme,
Your Life will be dying
Because
I shall not be pleasing You
In Your own Way.

44

My Lord Supreme,
What can I do?
What shall I do?
I am so helpless
And
Useless.

45

"My child, do not worry.
I have already
Forgiven you.
I am now preparing Myself
To help you embark
On a new Journey
And watch your heart's
Blossoming, singing
And
Dancing
Rainbow-sunrise."

APPENDIX

BIBLIOGRAPHY

–*When God-Love Descends,* New York, Agni Press, 1975. [GLD]

–*Lord, I ask You for one favour,* New York, Agni Press, 1975. [LAF]

–*Lord, receive this little undying cry,* New York, Agni Press, 1975. [LC]

–*Lord, I need you,* New York, Agni Press, 1975. [LNY]

–*My life-tree,* New York, Agni Press, 1975. [MLT]

–*My promise to God,* New York, Agni Press, 1975. [MPG]

–*Sound becomes, silence is,* New York, Agni Press, 1975. [SBS]

–*The silence-song,* New York, Agni Press, 1975. [SLS]

–*Silence-seed and sound-fruit,* New York, Agni Press, 1975. [SSF]

–*This is God's Home,* New York, Agni Press, 1975. [TGH]

–*Dedication-drops,* New York, Agni Press, 1975. [DD]

–*Union and oneness,* New York, Agni Press, 1975. [UO]

–*Three soulful prayers,* New York, Agni Press, 1979. [TSP]

–*My fifty gratitude-summers,* New York, Agni Press, 1981. [FGS]

–*The loser and the winner,* New York, Agni Press, 1981. [LW]

–*I meditate so that,* New York, Agni Press, 1982. [MST]

–*I pray so that,* New York, Agni Press, 1983. [PST]

–*I am ready*, New York, Agni Press, 1982. [IAR]

–*My heart's thirty-one sacred secrets*, New York, Agni Press, 1982. [MHS]

–*My God-Hunger-Dreams*, New York, Agni Press, 1986. [GHD]

–*The God of the mind*, New York, Agni Press, 1989. [GMN]

–*O my heart*, New York, Agni Press, 1988. [OMH]

–*O my mind*, New York, Agni Press, 1988. [OMM]

–*My Lord Supreme, do You have a moment?*, New York, Agni Press, 1990. [LSM]

–*God is kidnapped*, New York, Agni Press, 1990. [GIK]

–*European Poem-Blossoms*, New York, Agni Press, 1990. [EPB]

–*Every day a new chance*, New York, Agni Press, 1990. [EDN]

–*God minus*, New York, Agni Press, 1990. [GDM]

–*God plus*, New York, Agni Press, 1990. [GDP]

–*Twenty-seven Heart-Fragrance-Dreams*, New York, Agni Press, 1990. [HFD]

–*Each hour is a God-Hour*, New York, Agni Press, 1990. [HGH]

–*My life-boat's Dream-Reality-Shore*, New York, Agni Press, 1990. [LBD]

–*War: man's abysmal abyss-plunge, part 1*, New York, Agni Press,

1990.
–*War: man's abysmal abyss-plunge, part 2*, New York, Agni Press, 1990. [WMA]

–*I know why I am helpless*, New York, Agni Press, 1992. [IKW]
–*The beginning and the arriving*, New York, Agni Press, 1992. [BGA]

–*Beauty-discovery*, New York, Agni Press, 1992. [BTD]

–*Beautiful is my whispering soul*, New York, Agni Press, 1992. [BWS]

–*Friendship-birds fly*, New York, Agni Press, 1992. [FBF]

–*God the Eye and God the Heart*, New York, Agni Press, 1992. [GEH]

–*My God-Master*, New York, Agni Press, 1992. [GM]

–*My God-prayers and my God-meditations*, New York, Agni Press, 1992. [GPR]

–*I am sure*, New York, Agni Press, 1992. [IAS]

–*My mind-confusion out, my mind-illumination in*, New York, Agni Press, 1992. [MCM]

–*My God-commitments*, New York, Agni Press, 1992. [MGC]

–*Morning invites my heart. Evening invites my life*, New York, Agni Press, 1992. [MIH]

–*The Oneness-Heart-University*, New York, Agni Press, 1992. [OHU]

–*Peace: God's Fragrance-Heart, part 1*, New York, Agni Press, 1992.
–*Peace: God's Fragrance-Heart, part 2*, New York, Agni Press, 1992. [PGF]

–*Yesterday, today, tomorrow*, New York, Agni Press, 1992. [YTT]

–*Immediately start!*, New York, Agni Press, 1993. [IS]

–*Immediately start again!*, New York, Agni Press, 1993. [ISA]

–*Immediately stop!*, New York, Agni Press, 1993. [ISP]

–*My bondage-life is my self-invention*, New York, Agni Press, 1993. [BLS]

–*My eagerness-heart*, New York, Agni Press, 1993. [EHT]

–*My gratitude-heart-garden*, New York, Agni Press, 1993. [GHG]

–*My gratitude-tears and God's Satisfaction-Smiles*, New York, Agni Press, 1993. [GTG]

–*God the Mother and God the Father*, New York, Agni Press, 1993. [GMF]

–*A love-bathed heart*, New York, Agni Press, 1993. [LBH]

–*Love, compassion, forgiveness*, New York, Agni Press, 1993. [LCF]

[Suggested cite-key in brackets]

POSTFACE

Publishing principles

This edition of The works of Sri Chinmoy aims to obey the Author's wish: scrupulous fidelity to his original words, use of typographical style by him selected, specific spelling choices, end placement of any editorial content (i.e. not written by Sri Chinmoy himself), particular treatment of some personal nouns in special cases, etc.

Textual accuracy

The text of this edition has been checked to ensure faithful accuracy to the originals. Although much effort has been put in proofreading and comparing different versions of the text, this print may still present a few lingering errors.

The publisher would be grateful to be apprised of any mistypes, possibly with scan of the original page where the text is different. Please use original books only, specifying the year of publication.

Acknowledgements

Our deepest gratitude to Sri Chinmoy. His living presence can be felt breathing throughout his writings. It is a privilege to be involved with his works, in any form.

TABLE OF CONTENTS

When God-Love Descends	13
Lord, I ask You for one favour	27
Lord, receive this little undying cry	39
Lord, I need you	55
My life-tree	67
My promise to God	81
Sound becomes, silence is	93
The silence-song	131
Silence-seed and sound-fruit	145
This is God's Home	156
Dedication-drops	171
Union and oneness	187
Three soulful prayers	205
My fifty gratitude-summers	217
The loser and the winner	227
I meditate so that	235
I pray so that	245
I am ready	255
My heart's thirty-one sacred secrets	265
My God-Hunger-Dreams	273
The God of the mind	285
O my heart	295
O my mind	305
My Lord Supreme, do You have a moment?	321
God is kidnapped	331
European Poem-Blossoms	349
Every day a new chance	365
God minus	375
God plus	381
Twenty-seven Heart-Fragrance-Dreams	387
Each hour is a God-Hour	393
My life-boat's Dream-Reality-Shore	403
War: man's abysmal abyss-plunge	409
I know why I am helpless	419
The beginning and the arriving	429
Beauty-discovery	439
Beautiful is my whispering soul	445
Friendship-birds fly	453

God the Eye and God the Heart	461
My God-Master	471
My God-prayers and my God-meditations	481
I am sure	489
My mind-confusion out, my mind-illumination in	497
My God-commitments	505
Morning invites my heart. Evening invites my life	515
The Oneness-Heart-University	527
Peace: God's Fragrance-Heart	537
Yesterday, today, tomorrow	555
Immediately start!	565
Immediately start again!	575
Immediately stop!	585
My bondage-life is my self-invention	595
My eagerness-heart	603
My gratitude-heart-garden	611
My gratitude-tears and God's Satisfaction-Smiles	621
God the Mother and God the Father	631
A love-bathed heart	645
Love, compassion, forgiveness	653
Appendix	665
Bibliography	667
Postface	675
Table of contents	679

www.ingramcontent.com/pod-product-compliance
Lightning Source LLC
Chambersburg PA
CBHW030110240426
43661CB00031B/1356/J